IN SEARCH OF ELOQUENCE

Cross-Disciplinary Conversations on the Role
of Writing in Undergraduate Education

Research and Teaching in Rhetoric and Composition
Michael M. Williamson and David A. Jolliffe, series editors

Basic Writing as a Political Act: Public Conversations About Writing and Literacies
Linda Adler-Kassner and Susanmarie Harrington

New Worlds, New Words: Exploring Pathways for Writing About and In Electronic Environments
John F. Barber and Dene Grigar (eds.)

The Rhetoric and Ideology of Genre: Strategies for Stability and Change
Richard Coe, Lorelei Lingard, and Tatiana Teslenko (eds.)

In Search of Eloquence: Cross-Disciplinary Conversations on the Role of Writing in Undergraduate Education
Cornelius Cosgrove and Nancy Barta-Smith

Teaching/Writing in the Late Age of Print
Jeffrey Galin, Carol Peterson Haviland, and J Paul Johnson (eds.)

Revision Revisited
Alice S. Horning

Multiple Literacies for the 21st Century
Brian Huot, Beth Stroble, and Charles Bazerman (eds.)

Identities Across Text
George H. Jensen

Against the Grain: Essays in Honor of Maxine Hairston
David Jolliffe, Michael Keene, Mary Trachsel, and Ralph Voss (eds.)

Classroom Spaces and Writing Instruction
Ed Nagelhout and Carol Rutz

Unexpected Voices
John Rouse and Ed Katz

Directed Self-Placement: Principles and Practices
Dan Royer and Roger Gilles (eds.)

Who Can Afford Critical Consciousness?: Practicing a Pedagogy of Humility
David Seitz

forthcoming

The Hope and the Legacy: The Past, Present and Future of "Students' Right" to Their Own Language
Patrick Bruch and Richard Marback (eds.)

Toward Deprivatized Pedagogy
Diane Calhoun Bell and Becky Nugent

Rhetoric in(to) Science Inquiry: Style as Invention in the Pursuit of Knowledge
Heather Graves

Remapping Narrative: Technology's Impact on the Way We Write
Gian S. Pagnucci and Nick Mauriello (eds.)

IN SEARCH OF ELOQUENCE

Cross-Disciplinary Conversations on the Role of Writing in Undergraduate Education

Cornelius Cosgrove

Nancy Barta-Smith

Slippery Rock University of Pennsylvania

HAMPTON PRESS, INC.
CRESSKILL, NJ 07626

Copyright © 2004 by Hampton Press, Inc.

All rights reserved. No part of this publication may be reproduced, stored in a retrieval system, or transmitted in any form or by any means, electronic, mechanical, photocopying, microfilming, recording, or otherwise, without permission of the publisher.

Printed in the United States of America

Library of Congress Cataloging-in-Publication Data

Cosgrove, Cornelius.
   In search of eloquence : cross-disciplinary conversations on the role of writing in undergraduate education / Cornelius Cosgrove, NancyBarta-Smith.
     p. cm. -- (Research and teaching in rhetoric and composition)
Includes bibliographical references and indexes.
ISBN 1-57273-576-7 and ISBN 1-57273-577-5
  1. English language--Rhetoric--Study and teaching. 2. Report writing--Study and teaching (Higher) 3. Interdisciplinary approach in education. I. Barta-Smith, Nancy, II. Title. III. Series

PE1404.C637 2004
808'.042'0711--dc22
                                                           2004054384

Hampton Press, Inc.
23 Broadway
Cresskill, NJ 07626

Contents

1 **Meeting the Rhetorician's Challenge Through Cross—Disciplinary Conversation**   1

    Composition's Role When "English" No Longer Encompasses Writing Instruction   3

    Conversation as a Model for Cross-Campus Talk About Writing   9

2 **An Institution and Its Faculty: The Why and How of Our Study**   15

    The Teaching Life at a Small Public Comprehensive   16
    Searching for Written Eloquence: Programs and Problems   20
    Processes and Principals   22
    An Ending and a Beginning   29

3 **In Search of Recognition: The Dynamics of the Interviews**   31

    Developing Ordinary Language   37
    Facilitating Conversation: Moves Both Adept and Clumsy   51
    Interdisciplinary Study Through Conversation   61

4 **What Should Students Write? Distances and Proximities Among Classroom, Disciplinary and Workplace Genres**   63

    Defining Genre   63
    Identifying Genres   69
    Connecting Classroom and Professional Genres   80
    Considering Doubts and Possibilities   85
    Translating, Playing and Adapting   91
    Valuing Classroom Genres, Contexts, and Collaborations   98

5 Writing as Inquiry, Argument and Persuasion 103

Logic, Emotion and Aesthetics in Inquiry and Argument 106
The Shifting Circumstances of Ethos in Academe 117
What, Then, Should We Teach? 124

6 Expert Knowledge: Knowing That, Learning How, and Asking Why 135

Connecting Expertise to Practice 139
Asking Why or Learning How in Graduate School 148
Writing to Learn, Reflect, and Critique in the Undergraduate Major 153
General Education as a Supplement to Specialist Expertise 163
Learning Non-Specialist Functional Expertise 171

7 Connecting Correctness and Style to Writing Instruction Within and Beyond Disciplines 181

Teaching Writing and Teaching Correctness 181
Seeing Meaning as Stable or Variable 189
Connecting Style to Writing Within And Beyond Disciplines 202

8 Further Steps in the Search for Eloquence 215

Appendices

Appendix A
  Schedule of First Interview Questions 229
Appendix B
  Schedule of Second Interview Questions 231
Appendix C
  Transcript Analysis Sheet 233
Appendix D
  Technical and Scientific Writing: Assignment 4 237
Appendix E
  College Writing II: Evaluating the First Position Paper 239
Appendix F
  College Writing II: Second Position Paper Checklist 243

References 245
Author Index 251
Subject Index 255

1
Meeting the Rhetorician's Challenge Through Cross-Disciplinary Conversation

> It would have been nearer truth to say that no man can be eloquent on a subject that he does not understand; and that, if he understands a subject ever so well, but is ignorant how to form and polish his speech, he can not express himself eloquently even about what he does understand.
>
> —Cicero (*De Oratore*, Book I, xiv)

We suspect that every teacher of college composition can identify readily enough with the dilemma Cicero posed for rhetoricians more than two millenia ago. Through his alter ego Crassus, Cicero argued that rhetors could only master, and consequently teach, their craft by setting out to learn all that there was to learn in every subject. And this vast learning, once acquired, could only be shared and applied through a grasp of those linguistic forms capable of making the knowledge accessible to others. The briefest reflection would suggest that no one could become a master rhetorician in the course of numerous lifetimes, regardless of how successful medical science might be in extending the present one. Even if, somehow, we could emulate Bill Murray's TV weatherman of a few years back, just how many "groundhog days" would we need to live through before reaching such a goal? (Mastering jazz piano and increasing our empathy for our fellow humans pale in comparison.)

The obvious impossibility of Crassus' charge pervades the professional lives of the great majority of composition teachers, whether they seek to cultivate "good writing" in a 2-year or liberal arts college, or a public comprehensive university (Slippery Rock University [SRU]) like our own. Every faculty member in our English Department teaches at least two sections of writing each semester—regardless of training in literature, composition, critical or rhetorical theory—and our contractual teaching load is eight sections an academic year. Our writing sections, whether in first-year composition or for courses in an undergraduate writing program, commonly contain from 25 to 28 students. Life never seems so short, or art so long, as it does in the midst of one of our intensive teaching terms.

Throughout the years, English faculty have dealt with Cicero's dilemma by employing numerous strategies that may serve to limit or "discipline" the rhetoric of written composition, such as confining themselves to literary models and expressive modes, or focusing almost exclusively on style and usage. But the rhetorician's burden, as perceived by Crassus, cannot be long denied or suppressed. Rhetoric has no clear scholarly limits; its scope encompasses just about everything, and writing courses are supposed to prepare students for a range of majors. The medieval scholastics categorized rhetorical study as one of the trivium of liberal arts (Scholes 120) and there it remains, an anomaly within a contemporary Western academy that spins out ever more focused areas of study as readily as the silk worm spins out thread, or the Internet does Web sites. As purveyors of this "art," writing faculty find themselves in the permanently ironic position of both expert and novice, conveying the results of research within our own field that assert the distinctive character of writing outside it. We struggle to "keep up" with scholarship that increasingly takes us outside the English Department in search of expertise about writing, via recent investigations of academic and professional genres (Dias et al.; Berkenkotter and Huckin; Coe and Freedman) and of writing as a form of disciplinary and interdisciplinary practice (Geisler, Rogers, and Haller; Russell; "Rethinking;" Segal et al.).

There is no apparent end to this struggle, yet its Sisyphean quality may be the ultimate proof of its importance. It is important because we are forced once more, in very immediate and concrete ways, to confront the problematic relationship between linguistic form and subject-specific knowledge that so exercised Cicero. It is also important because it offers new perspectives on the current crises regarding what can and should be taught to undergraduates about the rhetoric of written discourse across the disciplines, and regarding the subject of English in its entirety. While considering the challenges endemic to our subject area and our specialization, it has become increasingly clear to us that composition studies cannot, and never could, live by English alone.

This book describes our response to the ancient challenge that a study of rhetoric poses, so forcefully articulated by Cicero, and to the current challenges facing undergraduate professors concerned about the role of writing in their students' educations. It depicts our efforts to employ dialogue as a kind of "action research" undertaken not just to gain knowledge but also to effect useful change in our teaching, our curricular structures, and our interactions with colleagues in other disciplines. Our initial chapters explain the perceived need for such dialogue, given our positions within an evolving public comprehensive university; the ways our conversations with colleagues in eight disciplines distinct from our own have influenced our analyses of the connections between knowledge and language; and the forms of talk that evolved during the course of those same conversations. Further chapters explore issues and themes that emerged from the dialogue, as well as their implications for future cross-campus talk. This book is, in essence, our search for a knowledge that can add value to our teaching of writing, and the teaching of our colleagues. It is a search for language that is inseparable from that knowledge, a language that forms the knowledge and makes it usable.

COMPOSITION'S ROLE WHEN "ENGLISH" NO LONGER ENCOMPASSES WRITING INSTRUCTION

The separation between knowledge (understanding) and its shape or form in language (eloquence), although the result of a cognitive, analytic operation, has an intuitive common sense born in everyday experience. We can put others' ideas into "our own words," shape our own words to fit a particular situation, and create something new out of "raw materials." These analytic distinctions pervade Western culture, in the separation of form from matter, essence from mere appearance, mind from body. From Aristotle's woodcutter to our childhood molding of clay to the conduit metaphor so well elaborated by Lakoff and Johnson (10-13), where ideas are packaged in words, we have accepted this distinction between knowledge and its expression.

Such a view cannot reduce eloquence to mere ornamentation, however. For we have also believed in the integral and reciprocal relationship between matter and form. Our epigraph from Cicero can function as a polyvalent metaphor for the distinctions between disciplinary understandings, for the role of writing practices within every discipline, and for the challenge English departments face in facilitating the writing and reading of texts across disciplines. Such a challenge is one that English departments have long avoided, simply because the separation of form from matter has both given English an identity and created strains within that identity. A concentration on the study of literature, in the form of writing deemed aesthetically valuable, made English departments "matter" in 20th-century American universities. But that concentration also served to ignore what English departments most often did within those same universities, and that was to teach writing as writing, as an end, as an activity, primarily to students who were novices within the realm of higher education. The separation of a subject matter primarily focused on literary study from the actual activity of most writing teachers within English departments has generated tensions within the discipline that have often been economic in nature. Scholarship in literary studies has been most valued, historically dominating graduate programs, but the great majority of available professional positions entail teaching composition, often as part-time and/or temporary faculty. Since the late 1970s, when the Modern Language Association (MLA) began to conduct surveys on job appointments, the number of new English PhDs reporting placement in full-time, tenure-track positions has seldom exceeded 50% (North et al. 238). In 1997, universities in the United States graduated 1,080 new PhDs in English ("Latest National Research" 1), while advertising for only 307 definite, tenure-track assistant professor positions in the MLA's fall Job Information List for English (Laurence and Welles 2).

These ongoing crises in both identity and professional employment have led to a variety of recent reactions. Literary critics may perceive their field as experiencing either a postmodern renaissance or a fin-de-siècle funk (Raymond passim). Rhetoricians such as Ross Winterowd may complain of the insular quality of literary studies and the restrictions such studies have placed on inquiry within the discipline (131-33). Robert Scholes, a prominent literary critic who has gradually embraced rhetorical studies as the most likely savior of his discipline, curses both postmodern and traditionalist literary studies, accusing the postmodernists of engendering a "hypocriticism" (81) that takes them further and further from the educational needs of their undergraduate students, and the traditionalists of occupying "merely a field, organized like a burial ground, around the textual tombs of the grand dead" (144).

To some, locating writing instruction within the discipline of English can be considered as not just a lifeline but also a burden and a perpetual bother, a source of both employment (often tentative and overburdened employment) and, as our colleagues remind us, of frustration and blame. It is a lifeline when department tenure lines are threatened. It is a burden and bother when those of us whose primary "area" of teaching and scholarship is rhetoric and composition are "held responsible" for disappointing student writing within our colleagues' major courses. "I don't see how some of our students could pass College Writing I and College Writing II," a sport management professor has told us. "These students are . . . coming up to a junior or senior taking my classes and I'm basically the one saying 'you're not going to pass here . . .' You can't write a memo. You can't put a sentence together" (Sport Management, June 12, 1998). Faculty members in other disciplines cannot understand how our focus could ever stray from these concerns. Unfamiliar with research in our field, they do not realize how the particular challenges of the disciplinary writing they assign, and of entering the culture of the university itself, contributes to breakdowns in meaning or syntax.

In truth, current research on writing in the disciplines generates the same challenging questions for both composition faculty and disciplinary practitioners: How and when should students be required to regard the practice of their major disciplines, at least in part, in terms of the production of its documents—to be imitated, manipulated, criticized, and modified? In what sense are these documents even apparent as "writing" once they are embedded in disciplinary cultures (Dias et al. 233)? If academic and nonacademic cultures represent different "worlds" of activity, and call for actions with different goals, are there transitional genres and methods to bridge the gap (Dias et al. 235)? Seeking to answer these questions places English faculty in the midst of research that truly matters, because the relationship between knowledge and form has perplexed us all for more than two millenia. Addressing these questions forces us to embrace our status as a "liberal art," one that radiates outward into every academic area, rather than to perpetuate with our non-English colleagues the mutually comforting delusion that language only matters in composition and literature courses.

The conceptual abstractions of academe authorize the separation of knowledge from execution and theory from practice, of which the separation of the teaching of writing from the teaching of knowledge content is but one example. Disciplines across the curriculum define themselves as content areas and responsibility for writing has fallen to English departments. Some members of English departments have even thought and still do think of the teaching of writing simply as performing a service to the many disciplines that increasingly require specialized forms and tools of writing in their practice. As composition teachers ourselves, however, we accept that no matter how many kinds of intelligence, and how many areas of specialized knowledge and ways to apply them there are, they all "live" in one body. The separation of form from matter, ends from means, theory from practice, and mind from body have created and perpetuated divisions within our own discipline and within the whole of the contemporary academy that limit necessary student learning and that we must therefore struggle against. Integrated knowledge—both theoretical and practical—develops and adapts interactively within environmental contexts, as Piaget's cognitive psychology has demonstrated.

This developmental, adaptive and contextual nature of cognition is evident in the way that evolutionary and comparative biology has taken up the implications of Piaget's work (Langer and Killen). Moreover, we perceive that the Russian activity theory at the heart of new genre study (Broughton and Freeman-Moir 42) lends itself to a developmental, adaptive and contextual approach to writing instruction that would place writing faculty in partnership with both academic and nonacademic practitioners of all the disciplines. For us, the search is for an appropriate way to implement such a partnership. Activity theory differentiates between actions and operations (ends and means), but also allows that these separate functions can occur simultaneously, while differing significantly from context to context. Can compositionists be effective actors within their own discipline, treating writing as an action and an end, while facilitating writing as means or operation within and across disciplines? Is there a way to conceive this distinction that does not imply the separation of mind from body, conception from execution, content from writing?

Dias et al. acknowledge that writing is an end before it becomes a means. For instance, at one stage holding a pencil is a goal of action. With experience it becomes an operation or means for writing words and sentences (26). Moreover, in every case such actions occur in an environment. If writing remains an action or end for writing faculty, we can work with others to make it a means as well. Piaget and the American psychologist James Mark Baldwin tended to emphasize the progressiveness of development. Such an emphasis encourages a curriculum that approaches writing first as a skill to be mastered, by focusing on writing as writing, and then abandoning that focus as a student becomes more capable of using writing as a means to some other end. Phenomenology, particularly that of Merleau-Ponty, seems to us more applicable to what we ourselves observe, because it suggests that stages in which writing remains an end can co-exist with its status as a means (Phenomenology of Perception 355). Every action is integrated in one body, a body that is embedded in the world. So when Dias et al. suggest that in school we should "engage students in activities that commit them to write as necessary means—but only as a means, not an end" (235), they appear to repeat Piaget's error of projecting the end of development onto its beginning, and defining early developments as immaturity or lack. Consequently, Piaget claims that perception victimizes the immature, while concrete and formal operations mostly correct perception's errors.

Writing instruction, we are led to think, should simultaneously treat undergraduate writing as both ends and means, as an activity that requires continual engagement and as an operation performed with a variety of ends in mind. Moreover, writing for all of us occurs within distinct environments that can never be wholly anticipated. In this sense, even recent research studies attempting to recontextualize genres as more than fixed forms may be misleading, if they imply that schools should focus on the deficiencies of student writers or should inculcate skills "detached" from workplace, academic, or private settings. Theory and research that reveal the situatedness of disciplinary and workplace discourse (Dias et al. passim) demonstrate what makes professional genres distinct (Segal et al. 74). There is always something new to learn, about the writing and about the disciplinary or professional practice of which the writing is a part. It seems equally plausible to us that neither school nor workplace should be restricted in its developmental role. Why can't workplace settings, for example, allow professionals to address writing as an end, in order to improve its use as a means? Isn't such an orientation reflective of what corporate training and technical editing may already strive to accomplish?

Thinking fully about writing as both form and content, language and knowledge, ends and means relieves composition teachers of collective guilt for the inadequacies of student writing and increases the possibility of cross-disciplinary collaboration. Academic and professional writing can only be satisfactorily learned when the learner is engaged in context-bound practice (Dias et al. 181). In a way, writing faculty are taken "off the hook." For once non-English faculty begin to complain about students' inadequacies in linguistic performance in their own discipline, further inquiry may help them recognize the futility of blaming English courses. Non-English faculty will have to confront the same realities faced by English faculty. They will need to explore the disciplinary contexts in which language is used, the practices of those who successfully navigate a given discourse, and the genres to which these contexts and practices give birth. Composition faculty know this trajectory themselves only because so many of them have traversed that same path during the last 30 years or so.

The price for such relief from guilt, of course, is necessary doubt about the "transferability" that currently allows English departments to claim composition classes prepare students to write in their major courses and professional settings. Recognizing that writing cannot be approached solely, or in sequence, as either form or matter, ends or means, gives both rhetoricians and content-area scholars necessary roles in undergraduate writing instruction. For us, the better part is to discover ways in which what we have learned about written texts and effective communication, through centuries of rhetorical and literary analysis, can be used to connect with, build on, and supplement each discipline's level of awareness concerning its own discursive practices. As we have tried to show here, we can continue to teach writing as a goal or action in collaboration with those who teach it as an operation.

Scholes' solution to the question of matter and form is for English as a whole to emulate rhetorical studies by adopting a canon of methods rather than of works (173). Focusing solely on those texts that have been deemed "literary" has served to place English on the curricular border, along with all those other "specializations" that hold out much better prospects to their students for future professional employment. But teaching methods derived from both literary and rhetorical theory, methods that facilitate both the generation and the critical consumption of texts, would place English at the core of the undergraduate curriculum because it would give students the ability to "cope with the texts in various media that constantly bombard them in their work and private lives" (Scholes 73). If Merleau-Ponty is right about the ongoing, integrative nature of human development, then a canon of methods will not make English the handmaiden or servant of other disciplines but their partner, because it is only in the context of a body assumed separate from the mind and world that the whole distinction between theory and practice, conception and execution, content and writing is feasible. Recent neuroscience research increasingly blurs such distinctions.

Embracing a canon of methods is an impressive idea, especially for those inside and outside English who are tired of the blame game. But which methods, derived from which theories, will be most useful to our students, given the limited time that they will be under our tutelage? Literary and rhetorical studies have certainly accumulated plenty of methods and theories over time. Moreover, those English faculty who are involved in composition and rhetoric already have become habitual, perhaps even compulsive, borrowers of instruments of textual analysis from other disciplines. This fact is particularly true within the area of genre studies, discussed earlier and in Chapter 4. Berkenkotter and Huckin, at the beginning of their study of the role genre knowledge plays in disciplinary activity, listed at least seven different influences on their methodology—"structuration theory in sociology, rhetorical studies, interpretive anthropology, ethnomethodology, Bakhtin's theory of speech genres (*Speech Genres*), Vygotsky's theory of ontogenesis, and Russian activity theory as it has shaped the movement in U.S. psychology called *situated* or *everyday cognition*" (3). We embrace this interdisciplinarity.

But which disciplines should have a bearing on the methods of textual analysis we in English teach? Michael Carter has characterized the compositionists' project as moving students from an application of "culturally generated" global strategies to eventual acquisition of local writing knowledge (281). Can we start students down the road toward analysis and generation of discipline-specific texts while relying solely on the theory and method of our own discipline as the vehicle? How much do we need to know of other disciplines before we can give our students what they need? These questions can only be answered as together with other faculty outside English we explore the contexts, successful practices, and genres in which disciplinary knowledge manifests itself.

Whether English faculty are wrestling with how best to link form and knowledge in their writing instruction, or how to redefine the role of their discipline within the 21st-century academy, it seems clear that neither activity will have much impact unless it is performed in concert with colleagues across the disciplines. Faculty at public comprehensive universities are particularly well placed in this regard. Much has been written about the difficulties of interdisciplinary inquiry, and seemingly less about its inevitability. At least for academicians at comprehensive public universities and liberal arts colleges, the great bulk of their professional interactions could be said to be interdisciplinary. They take place with faculty in their own discipline but in different areas of scholarship, with faculty from different disciplines, and with students who do not yet regard themselves as members of any discipline. Teaching 6 to 8 sections a year in liberal arts colleges and public comprehensives, or 10 or more sections a year in 2-year schools, both requires and produces "generalists" in the broadest sense of the term, even in disciplines seemingly less distended than English. Although our own interest may be in discovering how we can best use those interactions to strengthen our teaching of first-year and professional writing courses, already we are finding that our colleagues across campus, also charged with preparing undergraduates for intellectual futures both uncertain and demanding, have interests that dovetail with our own. Academicians outside of English seem to find the implications of taking the specificity of disciplinary discourse seriously only slightly less daunting than we do. They may conclude they could use our help, especially if we make it clear that we need theirs. For example, one of our colleagues in Health Services Administration heard of our lines of inquiry and welcomed guidance in creating criteria for assessing student writing. Even those believing in the "transparency" or arhetorical nature of their discourse—or in transparent notions of clear, effective prose—may have difficulty, if called on to not only produce but also teach such "good writing." For doing so may suddenly require explicit reference to concepts and methods largely implicit in their own practice. On the other hand, even if we can presume that our experience in assessing student writing can be of help to colleagues in other disciplines, we cannot avoid discovering our own ignorance of what is valued in the writing of, for instance, health services professionals. We become fascinating reflections of each other; paramount among their concerns might be how to make time for writing under the pressure to "cover content"; paramount among our concerns might be the challenge of relating student writing to fluid and ever-expanding areas of activity within which their writing might be put to use.

CONVERSATION AS A MODEL FOR CROSS-CAMPUS TALK ABOUT WRITING

Cicero admitted to himself in *De Oratore* that the rhetorician he envisioned was an ideal toward which to strive, all the while knowing that attainment was simply impossible. One worthy example of such striving has been the employment of traditional modes of academic communication, like the conference, the journal, and the book, for interdisciplinary ends. Debra Journet has advocated the creation of "boundary genres" that "sublimate differences" between disciplines "not just by articulating connections but also by recasting the knowledge claims of one discipline into the generic forms of the other" (57). The problem with all these interactions is that they are, for the vast majority of us, "special events," infrequent in occurrence and removed from both our campuses and the day-to-day concerns that shape our professional lives. They are also, regardless of the noble efforts of some conference organizers, almost always monologic, even when workshops occur on our own campuses.

These interactions do not suffice for two important reasons. One is that, in interactions between English compositionists and faculty from other disciplines about discursive practices, no one can claim expertise within the range of possible subject matter. The second is that such interactions will most likely impact on our students' education in a positive way when they are clearly related to those ongoing dialogues on our particular campuses regarding curriculum, pedagogy, and the assessment of student learning (as they are for the colleagues we have interviewed for this study). In short, we need interdisciplinary interactions that are extended rather than episodic and informal rather than assertive, ones in which the participants perceive themselves as professional equals. Our students must negotiate between their English writing courses and the writing demanded of them in their majors, and so must we.

With this imperative in mind, we have initiated discussions with faculty at our institution, but outside our department, about the role of disciplinary discourse, particularly written discourse, in the professionalization of our undergraduate students. These discussions are in the form of interviews that begin with a predetermined set of questions first developed as a student assignment in our courses in technical and scientific communication (see Appendix D). We allow these discussions to expand into free-flowing interchanges concerning the subjects the questions evoke. We think that such a scenario unsettles the power relations so often in place when professional writing faculty act as consultants either in business and industry or across the curriculum. Over a period of 18 months (from June 1998 to November 1999) we conducted 15 interviews with eight faculty members in the fields of computer science, elementary education, health services administration, health education, mathematics, nursing, physics, and sport management. This book is most succinctly described as a report of those interviews and their implications. As we have already stated, we regard what we have done as a kind of "action research" that seeks to accommodate the learning we desire to the academic context in which we function through face-to-face discussion, followed by reflection and possible collaborative effort.

On the local level, we had several hopes for the interviews. They could tell us of a variety of discipline-based classroom genres (see Chapter 4). For instance, health services administration students were asked to write personal and professional credos, as a mode for generating understanding of professional ethics. Although the faculty member we interviewed has acknowledged this as a learning activity, it was implicated as discipline-based as well when the professional credo emerged again as part of an institutional mission or vision statement assignment. We also hoped to discover what individual faculty within our institution consider normative, justifiable, or open to criticism in their professional discourse and in the discourse of their students. We hoped to identify some conceptualizations that are shared by the bulk of the faculty within our institution. Perhaps we could relate the criteria used by individual faculty while evaluating the products of their culture to the criteria we employ for similar purposes. In all of these endeavors, we examined how interviewees' responses to our questions matched up with our own expectations.

On a more global level, we hoped these interviews could reveal to us modes of conversation capable of accomplishing two significant goals. One goal, as already noted, is to discover talk that avoids either interlocutor assuming the "missionary position" for which some English faculty within the writing-across-the-curriculum (WAC) movement may be infamous (Segal et al. 83, Walvoord et al. 9-10). Can the talk reflect an attitude that regards "discipline members not only as 'informants' but also as full partners in an investigation they care about and see value in" (Segal et al. 84)? When cross-disciplinary teaching did take place during these interviews, we hoped that it was reciprocal in the sense described by James Crosswhite in his *Rhetoric of Reason*—through the recognition of claims as claims, as well as through a questioning that demonstrated a respect for the claim and the claimant, and that elicited reasons that help our interlocutors define their discursive actions, their disciplines, and themselves (77). "Rhetoricians from Aristotle to Chaim Perelman," Crosswhite pointed out, "have recognized that to argue with someone is to show a sign of deep respect" (96). In recognizing the claims made by those with whom we converse we take responsibility for them, meaning that we necessitate their possible incorporation into our own actions, into our sense of our own disciplines and of ourselves (Crosswhite 66-76).

Our second global hope is for numerous instances in which an "ordinary" language is discovered, one that allows conversants to feel comfortable that they understand each other. We are using J.L. Austin's sense of the "ordinary" here, as "a context in which communication is experienced as mostly successful" (Crosswhite 29); as a state conversants seek to maintain (Edwards 71) but might naturally fear to lose when speaking about writing from the perspectives of two distinct academic disciplines. Beyond the interviews, this book is also an attempt to discover ordinary language that, at least at serendipitous moments, can understandably represent thinking about writing and the teaching of writing to a cross-disciplinary set of readers.

Interviews that could happily transform themselves into conversations constituted a method recommended to us by the work of James Mark Baldwin, briefly alluded to earlier in this chapter. For in Baldwin the developmental nature of our capacity for representation in social development is more progressively elaborated than in Piaget, where the "mature" adult is clearly the scientist. The expansive discourses that have developed in English and cultural studies on the differences in perspective of those differently situated have indeed naturalized the expectation that communicating across "boundaries" is difficult. But in our on-campus conversation we co-inhabit embodied physical as well as conceptual landscapes—communicating face to face as much as mind to mind.

Baldwin reserved the term *recognition*, employed by Crosswhite to imply respect, for sensorimotor encounter—as opposed to recall, which Baldwin associated with first capacities for conscious representation in memory. Such primary encounters with others are akin to what Lakoff and Johnson call "basic-level" categories in language because they match physical objects quite well, through hands-on experience, but also invoke a whole range of affective possibilities in addition to verification. It may be more than ordinary language that sets conversants at ease, allowing for recognition and its concomitant respect, for a host of sensorimotor processes operate at the perceptual level that can break down preconceived assumptions about difference. This affective backdrop to our conversations could help to make ordinary language both effective and possible, even when our respective discourses did not see "eye to eye." Certainly, there has been little friction in our interviews, even when faculty members refer to their frustration with English departments for passing students who turned up in their classes with questionable proficiency, or for emphasizing self-discovery and personal narrative, it seems, at the cost of professionalism.

When we are able to engage effectively in a conversational model of cross-talk about discipline-specific writing, all parties to the conversation both speak and listen. Such a mutually respectful environment creates more complex understanding of the legitimate frustration both English faculty and others feel when students appear unable to demonstrate commonly expected characteristics of effective writing. Such a climate also creates understanding of the complexity of writing itself and of the way that the goals of separate areas of activity, such as learning and work, can affect operational means, such as spelling and grammar, that in other contexts may be "mastered."

As an explanation, theory and research on the complexity and situatedness of genres and writing in the disciplines is certainly preferable to one that implies college writing teachers are lax, indolent, wrong-headed, and/or incompetent. Discussing such theory and research also offers the possibility to mutually consider whether genres such as memos are more than fixed forms, how they arise in situations, and in what kinds of institutional cultures they may evolve or remain static. In cross-disciplinary conversation faculty members in English may find themselves admitting that they were drilled in grammar and can still recite rules. Faculty members outside English may acknowledge the rich reading culture that has contributed to their literacy, and how little students read not only because of the many alternatives our visual culture provides, but because of the work requirements they juggle along with their schooling.

Together we can at least move toward the Ciceronian ideal of the eloquent polymath. We can step out from our disciplinary shelters into an academic agora that allows cross-disciplinary interaction, learning, and teaching. Cross-disciplinary talk acknowledges the constraints imposed on contemporary teachers in higher education and seeks to work within those constraints in order to learn and to do.

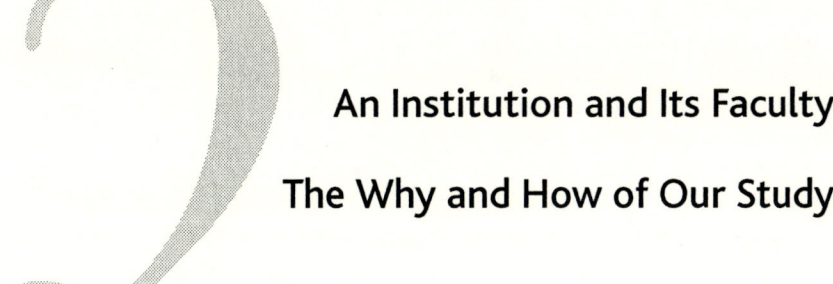

An Institution and Its Faculty

The Why and How of Our Study

> Lack of experience diminishes our power of taking a comprehensive view of the admitted facts. Hence those who dwell in intimate association with nature and its phenomena are more able to lay down principles such as to admit of a wide and coherent development, while those whom devotion to abstract discussions has rendered unobservant of facts are too ready to dogmatize on the basis of a few observations.
>
> —Aristotle (*On Generation and Corruption* Book I.2, 316a)

Within the social sciences there is a standard organization for explaining and justifying research. The writers begin by exploring the need for their study, reviewing prior scholarship and describing what gaps in the scholarship their work may close. This introduction is followed by an explanation of the "methodology" used to carry out the study, with the idea that others may wish to verify or disprove their findings by executing similar research. Reproduction and/or verification of the results are the main reasons for this careful and conventionalized presentation of material. The intent is to arrive at "truth statements"—the more generalizable the demonstrated hypotheses the more adaptable they will be to a discipline's chosen objects of study, whether they be schools or social groups, laptop users or labor unions.

Many in the field of composition and rhetoric have adopted the role of social scientist in performance of their scholarship. But we knew early on in our thinking that we would not. The intent of our inquiries seemed unsuitable to such a role. For one thing, our primary concern was to discover methods to facilitate interdisciplinary communication, rather than generalizable principles or truths. We were looking for ways to facilitate ongoing curricular development at particular institutions but not through the vehicle of general claims. If we were skeptical of analytical approaches to writing that isolated ends and means (actions from operations) we were equally skeptical of approaches to research that reduced contexts ("dwelling in intimate association with nature and its phenomena") to uses. The initial interview questions that we used were based on those we had provided our students to get them started in an assignment in which they interviewed academic and/or nonacademic professionals about writing in their fields—most often face to face on an interpersonal level. Such a dynamic, oral context is philosophically in tune with those perceptual contexts left out of most accounts of cognitive development we mentioned in the last chapter. But such a context is also key to understanding how easily adaptation from one context to another can occur, not through abstraction and application, but through lived interaction across varying contexts. This interaction is what we have called *action research*.

We hope faculty at other institutions, particularly public and private comprehensive teaching universities, 4-year liberal arts and 2-year colleges, can recognize our circumstances as being very much like their own and possibly identify with our struggles to both learn what we needed to know and to effect appropriate curricular change. But they also will be aware of differences in circumstances, both subtle and not so subtle, and of how their own approaches to similar challenges would have to fit their particular circumstances.

In the chapters that follow, we focus on the particular details of our cross-campus conversations and the contexts in which they occur, counting on reader recognition, identification, and adaptation of what we narrated, described, and sometimes analyzed, interpreted, and disputed, rather than reader acceptance of our conclusions as "truth statements."

THE TEACHING LIFE AT A SMALL PUBLIC COMPREHENSIVE

Our university began in 1889 as the Pennsylvania Normal School at Slippery Rock; a privately owned college-level institution that followed state-mandated guidelines for training school teachers. In 1916, the state purchased the school from its stockholders and in 1927, with the graduation of its first class of 4-year students, the institution took the name of Slippery Rock State Teachers College. By 1960, because degree programs were no longer confined to teacher preparation, the name changed to

Slippery Rock State College and then to Slippery Rock University (SRU) of Pennsylvania in 1983, when the institution was absorbed into a newly minted State System of Higher Education along with 13 other state-owned schools that had begun as schools for teacher preparation (*Self-Study* 1-2).[1] SRU has had to adjust to several financial challenges in recent years that may be partly or wholly familiar to those who work in similar institutions across the country. Tuitions are set by our system's board of governors for all 14 universities, and student costs have been rising steadily since 1983, in direct relation to gradual decreases in that proportion of institutions' operating budgets allocated from tax revenues by the legislature. SRU endured an 8-year decline in enrollments, from 1991 to 1999, and from a peak of 7,925 students to a recent low of 6,803 (*Self-Study* 11). A number of factors that might be considered out of the direct control of the university contributed to this decline. A steep increase in tuition for out-of-state students led to a sharp drop in enrollments from neighboring states such as Ohio, New York, and Maryland. In the meantime, declining population within the region intensified competition for students among both the public and private colleges of western Pennsylvania. Along with the enrollment declines came increased demand for noninstructional services and for an improved technological infrastructure. SRU lost 26 faculty positions between 1990 and 1999, in step with the enrollment decline. But there were also sharp increases in the number of professional nonfaculty (16) and technical/paraprofessional positions (13), and smaller increases in managerial (3) and skilled craft (7) positions (*Self-Study* 23).

SRU is now what the U.S. Department of Education's National Center for Education Statistics categorizes as a "master's" level institution, and it has been identified for accreditation purposes as a "comprehensive public" university (*Self-Study* 150). It has more than 60 degree programs, including 17 that grant a master's degree and one that grants a doctorate degree, in physical therapy (*Self-Study* 2, 73). SRU is one of 559 "master's" institutions in the United States, public and private, enrolling 3,237,198 students in the fall of 1998, or 22.3% of all the students enrolled in degree-granting schools of higher education. The great majority of these students (71%) attend public universities. When considering all of the institutions most similar to SRU in terms of faculty teaching workloads and teaching missions—that is, master's, bachelor's and associate-level schools—they enroll 69% of all students in degree-granting schools of higher education, as opposed to 27.6% in research and doctoral universi-

---

[1]The information in the preceding paragraph is taken from a recently completed *Selected Topics Self-Study prepared for the Commission on Higher Education of the Middle States Association of Colleges and Schools, 2000-01*. All in-text citations that refer to this source will be labeled *Self-Study*.

ties (NCES Table 216).[2] For us, the importance of these percentages lies in an awareness that the great majority of composition instructors in the United States are either full- or part-time professionally credentialed faculty, not graduate students. We are, moreover, similar to the majority of our colleagues in other disciplines, in that our primary professional commitment must be teaching, resulting in scholarship that often tries to connect our knowledge to the task of educating undergraduates.

As a primarily residential institution located in a small town and with a mission to offer higher education access to populations for which such access has historically been denied, SRU students are predominantly undergraduates (90.5% of fall 2000 enrollments), mostly from Pennsylvania (93%), and commonly of traditional college age (82%) (*Demographic* 19, 25).[3] SRU's mission is to be accessible; given time our students generally succeed academically. The graduation rate for the fall 1992 cohort of full-time, first-time students was more than 45% within 5 years and nearly 51% within 6 (*Self-Study* 150).

What is remarkable, and possibly anomalous among the more than 500 public and private comprehensives in the United States, is the job stability and security enjoyed by the SRU faculty. In the fall of 2000 only 8% of the 382 faculty members were part-time (*Academic* 18-19), nearly 92% were either tenured or tenure-track, and more than 50% were at the associate or full professor rank (*Demographic* 79). Because almost all the state-system universities are master's-level institutions like SRU, graduate assistant teaching is generally prohibited by the faculty contract. It is interesting to contrast these figures with those for public 4-year degree-granting institutions nationally, in which 26.6% of all faculty, excluding graduate teaching assistants, were part-time in the fall of 1997 (NCES Table 227). Such a state of affairs has to be attributed to collective bargaining between the 14 state-owned schools and a strong faculty union, bargaining that has been in place since the mid-1970s. Despite recognition by professional organizations like the Conference on College Composition and Communication (CCC) and the Modern Language Association (MLA) of the exploitation of composition teachers, such organizations have been

---

[2]National statistics concerning enrollments and faculty workloads are all derived from tables found in Chapter 3 of the National Center for Education Statistics (NCES) web page entitled *Participation in Education: Undergraduate Education*. All in-text citations that refer to this source will be labeled NCES.

[3]Much of the information about SRU students and faculty comes from two internal publications produced by the university's Office of Institutional Research and distributed in October 2000—*Selected Demographic Characteristics of Students and Faculty, 2000-01* and *Academic Information and Data, 2000-01*. In-text citations will refer to these sources as either *Demographic* or *Academic*.

clearly ineffective in improving working conditions. Our union, on the other hand, has done the necessary hiring of "lobbyists and attorneys to represent [faculty] interests to legislatures and university administrations" (Crowley 240).

If anything, this overall stability and security is even more pronounced within SRU's English Department, where 28 of the 30 faculty members in fall 2000 were tenured or tenure-track, none were part-time, and 19 held the rank of associate or full professor (*Demographic* 101). Crowley has wondered if the "university that recognizes and rewards" first-year composition teachers for "their contributions to teaching and curriculum design with equable salaries, tenure or security of employment, and promotion" is "mythical" (237). If so, then SRU and the other Pennsylvania state-owned schools belong in some kind of pantheon. In any given semester, nearly all the English Department faculty are teaching at least two sections of first-year composition. Moreover, faculty members choose for themselves the textbooks and syllabi they use in these courses, another deviation from Crowley's general assessment of conditions among composition teachers (222).

It is also important, however, to note that the expected teaching load for SRU faculty is 12 credit hours per semester; an analysis of work assignments reveals that more than 83% of the faculty carried such a teaching load in fall 2000, whereas less than 17% were either on sabbatical or receiving workload equivalencies to perform various administrative, curricular, or faculty development duties (*Academic* 20, 24). Nationally, 45.6% of the faculty in public comprehensive institutions were teaching less than 10 hours per week in fall 1992 (NCES Table 234).

Nationwide, the ratio of full-time equivalent (FTE) students to full-time equivalent faculty at public 4-year institutions in fall 1997 was 15.9:1 (NCES Table 225), whereas only 38.1% of the faculty at public comprehensives in fall 1992 had more than 100 students in their classes (NCES Table 234). At SRU, in contrast, the FTE-student to FTE-teaching faculty member was 21.3:1 in fall 2000 and the average number of students per FTE-teaching faculty member during the same semester was 113.18 (*Academic* 26, 29).

Within SRU's English Department, each faculty member generally teaches at least two first-year composition sections per semester, and sometimes more; these sections are often accompanied by a section of introductory literature. The literature course is also required by the university's liberal studies program. As in many universities, our class sizes are considerably above those recommended by professional organizations for first-year composition courses, or for any course that features writing as an integral part of instruction and evaluation. In recent years, the maximum enrollments per section for our first-semester composition course (College Writing I) have been 27 or 28 students, whereas the limits for the second-semester course (College Writing II) have ranged from 25 to 27. Maximum enrollments for the introductory literature course, in which most faculty use writing for both learning and evaluation, have been as low as 35 and as high as 45. These numbers have significance, we believe, when one considers our perceived need for dialogic, rather than programmatic cross-disciplinary interaction among faculty seeking to further integrate writing into our undergraduate curriculum. For variations in class size and the number of sections of liberal studies courses make general pronouncements about the quantity and kind of writing difficult.

SEARCHING FOR WRITTEN ELOQUENCE: PROGRAMS AND PROBLEMS

With two required first-year composition courses, an English Department faculty fully involved in the teaching of those courses, an undergraduate degree program in writing with professional and creative tracks and growing enrollments, and a WAC degree requirement in place, SRU has accepted the need to integrate writing into its curriculum. Nonetheless, SRU has found it difficult to make necessary budget commitments to the teaching of writing. Moreover, the student loads carried by the English faculty are even higher than the heavy loads carried by the university's faculty as a whole. The heavy enrollments in sections of lower division courses delineated above resulted in a department ratio of FTE students to FTE teaching faculty in fall 2000 of 23.04:1 and an average number of students for each faculty member of 115.51 (*Academic* 26, 29).

Additionally, one English faculty member "coordinates" the freshman English program while also running the university's writing center. These combined duties are carried out through a release of just three credit hours from the expected full-time teaching load for a semester. The freshman English coordinator chairs a committee meant to oversee the first-year program. Additionally, the coordinator is to initiate or encourage curricular innovation and faculty development in the area of composition studies and instruction. However, direction of the writing center, including maintenance of a large personal computer lab/classroom and the recruitment, training, and supervision of graduate and undergraduate tutors, takes most of the reassigned time. As noted in Chapter 1, we ourselves are convinced that much of that rethinking and overhauling could and should be stimulated through conversation with faculty in programs the composition courses are often thought to "serve." Such conversation is not only more attuned to our belief in the transferability of knowledge between academic and nonacademic contexts but also independent of reliance on budgetary commitments in a difficult economic environment.

SRU's plans for WAC began with great promise for changing curricular priorities, and faculty members were particularly active during the period from 1987 to 1995 in a statewide organization devoted to the movement. Unfortunately, the university was never able to provide an administrative structure or a dedicated budget to the program. "WAC programs require leadership by someone . . . who takes on the responsibility of coordinating the various elements and who is responsible for the day-to-day running of the program," two of the movement's most prominent scholars wrote recently. "They also require a budget to provide released time, stipends, outsider speakers, and other WAC activities" (McLeod and Maimon 581). SRU's program also would have benefited from a specific committee or alternative curricular body to screen and influence "writing-intensive" courses required of students for graduation.

WAC at SRU did begin with an infusion of administrative interest and external funding. In the summer of 1981 a faculty member from English and another from Modern Languages, along with the associate dean of the College of Arts and Sciences, attended a National Endowment for the Humanities (NEH) Summer Institute at Beaver College directed by Elaine Maimon. Shortly thereafter, a WAC committee was formed and two workshops directed by NEH personnel and Beaver College faculty attracted a significant number of SRU faculty, as well as local secondary school teachers. The two workshops and later attendance at a national WAC conference in July 1983 were all partially funded by NEH grants.[4]

In January 1984 the university's president approved a requirement that all undergraduates entering SRU the following fall and thereafter would need to complete two "writing-intensive" courses beyond the first-year composition courses to qualify for graduation. These courses, first offered in spring 1985, could be housed in any department and need not be a part of the student's major program. A series of internal grants were then used to finance five workshops for faculty, administrators, and graduate students. Well-known national WAC leaders Toby Fulwiler and Barbara Walvoord led four of these workshops, held between October 1984 and August 1987.

At the end of the August 1987 workshop, faculty from around the state formed the Pennsylvania WAC Association, electing an SRU English professor its first president. From 1988 to 1993, this group organized statewide conferences and workshops each May at various locales across Pennsylvania. State-system faculty professional development grants funded publication of the association's newsletter *Writing and Learning* from

---

[4]This and subsequent information about the WAC program at SRU is drawn from files kept by Dr. Barbara McNeal, president of the Pennsylvania WAC Association from 1993 to 1995, and by one of the authors.

1991 to 1995. Faculty from other state-system schools such as Clarion, Bloomsburg, Lock Haven, and Shippensburg were active in the state organization.

SRU faculty were most engaged on the state level from 1993 to 1995, when a second SRU English professor served as president and a member of the SRU Physics Department, also a respondent in this study, edited the newsletter. However, the annual conference scheduled for May 1994 was cancelled because of a lack of registrations and program proposals, and funding for the newsletter ran out in spring 1995. A workshop on performing WAC research, organized by the state association's last president and held at SRU in April 1995, was the final effort to organize state-wide WAC activities.

Some internal funding did sustain SRU's WAC activities through the mid-1990s. The provost's office sponsored a WAC reading group from 1992 to 1996 that often focused on emerging studies of the purposes, forms, conventions, and processes of writing within a variety of academic and professional areas (Bazerman and Paradis; Halliday and Martin; Nelson, Megill, and McCloskey; Russell, *Writing in the Academic Disciplines*). This reading by faculty from several departments led to a 1-day workshop in the fall of 1994 on the role of writing in acquiring discipline-specific knowledge that was sponsored by the College of Arts and Sciences. Our evolving scholarly interests also reflected an overall WAC trend of the time away "from emphasizing expressive writing to emphasizing students' command of the conventions of discourse communities" (Walvoord 62).

PROCESSES AND PRINCIPALS

When we looked around us in the years of 1997 and 1998, the two of us began to consider how we might pursue our goals by other means, under some rubric other than WAC. We became involved in the evolving "institutional spaces" (Walvoord 69) that WAC leaders like Walvoord, McLeod, and Maimon were recommending for sustaining interest in cross-curricular writing—assessment (McLeod and Maimon 580; Walvoord 65), general studies, and technology as a mode for innovative pedagogy (Walvoord 72). Through these activities, we began to meet faculty who had not been involved in the reading groups but who were clearly committed to teaching and who might be interested in enhancing that teaching through writing. Given our past experiences, we did more serious thinking about how dialogue might be initiated and sustained in a context of shrinking educational funding, a context in which the programmatic strategies that had been the foundation of earlier attempts at curricular change seemed less and less feasible.

It was at this point in our thinking that we began to settle on the plan of initiating and studying conversations with our cross-campus colleagues—first through carefully planned interviews and then with less formal dialogue responding to what the interviews had provided. In considering the form the interviews might take, we began with our own primary teaching concerns. We wanted to know how what we were doing in the first-year composition courses fit in with what students encountered in courses in their major programs. We wanted to know how our colleagues' experiences and observations concerning writing in their fields might fit into certain courses in the undergraduate writing major—Technical and Scientific Writing, Advanced Technical and Scientific Writing, Advanced Research Writing—or whether what we learned in the interviews suggested new courses for the program. Our reading and thinking had led us to conclude that disciplines were learned and professions practiced primarily through the medium of written language, and we were curious as to whether colleagues outside our department shared that conclusion. If they did, we wanted to know how that conclusion might be currently applied, consciously or unconsciously, to the education of their undergraduate majors.

We had more specific questions as well, regarding the kinds of writing students were doing and how closely that writing might resemble either what was assigned in composition courses or what students might encounter in professional practice or graduate school. We wanted to know if disciplinary knowledge was ever taught as "contested"—a theme often explored in our own sections of the second-semester first-year composition course (College Writing II). If so, to what extent did their students learn and apply the modes of disciplinary argumentation? We wanted to know what were considered appropriate levels of "expertise" for students receiving a bachelor's degree, and how prominent a role discipline-specific writing and reading played in that expertise. (For a copy of our schedules of interview questions, see Appendices A and B.)

In short, we had an awful lot on our plate before we even started to receive dollops of our colleagues' preoccupations, worries, and perceptions about writing and language use. We didn't need to test or even generate hypotheses. We needed to talk, to connect and communicate on a much more intense and detailed level with the faculty outside our discipline than had occurred even during the days of WAC workshops and reading groups. It may seem ironic that we had determined it was *talk* we needed in order to explore the roles *writing* was playing or could play in the learning of various disciplines. But what has happened in the interviews has tended to confirm both our instincts and the reasoning for our approach we explicated in the first chapter. Academics are surrounded by paper, and a good deal of it—minutes and memos, reminders and come-ons—is anything but edifying. Adding more print to the pile did not seem the best way to hold our colleagues' interest, even if we were convinced the material we had sent would draw them in, if only they could find the time to examine it. No. If our intent was to create an atmosphere of trust and respect (meaning, in this case, a willingness to "attend to" what someone from another discipline considered important), then there seemed no substitute for one-to-one, face-to-face talk between two respirating humans in a place as cluttered and as obviously "lived in" as the campus office of a working teacher. (See Chapter 3 for a description of the interviews' dynamics, and the lessons learned through conducting them.)

Moreover, we thought such talk was something that we, as professors in a teaching university, could contribute, just as Howard Tinberg had once been able to gather 2-year college faculty from mathematics, history, English as a second language, nursing, dental hygiene, and business in the same room to thrash out "what makes for 'good' writing in the disciplines" (6). Our experience as graduate students, our conversations with colleagues in other universities, our sense of the pressures visited on those whose primary concern must be to research and publish discipline-specific knowledge, all suggested that where we were was a more likely place than a Carnegie I institution for cross-campus talk about undergraduate learning to occur.

The demands of teaching have been the motivator for encountering faculty outside our departments on various occasions: through participation in WAC reading groups, or similar groups devoted to classroom pedagogy; through an interest in the impact of technology on teaching, or a desire to ensure that campus assessment of student learning was faculty-driven. From these acquaintances, for the most part, we chose our interviewees. We wanted to draw from a variety of disciplines, of course, and to include faculty from all four of the university's colleges at the time—Arts and Sciences, Education, Health and Human Services, Information Science and Business Administration.[5] But the primary reason for choosing the professors we did for our interviews was their obvious engagement with their teaching. They would represent their particular disciplines, epistemologies, or ideologies through the prism of that engagement. Additionally, it is important to note that our main concern at this point was to discover effective modes of conversing across disciplines about those things we considered important to undergraduate education, rather than to have a roster of conversants that covered the widest possible spectrum of disciplines possible.

Our interviews began in June 1998, with faculty members from the Sport Management, Health Education, Nursing, and Physics Departments.

---

[5]A subsequent reorganization of the university's colleges, effective in fall 2001, altered their makeup somewhat. However, the departments of our interviewees are still to be found in three of the colleges, whereas English is in the fourth—the College of Humanities, Fine and Performing Arts.

Once a date and a time was established via phone conversation, each interviewee received through the mail a schedule of the questions for the first interviews and a release form providing us with permission to use what was said while preserving participants' anonymity. Each interview was audiotaped and lasted anywhere from 75 to 90 minutes. During the interviews we also took extensive notes. Once all four initial interviews were completed, we listened to them together, making some modifications in our schedule of questions for the follow-up interviews and preparing specific questions for each colleague based on the first interview. For instance, in the case of the mathematics professor, after a discussion of similarities between English and mathematics emerged from our conversation, we asked a specific follow-up question about when and how the professor came to hold these views regarding the relationship between the two fields and whether it was also held by those who had taught him. We also asked whether or not he thought there were ways that first-year writing courses could help math majors write mathematics. When the computer science professor indicated that her students wrote documentation, we asked her to describe a systems or program documentation assignment in detail and to give us a copy. (This same pattern was followed during the round of interviews with four more colleagues that took place in the summer and fall of 1999, although the schedule of questions for all follow-up interviews was not altered after June 1998.) Participants received the follow-up interview questions before meeting with us the second time, but not the questions prepared for each one specifically.

In 1998, the only ambitions we had for our study were to initiate the kind of talk we envisioned and to meet our modest local goals. Doing a book-length treatment of our work only occurred to us in early 1999, as we began to recognize the scope of our interviews and of the questions that motivated us. One of us subsequently applied for a sabbatical in fall 2000, which was granted in May 1999, around the same time we received an internal grant from the university to hire a transcriptionist. This grant was a tribute to the kind of cross-pollination we had been driven to by the demise of campus WAC activities, as it was based on the argument that our interviews could lead to improvements in the assigning and assessing of student work in various departments.

In the summer of 1999 we began to write, working to clarify our purposes and to construct meaning from what the interviews were yielding, not to mention the years of reading the two of us had done in rhetorical theory, composition studies, developmental psychology, and phenomenology. Meanwhile, we also conducted seven more interviews between July and November with faculty from the Computer Science, Elementary Education, Health Services Administration, and Mathematics Departments. When the spring 2000 teaching term came to an end, we reviewed the audiotapes of all 15 interviews to ensure that the 217 pages of single-spaced transcripts now in our possession were clear and accurate. Then we developed a grid for analyzing the transcripts, using categories derived from the questions we had placed on our interview schedules, from our growing sense of what the interviews appeared to be telling us, from the interests that guided our scholarly reading, and from the possible book chapters we were beginning to project. Under the subject area "Chapters," subcategories on grammar, rhetoric, logic, expert knowledge, and conversing about language emerged. Under the subject area of "Modes of Conversation," a set of difficulties (assumed knowledge, semantic dissonance, negative responses, one-way communication, contradictions) and successes (repeating to confirm, agreement, recall of earlier discussions, free exchange, coining common language, sympathy statements) developed. A final subject area of related issues included subtopics such as student meta-awareness, disciplinary knowledge creation, role of liberal studies, genres, and student growth (see also Appendix C).

By this time we had not only lived the interviews, but had also listened to them and read the transcripts of them several times. We struggled—with some success, we believe—to ensure that our analyses of what was before us were not strictly controlled by a set of *a priori* categories. Passages from the transcripts would frequently be placed in more than one category, with the page number and lines inserted in particular cells on the grid. When preparing to draft a chapter we would first list all the categories that might be appropriate to the chapter's subject matter. Then we would plow through each transcript and list the passages from each one that fit into the designated categories. As we did so, the themes and structures of a chapter would begin to emerge, as would new categories. Sometimes our re-examination of the transcripts led us to segments we had not originally thought appropriate. Even while composing we would recall material that seemed "right" for our discussion of the moment, the appropriateness of which we could not have earlier anticipated.

Drafting of our current Chapters 4 through 7 began in early July 2000. We had decided the previous summer that, in keeping with what we saw as the dialogic nature of our entire enterprise, we would ask our interviewees to read and respond to certain chapters. They would provide us with our first reader-responses, and would have the opportunity to see how we were using and building on the interview material to explore problems and questions regarding the teaching of undergraduate writing that seemed to involve both English composition teachers and themselves. This approach still seems to us an excellent idea, but it also put us under a self-imposed gun. (Given our limited time for composing, our plan for respondent reading of chapter drafts may have been a useful incentive for getting on with it; it also heightened the tyranny of deadline writing.) We felt the proposed chapters needed to be in our colleagues' hands well before the mid-term point of the coming fall semester, in the hope that they would not already feel overwhelmed by their classroom and service obligations, and could give the material something approaching the attention we thought it deserved. That hope gave us a time frame of around 11 to 12 weeks in which to write relatively polished drafts of four chapters.

Understandably enough, several key decisions were made during this intensive period of writing. Early on, for instance, we decided to present material from the transcripts in generally large chunks, rather than resort to much paraphrasing and summarizing. We wanted to preserve the voices of our colleagues, and to give our readers a feel for the kinds of discussions that the interviews had spawned. Although arguments we wanted to develop would appear in each chapter, we wanted those arguments clearly related to both the content and the communicative dynamics of the interviews themselves. In other words, we wanted the interviews to generate much of our written discussion, even as we ruminated on, and sometimes explored possible solutions to various issues we had either anticipated or been surprised by.

There were also alterations in the focus and structure of the four chapters we had settled on for initial drafting. In our original plan these chapters had been tentatively entitled Grammar, Logic, Rhetoric, and Expert Knowledge. The first three of these chapters were meant to relate what our colleagues told us of the language practices found in their disciplines and classrooms to the educational trivium of rhetoric, dialectic and grammar that had emerged among the Greeks during the fourth century BC (Wagner 9). Such an arrangement would reflect our concern, similar to that of Scholes, that English clearly re-establish itself as a Liberal Art and as an integral element in any university's program of general studies. But once we began to thoroughly examine our transcripts and to write, our scheme seemed too reductive and misleading. Entitling one chapter "Logic" would de-emphasize the sense of argumentation as containing a variety of audience appeals we saw emerging from both our interviews and much contemporary research into disciplinary and workplace writing. Entitling another "Rhetoric" would suggest that rhetoric was merely equivalent to both persuasive appeals and linguistic form. Such an arrangement might be pleasing to those who still agreed with the 16th-century French scholar Peter Ramus that rhetoric should be separate from the invention and organization of texts, while focusing solely on style (Corbett and Connors 502). But it would do violence to our own view of rhetoric as an art encompassing all "the available means of persuasion" (Aristotle, "Rhetoric" 595), including both argumentation and style.

Moreover, the original chapter titles might serve to de-emphasize our abiding interest in the teaching of genres, along with all the contemporary scholarly activity accompanying that interest, such as dialogism, activity theory, and genre theory. Our thinking had gradually settled on the notion that we would first talk in order to connect with and learn from our colleagues in other disciplines; we would then write in order to reflect on the interviews, our initial questions and concerns, our reading and thinking about how and what to teach undergraduates about writing. In fact, our question schedules had contained no specific interest in issues of usage and style, but the concerns of our respondents appeared to make a chapter devoted to those issues imperative. If English studies were to truly take their place as a 21st-century liberal art, they would hardly do so by ignoring such concerns.

Eventually we arrived at the arrangement you see in this book. Chapter 3 explores the dynamics of the interviews themselves: how we negotiated meaning, made personal and professional contact, acknowledged and discussed individual concerns, and discovered areas of possible mutual action. In the subsequent four chapters, as we've said, we simply jump into a snake pit of issues, problems, and questions that may confront any one seriously working through how best to help undergraduates grow and develop as thinking, astute, and effective practicing writers and professionals. Sometimes we find ourselves arguing with our colleagues; at other times we acknowledge the sobering realities of their perceptions. Sometimes we explore strategies or attitudes that might help either them or us; sometimes we consider, painfully or otherwise, just what we might do about our own assignments and courses. Always we hope to convey the valuable fermentation that can be triggered by direct, embodied conversation across disciplines, as distant as a humanities-oriented English often seems from those of our respondents.

Chapter 4 reviews what we learned about classroom, disciplinary, and professional genres from our colleagues, reflecting on how best to approach the teaching of genre, drawing on the perspectives of activity theorists, researchers into academic and nonacademic writing, writing center and WAC scholars, and the phenomenology of Merleau-Ponty. Chapter 5 considers the scope of inquiry and argumentation as discussed in the interviews, along with the difficulties and challenges of teaching written disputation to our students. Where should knowledge be presented as "contested," it asks, as it ruefully acknowledges how limited such a presentation must be in first-year composition. Chapter 6 examines the kinds of professional and extra-disciplinary "expertise" our colleagues would like undergraduates to eventually possess, and the role of writing in gaining and executing such expertise. Something of a culmination, this chapter also raises interesting and difficult questions regarding the meaning of expertise for both citizens and beginning professionals within a complex world of fragmented knowledge, questions that we feel anyone attempting to organize a general studies curriculum should address.

Chapter 7 addresses the concerns of our colleagues regarding style and "good grammar," concerns that were not necessarily primary to us at the beginning of our study but that professors in other disciplines seemed to commonly associate with writing in their classrooms. We relate their observations and worries to the points of view of experienced composition teachers such as ourselves, as well as to recent scholarship in linguistics and in educational studies. Our final chapter reviews some of the major themes or problems explored within our book, while considering their implications for an undergraduate education in rhetoric. The impact of exchanges among professional equals about writing may be most apparent in this chapter, as we ponder the possible implications of those exchanges on our own first-year composition requirement and on our English curriculum more generally.

AN ENDING AND A BEGINNING

By the end of September 2000 we had completed our drafts of Chapters 4–7, and were ready to obtain responses from our colleagues participating in the study. It was just about 3 weeks before mid-term grades were due, a little later than we had originally hoped. But although we knew the period of writing that had just passed must be intense, we were determined that it not be rushed. Accompanying the four chapter drafts were a cover letter, individual sheets for writing responses to each of the chapters, and a copy of the first two pages of the book prospectus we had composed in the summer of 1999. Each interviewee was instructed to read the chapters and to record their thoughts regarding each one on the response sheets. Once the chapters were read and responses were written, the interviewees met again with the person who had conducted their first two interviews. These meetings took approximately 20–30 minutes and were audiotaped but not transcribed. In these final face-to-face discussions, respondents were invited to ask questions and add any reactions to the chapters they had not managed to record on the sheets. Materials from those sheets (designated within parentheses by the subject area of the professor who wrote on them) and the audiotapes (indicated by the phrase "Draft Response Interview") now appear in various places within our chapters, building on or adding to what we had learned in the main interviews.[6]

---

[6]All quoted material from the main interviews indicates the subject area of the featured professor and the date on which the interview took place. All interview material is *italicized*. **Bolded** print indicates statements by the author conducting the interview and non-bolded print indicates statements by the interviewee.

In gathering together these materials, we could see that we had again counted on the good will and graciousness of colleagues in the midst of a fully loaded teaching semester. One was immersed in the writing of two grant applications. Two others were busy pulling together materials for agencies that evaluated and accredited their major degree programs. One of those was able to read and respond to our chapters during the tedium of a week on jury duty. Nevertheless, all eight faculty members made time for us. and their honest responses have contributed greatly to revisions and, we hope, improvements we have made in our manuscript.

We could have finished our work without the complications such cross-disciplinary reader responses were bound to create. But, while we believe the primary readers of this book will be composition specialists like ourselves, who are concerned with the way what we teach about writing connects to the writing our students later perform, we also hope that significant segments are accessible to colleagues outside our field, and can be used to stimulate further dialogue of the type we seek to model here. Moreover, failing to seek out those responses would have been, for us, a violation of the spirit that has compelled us to undertake our cross-campus talk in the first place. If we are to continue our conversations, then we must first see how respondents interpret our initial accommodations of the interview results to ancient and persistent challenges involved in teaching the art of eloquence, to a literature of educational and composition studies, and to a phenomenology we hope will serve as a counter to current divisions of academic knowledge.

Although much writing and thinking remained, the gathering of our colleagues' responses to chapter drafts essentially marked the end of this particular study. For us, it has been a stimulating journey, inviting us to freshen our thinking about issues regarding writing and teaching that have preoccupied us for years. The discussions with our colleagues have been a pleasure throughout, and even the writing of this book has proven to be a deeply satisfying and enjoyable experience. We hope the readers of what follows perceive the value cross-disciplinary talk about writing might have for their campus, for the learning that can occur and the connections that can be made, to the eventual benefit of our students. How can we expect students to link the various disparate elements of their undergraduate educations, to grasp both the vastness and the limitations of human knowledge, unless we attempt to forge such links ourselves? We are convinced of the necessity of our conversations, and plan to pursue them further by all possible means.

3

In Search of Recognition

The Dynamics of the Interviews

> . . . if there were not some community of feelings among mankind, however varying in different persons—I mean to say, if every man's feelings were peculiar to himself and were not shared by the rest of his species—I do not see how we could ever communicate our impressions to one another.
>
> —Plato (*Gorgias*, 481)

What we fear the most, as we set about describing how our interviews unfolded, is that, to borrow a metaphor from Bakhtin, we will end up transposing a "symphonic . . . theme on to the piano keyboard" (*Dialogic* 263). The conversations were so rich and varied that it seems we cannot avoid reducing them to something much more paltry within the pages of this book. Writing allows us to spin out long thoughts, to do things like closely examining the nature of "genre" (see Chapter 4) or differentiating among the meanings of "grammar" (see Chapter 7), things that in talk might only manage to bore a companion silly. Conversation is multivoiced, on the other hand, ever shifting in rhythm and pitch and intensity, able to engage participants in an immediate, palpably physical manner that the most adept writing may emulate but not duplicate. The interviews have taken the complexities, frustrations, and passions of our teaching lives off the page and into the presence of another.

If we could sum up the value of the interviews, it may be in the establishment of an embodied identity that has become attached to our contemplation of such words as "discipline" and "profession." Again, we want to make sure that no one mistakes any of us as representative of some field of study. And yet, it is inescapable that we *are* English at a smallish comprehensive state university, just as our colleagues *are* Nursing and Physics and Health Education, and so on. We are also, in conversation, much, much more. Our purpose remains to build on the recognition that each of us is *this* and more than *this*, members of professions but members and professions interacting within a peculiar environment, and within peculiar historic, political, economic, social, and academic processes. Through this recognition we may act in a knowing way for the learning of our students.

When we initiated our interviews we knew that understanding, much less agreement, might sometimes prove an elusive thing. Our differing perspectives, evolved through both distinct experience and purposeful professional training, have proven their value within our culture. If composition and rhetoric are to be re-identified as liberal "arts," then it will probably happen through a kind of creative tension with other disciplines, where writing and rhetoric are always present but uniquely so (Leff 32). Continuing our cross-campus talk may even result in more frequent disagreement, not less, because "to argue with someone is to show a sign of deep respect" (Crosswhite 96). To disagree, one must recognize the presence of another. We accept James Crosswhite's idea that making claims to others is to recognize our "connections" with them and a "responsibility for oneself." We "acknowledge the claims others have on us" by making our own "claims explicit" and therefore "hearing them as questionable" (73-74). We place ourselves in danger, then, of being changed into both a person and a discipline different from what we once were (75). The alternative, unfortunately, is an "indifference" by which we will remain "departmentalized," one point in an academic circle with neither a center, nor a common meeting place, such as the agora of ancient Athens.

To admit that we might be changed by a conversation with a colleague is to say that we will listen to what they have to say, and too often it is speaking rather than listening that has been associated with those who teach. For Aristotle in *The Metaphysics*, as for Plato in the *Dialogues*, it is those intent on a truth beyond appearances who know and can teach. Socrates teaches much but listens rather little, constructing the argument to bring the other to his conclusion. But we also know by trusting what we see and by our attentiveness to what others can tell us, not just to what we ourselves find out. To know we need to listen to the experiences of others as much as we speak about what we have found.

For the well-known biologist Barbara McClintock, it is those longest in the academy who become most one-sided in their thinking, even blind to their assumptions.

[McClintock] found no difficulty with young scientists, but she felt that with too many of her colleagues age brought on a hardening of mental arteries. Years of reading the literature, or listening to seminars, make it more rather than less difficult for them to become aware of their assumptions, to hear something new. (Keller 178)

The mode of scholarship to which McClintock refers can become a stumbling block, for the listening has been all in one direction. Notice how the very idea of truth seeking can suggest the taking of a narrow, linear path, and can turn us away from the circularity of conversation. In such a mode, one can argue only by displacing the point one has arrived at, as a prelude to "progressing" farther.

Wishing to be more inclusive, some disciplines have hoped to avoid the implication that truth is singular or "universal," as we used to say, by acknowledging the ground from which they speak. But such an attitude does not really remove the difficulty of acknowledging the presence of, or listening to, another. Too often, this posture persists in offering only a vantage point for recognizing individual, or relatively small, group linear trajectories (i.e., "where I'm or we're coming from," or "my or our view or stand point"). This idea of multiple perspectives has been the only alternative to having a god's eye view of things. Its logic assumes either that we cannot see another's point of view at all, or that we can only do so by imaginatively placing ourselves in the other's perspective, rather than really listening to someone next to us.

With such an understanding of multiple perspectives, there really is no conversation, but rather a multiplication of "individual" points of view. Such a line of sight acknowledges the object, but not other subjects, as if it were beyond us to really listen to each other. Our conversations with our colleagues belie such an attitude. For Merleau-Ponty, a "perspectival" attitude, or intellectual line of sight, makes the world "flat," whereas a "perceptual," lived attitude gives the world we behold "depth" and texture. This model of face-to-face encounter seems more congruent with what we have experienced in conversation with our colleagues. Here the shared background of the world is lived, not an intellectual or disciplinary landscape, and an object is most fully understood when those looking from each direction speak and are heard by all others. The usual metaphor of the pursuit of truth along a disciplinary path opens up and transcendence is lateral. In the flesh, we live among things, and "alter ego"—"lateral consciousness thrown outside itself"—closes up strict linearity and allows for face-to-face encounter (*Visible and Invisible* 243).

Sociologist Dorothy Smith suggests a difference between conceptual space and concrete place when she asks:

> Can we . . . come to rest in an acceptance of the intrinsic many-sidedness of our worlds and therefore of the many stories that may be told of it, of which ours is only one? . . . suppose we pose the problem at a more mundane level where we are not grappling with notions of truth. (121)

Her idea is to begin disciplinary inquiry by listening to those who will be the subjects of inquiry, and formulating questions based on those outside the discourse. In some ways, we have done the same thing by starting with colleagues outside our discipline and by meeting them face-to-face in conversation. We can return to the perceptual ground of lived experience—a ground that disciplines ordinarily hold suspect and doubt—as a condition of doing inquiry. Multiple points of view signal habitation of a shared ground not threatened by the angles of different perspectives, even though the existence of those different perspectives is openly acknowledged. One's view is less complete the more one has not heard from every direction. A phenomenology of lived experience comes close to Crosswhite's idea of mutual respect.

If we choose to continue our conversations, then our salvation is in the dynamic nature of the activity, where neither disagreement nor commonality lasts. In talk, "mutual understanding" is *"practically managed . . . rather than a series of actual mental states that precede and result from it"* (Edwards 20). Within our interviews, the presence of the other ensured that dissonance was often quickly recognized and that concepts couched in some particular form could be just as quickly modified. We were glad that our colleagues, for instance, could feel free enough to criticize their counterparts in English for passing through students still capable of careless prose, or for emphasizing personal expression at the possible expense of proper usage (see Chapter 7). We were also glad that our presence ensured the discussion would not stop there, but would push our colleagues into further thinking about their assertions. The following is an exchange we had with the sport management professor subsequent to his criticism of English for allowing students to pass the first-year composition courses.

> **. . . You might decide that what we're going to do is focus on something like . . . public discourse, because maybe we can do that. We can't anticipate the type of reading they're going to do in Sport Management. We can't anticipate how specifically they're writing in Sport Management. . . .**
>
> *You have so many people coming from so many areas and each area has a different expectation. . . . I want to establish a linkage between these other programs—Communication, English, Computer Science; that we have our students taking, to where I*

> can go in and say, "Now look, this is what we would like to see."
> Is it possible? What do you feel? Because I think that's important.
>
> (Sport Management, June 12, 1998)

Our presence, we believe, took the sport management professor from a simple expression of frustration with student writing to an exploration of possible avenues of mutual assistance, even though that assistance might lead to an outcome somewhat different from the one he originally had in mind. And this came from the health services administration professor immediately after his complaints that concern about sentence fragments, verb tense, and misspellings appeared to be taking a back seat to work on self-expression and persuasive argument.

> The challenge is, I think it's real hard to do in 4 years . . . there's been an exponential growth of knowledge that at the level of this institution, which is an undergraduate institution; I think it's just a real tough job. And I think what we have is people gravitate toward what they do well . . . maybe in terms of the way the university serves our undergraduates . . . it's appropriate to say that people out there . . . are talking about expression, as opposed to someone like myself that's talking about tool use and content. I think we . . . probably overall get the job done pretty well . . . I'm proud of the students that we graduate out of the program and I think part of their strengths doesn't just reflect what I've taught but what faculty outside the health service administration program have taught them as well.
>
> (Health Services Administration, July 1, 1999)

The statements just presented may be considered mere olive branches, as strategies for either softening a blow or preventing further conflict. That's fine with us, because the manner in which the speaker forms such ameliorative utterances, given the presence of another, creates possibilities for further discussion, whether the speaker balances criticism with praise or seeks alternatives to a current mode of action. Do we really meet face-to-face on the ground of disciplinary specialties, saying, "Here is a physicist, or a philosopher, or a social scientist, or a computer scientist, or a literary theorist, or a compositionist?" If we do share disciplinary perspectives, are we destined to see eye to eye? The sorting operations of such categorical imperatives are part of analytical thought, not face-to-face interaction. Putting labels on ourselves, and others, constitutes a precipitate abstraction of what it means to be sentient and embodied—to converse face to face. Here we are caught up in the presence, not some essence, of another.

The dynamic fluidity of such exchanges can dissolve more than disciplinary boundaries. In fact, it is when we lose sight of the flesh-and-blood person face to face that we do not see eye to eye. A gaze that acknowledges the presence of another acknowledges someone who looks back. Having "someone who looks back" serves to guarantee that critical positions will neither fester nor remain unexamined; thinking moves forward because a possible challenger to the correctness or accuracy of a position has been recognized. In *Subjectivity without Subjects*, Oliver adopts the strange concept of "witnessing to the recognition of non-recognition" in order to respect difference and to battle her way back from the assumption that we see categories, not "flesh and blood" people, places, and things (176-78). But both James Mark Baldwin and Merleau-Ponty acknowledge that we are only a mental representation of ourselves, when we ourselves are not present to each other. There is a whole other dynamic in the realm of sensory perception that can surprise our assumptions about difference.

For Piaget, the stage of "deferred" imitation, what he called "true" imitation, was imitation in the absence of the model (see Chapter 4). He valued its priority precisely as a sign of the child's development of representational capacity on the way to becoming a little scientist, which he equated with becoming an adult. Such an adult was able to represent all of reality formally and mathematically, and supposedly had surpassed the false illusions of perception. Could it be that there is another road to truth than this narrow path that privileges individual consciousness, as if words were all we know of each other?

Rather than seeing argument as a good, as a sign of respect, an acknowledgment of the presence of another, and as a spur to further thought, our culture has developed an aversion to the word and sometimes to the activity it represents. It takes only conflicting battles among individual viewpoints, with each seeing from a different perspective, as its model for argument. For some, this pejorative connotation could be due to a tacit realization that argument can threaten a comfortably frozen self-identity. But for others, "argument" has come to be equated with intellectually aimless attacks, destructive rather than transformative. It's a word for which rhetoricians have a fondness, but others may prefer different terms carrying a more positive emotional freight. Like Lakoff and Johnson, philosophers of ordinary language, our colleagues may offer kinder substitutes for the metaphor of argument as "war" (89).

> *I think that if you make it too difficult for the students to understand what you're trying to say, then you've kind of lost them. Again, I think we end up with that sort of theory, and if it's not practical, then at least from where we're looking in, for the most part, I don't think it's relevant.*

. . . does this stuff get argued about when you go to conferences?

Yes. Not necessarily argued, but discussed.

What I mean by argument, is somebody putting forward a position like you just did, that it's got to work a lot better if somebody does research in which the information . . . from research is intelligible to somebody who is a practitioner in the field. I think that's what you're saying.

That's it.

Okay. You're taking a position . . . somebody else might come and say, "Wait a minute. If we're going to be a legitimate academic discipline we've got to make sure we employ rigorous scientific methods. We have to make sure that when we present conclusions about something in sport management that it's going to be couched in these particularly rigorous statistical methods of how we did it or whatever."

That's the controversy; not controversy, but there's a lot of discussions going on the last four, five years. It's almost like; it's almost some of the group wants to break away. In fact, I know they do.

Why do you hesitate from calling it a controversy, then?

It's, because I don't think it's; I guess when I think of the word controversy, I think of people losing control. And right now it's a healthy discussion, I guess is what I would call it.

(Sport Management, June 12, 1998)

DEVELOPING ORDINARY LANGUAGE

During conversation we can be content with the term *healthy discussion,* if it appears that by the term the conversants mean disagreement that does more than encourage a lack of recognition of the other. Instead, conversants see a complex and valued interlocutor beside them, one whose ideas are propelled forward by motives both practical and altruistic. The interviews contained many such exchanges; struggles to discover an "ordinary" language, as we said in Chapter 1, a mutually grasped meaning for terms introduced by either us or our colleagues in other disciplines. Merleau-Ponty, in acknowledging that motives are external as well as internal, reminds us of the way that the ideas of others can solicit our responsiveness, rather than provoke our reaction (*Visible and Invisible* 244-45). We assume this is a necessary feature of any serious conversation between people from different disciplines, although it could also be a feature of conversations even within a discipline. Such shared meanings need not seem permanent to be useful, but may need renewal in subsequent conversations. Those engaged in discursive psychology assign the label "indexicality" to this "feature of talk-in-interaction in which the specific sense and reference of a word is relative to the precise context of its utterance" (Edwards 100).

Another possible occurrence in our talk was that no shared meaning could be discovered, but the conversants chose to let their dissonance stand instead. Perhaps in some future time the conflict in meaning could be resolved, but not presently. In both interviews with our mathematics professor, a question came up as to whether students' difficulties with word problems could be more appropriately called a "math problem" or an "English problem." Our own tendency was to avoid the dichotomy and to see the problem as one involving the use of language in mathematics. But one could tell by the end of both exchanges that the mathematics professor still wasn't "buying" that perception.

> *. . . all math courses have word problems in it. There's always a student who says, "I can do the math, but I just don't know how to set the problem up." I almost lose my temper. But I tend to tell them, "That's not a math problem; it's an English problem." You've got to be able to read words and know what they mean. You know, when the problem says something like, "A farmer wants to fence in a rectangular plot of land." You should be able to look at that and know you're going to draw a picture of a rectangle. When you don't, that's not a math problem; the problem somewhere is that you can read the words but you're not putting forth the effort in actually listening to the words and seeing what they mean.*
>
> **That's interesting though. Because that gets to the nub of a few things that concern us, which is, we can compartmentalize these things. We can say, "Well, that's a math problem; that's an English problem." But the difficulty is that mathematics; we wonder if mathematics poses particular kinds of English problems. For instance, we may not be able to anticipate or grasp how we can help our students with that particular type of English problem. You see what I'm getting at?**
>
> *Well, I think part of it is going the other way, not from reading a word problem and coming up with mathematics, but going the other way, going from mathematics and talking about your solution. There is a real need for students to understand how you present something like this. You are not supposed to be writing the great American novel. You should be using nice short sentences that are to the point but convey everything that you need to say.*
>
> (Mathematics, August 6, 1999)

The difficulty appears to have been momentarily resolved by the acknowledgment that there are problems with language endemic to mathematics, such as the verbal presentation of a mathematical proof. The student can't write or orally present this material in a style or form that may be permissible in an English course ("the great American novel"). At the same time, the mathematics professor may still very well see the student's failure to grasp what mathematical procedures are necessary for the solution of a word problem as a manifestation of poor reading ability, and therefore something that belongs within the purview of our discipline rather than his. Such an interpretation seems borne out by the following exchange from our second interview, although it's also important to note that this interview occurred more than 3 months after the first.

> *... we're starting to get into word problems. That's where you definitely see it, because what you hear is, "I can solve the equation, but I have trouble setting it up." I always tell them, "That's not a math problem; that's an English problem. You don't know what you're reading. If it says something like a rectangular backyard, you've got to be able to process that and say, okay, that means it's a rectangle and rectangles have length and width and I know all these nice things about rectangles." And people won't do that. They see rectangular yard and they're thinking back to when they had a swing set.*
>
> **Yeah, there you go. There's that ambiguity coming in there. But see, I would argue that that is a math problem as well. It's a math problem because, somehow or other, they're not perceiving they have to use language in math.**
>
> *I think then that's not a math problem; that's a teaching math problem. I'll agree with you one hundred percent there.*
>
> (Mathematics, November 12, 1999)

We escaped the disagreement this time through the coining of a new phrase ("a teaching math problem") that at least seems to shift responsibility for the student's failing from the English teacher to the math teacher. But we are still left with a gap created by an association of language use with "teaching" rather than with mathematics. More conversation between this professor and ourselves might eventually cause one of us to shift, but in the interest of moving on to other matters, the question is abandoned at this point. It's natural to wonder how long talk could be sustained if we persisted in focusing on a particularly stubborn problem regarding meaning.

Many of our struggles to develop an "ordinary" or "common" language began with the questions we had scheduled and continued on into explorations of distinctions current in the particular discipline of our respondent. The interview format is designed, of course, to be "asymmetrical" (Edwards 127), with our non-English colleague expected to do most of the talking. Questions about the meaning of terms used in our schedules, which the interviewees had received in advance, allowed for a shift in responsibility back to us. One source of initial confusion, for instance, involved the terms *academic*, *nonacademic*, and *practitioner* found in Questions 2, 3, and 4 of the "Schedule of First Interview Questions" (see Appendix A). Was a health educator teaching in a high school an "academic?" What about a physicist doing basic research within the research and development (R&D) department of a large, publicly incorporated power company? If our health education professor taught a liberal studies course aimed at educating students regarding healthful behaviors, was he at that moment functioning as an "academic" or a "practitioner?"

Am I an academic. . . ?

Yeah.

Okay.

This is an interesting distinction. I'm thinking that we didn't really even think about it because we'd have to say, I guess, in one way that somebody that's doing health education in schools is an academic setting too, but not academic meaning higher education.

That's a good question. What we are attempting to do with a number of undergraduate programs here, but I can speak directly to the community health and the school health programs, is that we are preparing people to carry out these things in terms of behavior change, social systems change, environmental improvement, and so on. We are preparing people to do that with other populations. Now, it just so happens with Community Health they're going to be dealing with all populations . . . in fact, the distinction has been made within health education that, yeah, you have the higher faculty and then you have the practitioners, but like you said, there's an argument for saying we're all practitioners. For example, I teach courses in personal health which are for non-majors. I teach a course in human sexuality, which a lot of non-majors take. Well, we're teaching those courses to help people make healthier decisions about a lot of life issues. Not always with the intent of preparing them to teach those topical areas to somebody else.

(Health Education, June 16, 1998)

If our questions were meant to survey a given population for the purpose of supporting or falsifying various hypotheses, then they would obviously have to be rewritten to eliminate a monumental "validity" problem (Sudman and Bradburn 17). Our respondents were sometimes either initially confused by the terms *academic, nonacademic,* and *practitioner,* or prone to giving the terms interpretations quite distinct from each other, interpretations that seemed to best fit what went on in their disciplines. But with our dialogic approach, we can note the positive effect the terms had in prompting our colleagues to explain important distinctions within the practice of their disciplines. These distinctions sometimes proved valuable when we discussed the various kinds of professional discourse generated within a discipline as well. We can trace, for example, how initial reactions to the second question in the first interview by both us and the physics professor led to further refinements in explanations regarding both laboratory and discursive practices. At first, an equation was made between "academic" and "theoretical" work.

> *Does academic mean just in an educational setting?*
>
> **Well, no. Actually I would like you to tell me what it means for your field. I guess . . . probably in a science field it might even be that R and D takes place in industry or in nonacademic settings, but still has that theoretical character we associate with academics and the humanities.**
>
> *. . . if you looked at the different kinds of organizations in which physics research could be done, whether it's experimental or theoretical, it's not confined just to the universities . . . if you look at the way things are organized, there's the university environment, and there are outside organizations, some sponsored by government, government laboratories that tend to become at-large, and then there are private companies/industries that do research that is pretty variable on the continuum from applied to basic. Some industries spend a significant amount of money in basic research and others don't. So . . . a person that is trained in physics could work in all three of those areas—the university, the government lab, or the private and be doing what could be considered academic research in all three.*
>
> (Physics, June 22, 1998)

At this point, the distinction between "academic" and "nonacademic" appears to be completely muddied, at least if we think of these two terms in a framework of "place," or of geographical distance. But now there are additional terms in play to confuse us. Are we saying that academic research is "basic" rather than "theoretical?" Is basic research also theoretical, or can it be theoretical or experimental? Clearly, we have to do more conversational "work" here to get these questions answered. And this work occurs, several minutes further into the interview, triggered by a lingering tendency on our part to equate theoretical with basic and experimental with applied.

> *... how would you describe the difference between an application then and theory. Can you give me examples of what you consider applied physics and what you consider theoretical physics?*
>
> *Well, actually I'm not sure that those two things are exactly related. I mean, because ... what we would say is the classification would be experimental and theoretical, and applied could have experimental or theoretical components. So, from my point of view, applied means ... that the ultimate goal is not just the development of knowledge, but is something that is going to be useful in the sense that it results in some benefit to mankind. You're going to make a piece of equipment or the theory is going to allow somebody else to make something, something physical that could be used. So basic research can have experimental or theoretical components, and so can applied. So it's really what is the end result. So the basic research is just concerned with the discovery of knowledge for the sake of the discovery, and applied research some goal to help society in some way.*
>
> (Physics, June 22, 1998)

All this work put into definition begins to pay dividends just a few moments later, when we get to Question 7 in our schedule, asking what "professional materials" an "academic" or a "nonacademic practitioner" in physics would read. The professor replies that "the distinction between academic and nonacademic" is not appropriate, because theoretical physicists will read theoretical material and experimental physicists will read the experimental kind, regardless of whether they view themselves as academics, or as involved in basic or applied research (June 22, 1998). It would appear that the distinctions we introduced toward the beginning of the interview are inoperative, but they have circuitously led us to distinctions regarding professional discourse that are useful. A similar progression occurred in the first interview with the mathematics professor, who also suggested quite early on that the distinction between academic and nonacademic would be much less useful than one between "pure" and "applied" mathematics. "Pure math has more to do with conjecture and proof and not necessarily of physical objects. Applied math usually has its basis in some real problem that's ... to be solved" (August 6, 1999). At the same time, there can be blurring in actual disciplinary practice. For instance, when we asked if the recent solution of Fermat's Theorem was an example of "pure math" the professor agreed, but then added:

In Search of Recognition: The Dynamics of the Interviews 43

> . . . the two interrelate because in talking about Fermat's Last Theorem, which is a number theory problem, the number theory is strictly a pure discipline. But on the other hand, number theory has led to lots of studies on prime numbers. . . . It is prime numbers that are used in what's called Public Key Encryption System, which is what lets your MAC card be a secure instrument. Lets you beam credit card numbers around and know that nobody's picking them off in cyberspace because it's converted it into a code. Fermat's Last Theorem itself, I think it's a totally pure mathematics problem, but since it took 350 years to solve, it brought on a lot of different studies that end up being applied.
>
> (Mathematics, August 6, 1999)

Nor can we equate "pure math" with "academic" settings and "applied" with work in industry and government.

So you resist . . . splitting up into academic and nonacademic, because you feel that they cross over so often that the boundary is so fuzzy?

Yeah. I would consider the National Security Agency one of the larger private [sic] employers of mathematicians. But even through their work is based on codes and breaking codes, they hire a lot of pure mathematicians based on their attitude that even if we don't know an application now, eventually we'll find an application for what you're doing. The same thing when you're in academics. You could be in applied math and do your research in applied subjects and still be an academic person. So I tend not to break it up along those lines. I will admit there are much fewer pure mathematicians in industry but they do exist.

(Mathematics, August 6, 1999)

As is seen in Chapter 5, the last scheduled question for the first interview, on "rules of evidence" and "modes of proof," led us down several interesting paths. One thing that was clear, however, is that we were using language in that question that was not quickly recognizable to our colleagues. We may have thought we were directly addressing elements of disciplinary argumentation used to determine the acceptability of knowledge proffered by scholarship in a field. But the sport management and health services administration professors responded to the question by discussing the accreditation processes for academic programs (June 12, 1998) and health care institutions (July 1, 1999), respectively. Both professors did discuss argumentation within the knowledge-generating discourse of their disciplines at other points in their interviews (e.g., the sport management professor carefully explained what he meant by "practical research" and "descriptive statistics" for example, but not in direct response to the one question we thought would lead to discussions of critical thinking about disciplinary knowledge).

In other interviews, it was the back-and-forth immediacy of dialogue that led us to discover bases for disciplinary knowledge our strict adherence to notions of academic argumentation had not anticipated. The nursing professor described kinds of direct perception as "evidence" for making clinical judgments, rather than discussing some stable rules a professional would follow in judging evidence.

> **It seems to prejudice the questions a little bit for us to ask it in that way.**
>
> Well, I tell you, I immediately went to . . .
>
> **Right. You just simply went to what you consider as evidence, but you wouldn't; you didn't use the word "rule," for instance.**
>
> No. No, although we write computer programs that use the word "rule" in heuristics.
>
> **Right.**
>
> Rule of thumb. If this, look for that.
>
> **And you used the term "diagnostic reasoning". . .**
>
> (Nursing, June 17, 1998)

Curiously enough, it is the Greek-derived "heuristic" that appears here as the rhetorical term with which the nursing professor seems comfortable. We may never have thought of including that term in a question about the development of discipline-specific knowledge. Through the same conversational process, the phrase "mode of proof" was given a decidedly practical interpretation by the computer science professor.

> **. . . I guess ultimately you're saying, with the grammar of the programming language set-up, a mode of proof is that it runs. That's another . . .**
>
> And not that it just runs once. That it runs all the time with not only the test data, but the data that's supplied by a user.
>
> **Okay.**
>
> So that would be the mode of proof.
>
> **. . . Now, what would they mean by . . . it runs, but it's not relevant?**
>
> Meaning, I get output.

> **You get output, but...**
>
> It's disorganized. I can't understand it, or it's wrong. [Laughing.]
>
> **Okay, all right, so the program can conceivably run, but give you erroneous data.**
>
> Right, or just print out column headings.
>
> **Okay. I gotcha. All right. So that would be one mode of proof for a practitioner. Are there other things?...**
>
> (Computer Science, August 12, 1999)

The schedule of questions for the second interview (see Appendix B) seemed to generate less work toward discovering an "ordinary" language, and might be considered less rich for that reason, even if more readily accessible to our colleagues. Difficulties with the word "genre" in Question 5 are explored in Chapter 4. Two professors needed brief reminders of the denotative meaning of "pedagogies" in Question 4. In the case of the mathematics professor, we anticipated his question for two reasons. One was that he had chided us at the beginning of the first interview about our use of "fifty-cent" words in the question schedule. A second involved a prejudgment or assumption of ours that professors in his field may not be as familiar with the language of educational studies and teaching "method" as others might, a prejudice our mathematics professor sometimes seemed to consciously reinforce.

> **Let's go on to number 4. Which is, could you list the different pedagogies; that's a fancy word for teaching, right?**
>
> Actually that was going to be my first question to you. Give me a good definition for that.
>
> **... different methods that you will use in the classroom to help the students learn the material, and how frequently you use them.**
>
> Unfortunately, 99% of the time it's straight lecture. Part of that is my hazing attitude, which is that it was good enough for me and that's what I'm comfortable with and that's what I'm going to do.
>
> **You guys are going to pay for my youth.**
>
> That's right.
>
> (Mathematics, November 12, 1999)

There is a certain playfulness to this exchange, of course; other parts of his interviews indicate that our colleague in mathematics approached his teaching with considerable seriousness, and that the "ninety-nine percent" figure for "straight lecture" is most likely a gross exaggeration. At the same time, our mathematics professor and others among our respondents did perceive a "disconnect" between the focus of their doctoral programs, as well as the focus of their disciplinary colleagues in the research universities, and the necessary teaching work of the institutions in which they now found themselves. The gap between professional training and professional practice within many areas of higher education, including literature and composition studies, has received considerable notice of late, but may be most obvious where teaching occupies almost all of a faculty member's time between September and May. Our question about "pedagogies" simply reinforced the sport management professor's belief in the need for doctoral programs to reflect this reality.

> *Now, by pedagogies do you mean like group work, lectures?*
> **Any kind of teaching approach.**
> *. . . I'm very much a believer in . . . critical teaching, whereas I like to see myself more as a facilitator than as a "leading expert in the field" type of thing . . . one of my concerns about my doctoral program was that . . . I didn't take any pedagogy class with it. So it seemed funny to me, because I was a high school teacher for a couple years and we took a lot of method classes and everything else at the undergraduate level and yet when you prepare for your doctoral program, where you're actually teaching people in college rather than in high school, I would think that the quality of learning how to teach would be better. But there wasn't any pedagogy classes. So we never learned how to teach. And that was one of my concerns. That was one of the things on my evaluation when I got done with my doctorate; . . . that it seems to me you should teach us how to teach if that's what we're going into.*
>
> (Sport Management, July 27, 1998)

Our physics professor saw himself as something different, as not the "prototypical physicist," as "left of center" because early in his career as a teacher he developed an interest in pedagogy, in the study of teaching.

> *. . . my realization that pedagogy is scholarship is not in the mainstream and I don't know why I've come to this; I'm glad I have, but it's not something you can just tell people, because we really tend to teach in the way that we've been taught. There's this emulation throughout your career (and not that other people are teaching badly at all) but . . . that you can learn about it, that you can view it as a form of scholarship is . . . a powerful notion. Because it presents the idea that it's not static, and there's change, and there's innovation, and there's room for individual contribution. Not everybody thinks that way and probably even in the humanities, unfor-*

> tunately, they don't think that way either. Even though you have this tradition of teaching more built into the discipline.
>
> (Physics, June 22, 1998)

Teaching matters to the people we interviewed, and we had no qualms about selecting our respondents on the basis, as mentioned in Chapter 2, that we could talk to them about teaching. Given our interests, their concern for teaching could almost be considered a *sine qua non* for their selection, even if that concern made them something other than "representative." Once we got past the diction of our questions, and some of the more important distinctions made within a discipline, it was our colleagues' focus on teaching that probably created the most conversational effort to discover or generate common understanding.

One of the greatest challenges facing a teacher, for instance, involves discovery of an approach that will provide students with the knowledge and habits of mind a discipline demands while simultaneously inculcating in students the ability to learn independently. Amidst all the recent interest in the assessment of student learning among educators and politicians and parents and taxpayers, we hope one measure of pedagogical success is always taken into account—that is, the decreasing reliance of a learner on a teacher. It is awareness of this challenge that has led our colleagues and ourselves to abandon the comfort of the lectern for more experience-based teaching practices. At one point, our physics professor claimed "self-reliance" as a trait his discipline may impart to its majors in greater quantity than perhaps is the case with some other disciplines, while admitting this trait was "a really hard thing to teach overtly."

> ... the physics major, even though they might have as much specialized knowledge, I think they're going to have the ability; they're going to an internal feeling that they can go beyond what they learned, because that whole kind of mind set that a physicist has, that if you don't know something you know how you can learn it. You've got the confidence that you can learn something new, whether it be a computer program, whether it be some mathematical technique, or whether it be some new area of physics, that you can ... use your training; you've learned how to learn. I'm not sure we always accomplish that, but I think that's an important component of what we do.
>
> (Physics, June 22, 1998)

Given the significance of the "self-reliance" trait for most teachers, we were not letting this claim pass without further exploration. So, after listening to the tape of the first interview, we developed a question for the second interview we hoped would increase our understanding of how the study of physics might inculcate independent learning in students. Our technique was to contrast the "apprenticeship model" the professor said was generally followed in graduate studies in physics, including its sense of the student generally "emulating" or "following" the example of her or his professors, with the notion of "self-reliance."

> **. . . You seem to both agree that there's this apprenticeship model, and then you really spent a fair amount of time talking about how you thought graduates from the program are more self-reliant in some sense. We were curious about those things seeming to be a bit opposite.**
>
> Yeah, I can see that. I guess. That's a good observation. I'm not sure how I can see them operating together very clearly.
>
> **Well, why don't you first just recapitulate what you meant by saying they were self-reliant, if you can? . . . My feeling was that it had more to do with the ability to not just work with facts that were already in place, but to discover new knowledge, or discover plausible knowledge, as opposed to applying fixed, already discovered knowledge. So you had a kind of confidence.**
>
> Yeah, I don't think it always relates to the actual knowledge, but it relates to methodology too. . . . I view a good physicist as somebody who could essentially teach themselves enough about some new subdiscipline that they never studied before in order to make some progress on some problem. Clearly, it's going to be difficult to become world class if you're self taught, but I think to at least know where the literature is, how to use the literature, and you have the confidence that because you learned this technical material somewhere else you can apply that. So, I don't know how to articulate it, but somehow I don't see these two things as opposite. . . .
>
> **I suppose one way to think about synthesizing the two things is that if your apprentice model is indeed self-reliant you internalize, even though the process . . . is a kind of imitated process, since that is part of what you are imitating . . . is in fact this discovered self-reliance. . . .**
>
> I think that's true but I'm not sure if that's the whole thing . . . the classroom experience doesn't prepare you for the act of researching. It provides the framework and it provides the basis and it provides you tools, and it provides you a breadth of information in knowing resources . . . but a classroom experience is not a research experience in the sense that you have to define your problem and discover the methodology for solving any particular answers. . . . It's not clear how you can apprentice true research in the classroom. . . . This is really hard because it's kind of general,

but do you see what I'm getting at a little bit? . . . I think that being self-reliant can . . . help you be an effective apprentice essentially because you have things at your disposal that you can use in the process of learning, being shown how to solve research problems. One of the difficult things right away is to define and come up with a succinct definition of a research problem . . . there's a starting point and there's a goal, but the path between them is not clear. But . . . you know that the path is going to involve, in some way, elements of your discipline, the content, the experimental techniques. . .

(Physics, November 16, 1998)

By identifying a seeming contradiction, we pushed our colleague into further articulation of what he thought an education in physics did for students. We recognized his claim, placed it next to another claim, and then wondered aloud about their compatibility. As one of us was sitting across from him, awaiting a response, there was no escaping the question, difficult as it may be to answer without leisurely reflection and the luxury of trying out responses until the most convincing one emerges (even if the conviction is fleeting). Our physics professor was momentarily flummoxed, providing a trial answer and knowing immediately that our question demanded more of him. Then it was time for us to demonstrate some fellow feeling, and to offer up a fumbling explanation of our own, one that anticipated our claims for imitation as leading to an assimilated mode of action, found at the end of our chapter on the teaching of genre (see Chapter 4). But in the midst of conversation we were not so succinct or precise; we were improvising steps as we traversed the floor. The tables were turned; the physics professor found our suggestion admissible but hardly adequate. Still, he could not leave things that way; negation had created a vacuum which he alone, as the originator of the initial claim, had to fill. And so we got what we searched for, an explanation of what he meant by the quality of self-reliance gained through the study of physics, albeit a somewhat clumsy, halting explanation he could no doubt polish, just as we did ours when we frequently revised Chapter 4.

The challenge of teaching in order to free students of the need for teachers would come up again, in a variety of guises. In one interview with our elementary education professor she described a division between "content-area reading" and "reading a narrative text," a division reflected in the existence of two different methods courses in the majors program, one for the "narrative stuff" she taught and one for "the study skills stuff" someone else taught. As we discussed this division, both of us arrived at a concern that this "dichotomy" may hurt students' ability to adapt to a variety of readings as they progress through the grades.

... I guess our hope is students will be able to translate what they learn in both reading courses and make sense out of it, but I know in secondary they don't take a reading course in developmental reading.

Exactly, because that seems to be focused on in elementary, because that's supposedly where students ... learn how to read. It's interesting to even say "how to read," where we're always learning how to read.

In that dichotomy too, in the field of learning to read suddenly becomes reading to learn, which I think is a real false dichotomy. I don't think it ever separates out, but it's a real common ...

... Learning to read versus reading to learn.

As if you're not reading to learn when you're learning to read.

(Elementary Education, November 18, 1999)

Contributing to this sense of distance between the two areas of our colleague's field was a clear dislike for the "rigidity" of common approaches to content area reading—"this strategy, this strategy, that strategy"—approaches that could easily be construed as failing the student because no strategy in the quiver may function as an adequate template for some future reading the student may perform. These areas were even represented by two separate professional organizations, with one peopled by those in the "language arts ... writing and literature and spelling and handwriting, grammar" and the second by those in "reading ... how to read, the mechanics, the process."

And the language arts people are always the English kind of people and the reading are always the, I guess, more sort of mechanistic, behaviorist, if you agree. I'm putting it in real black and white terms there. There are many, many gray areas. But traditionally if you were going to think of stereotypes that would be what you'd put there. Hedge, hedge.

Language arts people walk around in tweed jackets and reading people have the pocket reinforcements.

(Elementary Education, November 18, 1999)

The identification between ourselves and the elementary education professor with a specialization in the "language arts" was obviously strong, to the point of having read a few of the same professional journals and many of the same professional books. That identification sometimes led to quick one or two-sentence exchanges, because recognition of common experiences and perceptions was frequent. But it did not preclude disagreement over words or concepts, which could either be resolved or serve as a catalyst for discussing further distinctions, as we've illustrated previously.

> . . . I think we often get on bandwagons in education. The idea of calling it literacy, rather than language arts or reading. The evolution of the word literacy is interesting anyway. I'm not sure it's always real appropriate, but commonly used.
>
> **The way I see it . . . at least with the word literacy you can always change it to "literacies" and that would be where we could get back into this, because then you're talking about different reading to fit different instances for reading, right? There are different literacies. That's why people say you're math literate or you're. . .**
>
> Culturally literate, which we talked about. That's true.
>
> **It gives you that flexibility, I felt.**
>
> Maybe it's a good idea to use that word, maybe not. It just came into vogue. If we're just using it to say, now it's reading and language arts combined, I don't know.
>
> **You mean reading and language arts used to get split?**
>
> They are at this moment.
>
> (Elementary Education, November 18, 1999)

Accommodating such academic compartmentalization, and sometimes overcoming it, are twin goals of our project, of course. We hope, in the fairly diverse sampling we have provided above, that we have begun to convey a sense of how we reached at least momentary understandings, and carried our conversations forward. We have not been afraid of semantic dissonance, nor of claims that engender further challenging claims. The important thing was to keep talking, and our next business is to further explore various ways the talk was sustained, as well as a few missteps that might have interfered with discovering an ordinary language.

FACILITATING CONVERSATION: MOVES BOTH ADEPT AND CLUMSY

The beauty of conversations in which the participants truly wish to keep the talk going is that not much can stop the dialogue from progressing. Because the motive to converse is strong, participants either ignore minor irritations within another's utterances, or engage in what conversation analysts call "repair . . . a rather useful procedure for *treating* rejected offers as misunderstandings, and thus for managing psychological issues of intention-in-speaking, motive, or 'face'" (Edwards 103). As we listened to the tapes of our interviews, and closely read the transcripts, we painfully took note of the interruptions, the lame forays into humor, the quickly discredited assumptions made by our colleagues and ourselves. But because we weren't playing "gotcha," or hoping for the slightest excuse to push a trap-door button, these moments were generally ignored or forgotten.

Still, a little self-reflection won't hurt us here. We might hope to at least avoid some pitfalls in the future, by virtue of an awareness of the mistakes we have committed in the past. Sometimes, for instance, we piled on the questions like stacking one box after another into a stock worker's aching arms. In this exchange, the Health Education professor calmly turned aside a torrent of words accompanying one question we had placed on our schedules.

> **Let's look at number 6. How do you expect your students to apply what they've learned in your courses once they've left them? Obviously, in part this is connected to some of the stuff we previously talked about in those practitioner questions this morning, but also it could apply to the courses that you teach to general studies students as well and what forms do you think those applications will take.**
>
> Back to the first question, what they've learned in the courses once they've left them. . . .
>
> (Health Education, June 16, 1998)

At the end of the physics professor's second interview, he expressed a perfectly understandable weariness in this way:

> **All right, I think that's it, unless you have any final words. This time it's really the end.**
>
> I'm all talked out. [Laughing.] I lost my focus here a couple of times. Your questions were so long.
>
> **I should have read them. Well, I think they repeated themselves though . . . .**
>
> (Physics, November 16, 1998)

Another sin we committed was to either supply an answer while asking a question or to seriously limit the range of answers. We seemed to be feverishly anticipating problems our respondents could have with our questions. Part of this worry may have been rooted in earlier exchanges with previous interviewees. Therefore, the assumption in operation here was probably counter to the spirit in which we initiated the interviews, suggesting as it does that people would tend to respond in similar ways to our questions.

> **So the first question is: How would you characterize your discipline? And the way we've generally thought of this is as a knowledge base or a practice. Or, in other words, do you think it's more an applied, or is it more of a content area, or some of both, or if there's some other way that you would like to characterize it?**
>
> (Computer Science, August 12, 1999)

In a way this seems a very "teacherly" reaction, trying to incorporate previous experience with students into the next presentation of a lesson. Actually supplying a specific answer was more like being guilty of thinking out loud. Suppressing this urge would heighten the chances of receiving a response unadulterated by the questioner's push in one direction, although in this next exchange it appears our mathematics professor managed to ignore the pressure.

> **Number 3 . . . seems to work into just what you're saying. Do you make distinctions between academic and nonacademic practitioners in your discipline? How would you describe those distinctions? . . . I think you're including in academic . . . a lot of mathematicians who might be at research universities and spending most of their time actually doing pure mathematics, and maybe another way we can make a distinction . . . is mathematicians who are teaching and mathematicians who are not teaching.**
>
> Yeah, well, you just gave the distinction there.
>
> **Yeah, I know. I answered my own question.**
>
> As far as what they will do outside of their teaching, I don't think there is a distinction.
>
> (Mathematics, August 6, 1999)

The most serious consequence of our ill-considered moments, obviously, is a loss of what the other might have said if only we had succeeded in managing our own statements more purposefully. When conversations are taped and transcribed, as ours were, you can relive your own awkwardness, not to mention the strangely disconcerting drone of one's own voice, over and over again. (In responses to our chapter drafts, a few of our respondents found the awkwardness of their transcribed statements disconcerting, although they didn't have to suffer the added dyspepsia of actually hearing those statements.) Naturally, one wonders what might have been. A painful subject and one we will stay with only for the examination of one more category of conversational clumsiness—interruptions. To be kind to ourselves, interruptions can be construed as a sign of empathy, of being on the same wavelength, of successfully anticipating what the other will say and wishing to aggrandize their statement with something that can expand on it. True enough, but such blandishments do not erase the accumulation of "little murders" that interruptions can effect, killing off another's thought before it can emerge into the conversational atmosphere. As in this exchange with the elementary education professor, concerning possible ways to relate a universally required literature course to reading methods courses:

> *That might be an interesting avenue to pursue, to see if there are direct connections between Liberal Studies classes and others. . . .*
>
> **Maybe even have them doing Interpreting Lit while they were doing Children's Lit.**
>
> *Cause there's so much that's common; obviously it's literature, but there are opportunities in theory.*
>
> **But that would be interesting; that goes in with the whole idea of things like feminist readings or how should you read Dick and Jane. I don't know if they still do Dick and Jane.**
>
> *Only as an example. Now it's Mario and the names are much more modern. They're ethnically . . .*
>
> **Yeah, Dick and Jane were basically white bread, all the way. . . .**
>
> (Elementary Education, November 18, 1999)

Discursive psychologists have observed that "successive speakers completing each other's talk, or . . . talking in unison" are ways to create "a sense of consensus" (Edwards 131). But consensus may not be desirable, when the idea is to expand our knowledge of some area with which we are only passably familiar. If only we had let her talk, how much more could we have discovered regarding contemporary basal readers, a subject about which the elementary education professor had to be more well versed than we? Perhaps this was the greatest danger of close identification for us—the sense that we did know how someone might respond, therefore eliminating the possibility of surprise.

All that aside, there appear to be more "moves" made by our respondents and ourselves that can be considered positive contributions to the building of meaning and a sense of connection than there are "moves" with a deleterious effect. One obvious technique was the use of single-word or briefly phrased affirmative statements, used as responses to whatever was previously said by the other. Although such statements were more common in some interviews than in others, they appeared in every one to some extent. In a few interviews, affirmative statements were quite frequent in the opening moments, when the conversants may have been intent on establishing both momentum and comity.

> **Do you make a distinction between practitioners and . . . theoreticians in the field, or people so-called "in the discipline" and then practitioners?**
>
> *Yeah, because you could be in this field with anything from an associate degree to a postdoctorate. There are distinctions in terms of where people are, but even though people who might be called academic personnel are expected to be grounded in practice.*
>
> **Is that because clinical practice is part of everyone's training, or would they expect you to have been on a job somewhere?**
>
> *Yeah, because you are preparing people to go back into the job, you're expected to know the job at some level. And some parts of nursing have an actual requirement that you have so many hours of clinical practice. And all of us are strongly encouraged to do practice.*
>
> (Nursing, June 17, 1998)

A variation on this conversational device was an interviewee identifying a particular question posed by the interviewer as "good," generally translatable as "appropriate" or "thought-provoking." Such reactions were particularly noticeable in interviews with the physics and elementary education professors.

Similar to affirmation was something we've called "repeating to confirm," a label descriptive enough to require little in the way of further explanation. Both interviewers and interviewees used this device to slow the pace of an interview, mostly with the intent of making sure a heavy load of new information could be absorbed. We "repeated" to ascertain the accuracy of a name, or the meaning of a discipline-specific acronym or term. Other motives might have been to encourage further response, or to overcome hesitancy on the part of a colleague. In the following passage, we used repetition and deliberate speech to draw out the computer science professor on common workday activities of a systems analyst. She, in turn, completed certain of our sentences as a way of cooperating, and perhaps because she considered the slow pace too excruciating.

So they'd be working with . . . they'd probably be internal people that are asking them to get a certain kind of information out of the system?

Right, right. Or to say . . .

. . . to design . . .

Yeah. "We have this need that's not being met by the current system. Can you customize the software or get different software to help us?" With scheduling activities, let's say.

So whatever kind of information that company acquires, ways to . . .

Massage the data. [Laughing.]

Okay. Now would . . . people with strictly computer background be asked to . . .

To work with users?

Not to work with users?

Probably not. They would probably be more information systems people. The computer science people would probably be the . . . The info systems people would be liaisons between the really technical people and the management people. . . .

Okay, but none of those would be . . . well, those would be users of the system in the company but . . . then the clients . . . ?

Or the clients.

Or the clients of the company. Okay.

(Computer Science, August 12, 1999)

Another approach both we and our colleagues used was to draw from our common or shared experience or knowledge. The most obvious way this was done was through reference to utterances earlier in a current interview or in the first interview if we were involved in the follow-up. Such references occurred with great frequency, usually to establish some idea as a "given" on which further talk could be based, or to either secure or challenge some idea's status as a "given." Less common were references to interviews with other colleagues, but we tried this on occasion as a way to propel an interview in a particular direction. As mentioned previously, we had also shared common experiences with some of the interviewees prior to execution of this particular project, and these experiences were employed during the interviews for a variety of conversational purposes. One of us had participated for years in reading groups and other WAC activities with the physics professor, and had attended a workshop on assessment of student learning with the health education and sport management professors. The second author had worked with the health services administration and nursing professors on development of projects and writing assignments for both their courses and our own technical and scientific writing courses.

One approach, given the disparate disciplines of the conversants, was to take note of general knowledge that both shared. For example, we shared an awareness with the health education professor of a common school district practice of having football coaches teach English and health classes. Making note of this phenomenon led to a clarification of who actually became certified health education specialists (CHES) ("I would not see a school health person getting CHES certified," June 16, 1998). We brought up "Einstein's thought experiment" to assist the discussion of whether Physics was more of a theoretical or an experimental science (June 22, 1998). The mathematics professor and his interviewer made note of their educations in Latin (November 12, 1999), whereas the elementary education professor shared with us her recognition of a common behavior among "more experienced" faculty.

> . . . probably like every department, we find reasons why, we tried that once and we can't do it this way.
>
> **The old person who's been here for awhile; we did that 20 years ago, it didn't work. Why bother?**
>
> Of course, we have a lot of new people and I'm afraid I know they've heard that from us. They do; I'm sorry.
>
> **They start rolling their eyes.**
>
> I know; I remember that.
>
> (Elementary Education, November 18, 1999)

This shared knowledge included current events. The attractiveness of internships with the ESPN cable network was discussed with the sport management professor, as was the sexual abuse of young workers by custodians at Toronto's Maple Leaf Gardens. That story had been recently in the news and it fit neatly into a discussion of interns writing sexual harassment policies (June 12, 1998). Andrew Wiles' solving of Fermat's Last Theorem featured in different segments of our interviews with the mathematics professor, while a discussion of the Lee spy case at Los Alamos grew naturally out of a discussion of changing publication opportunities for mathematicians at the National Security Agency (August 6, 1999). Even knowledge of details of someone's personal life could provide illustrations of a point, as in the following discussion of the lack of software documentation, in which computer work by the interviewer's son for a company that compiles actuarial statistics came into play.

> *. . . people in business are more inclined to just want to get whatever it is done up and running as soon as possible, and perhaps not even . . . be that concerned about documentation, which is frightening because for years and years that's one of the problems in the field . . . that people don't document their work in plain English . . .*

Or at all?

Or at all.

That seems to be the case where my son is working now. He's creating systems and they aren't documenting as they go.

Because they don't have time. [Laughing.]

(Computer Science, August 12, 1999)

The sharing of common knowledge naturally led to a few jokes, as in the health education professor's gentle ribbing about the popularity of required courses in our Liberal Studies program. ("I know your English majors love general studies . . . but I tell our students, 'This will make more sense to you after you're gone'," July 16, 1999). The same professor drew on mutual knowledge of budgetary tensions while justifying his heavy use of the copy machine for a particular course assignment.

> *You know, we're always asked to cut back on the number of copies. I figure somebody else is going to cut back. It's like if I lose ten pounds, somebody else is gaining ten pounds, cause the planet weighs the same. . . . Is the planet losing weight? No. I don't drink, but somebody else must be drinking my 6.00 gallons of hard liquor every year to make up for it. So I figure if I Xerox more, somebody's going to be Xeroxing less, somebody without tenure.*

(Health Education, July 16, 1999)

Humor is so determined by culture, of course, that any successful use of humor clearly demonstrates the achievement of an ordinary language.

(Any professor who has attempted to share with students something thought personally hilarious, only to be met with blank stares, knows exactly what we are talking about.) So humor both demonstrates and helps achieve commonality. At the same time, we were careful to use it sparingly because of the risks that exist, even when the joke is completely understood. For instance, we weren't quite sure just how appreciative the mathematics professor felt toward us by the end of the following exchange.

> . . . *Pure mathematicians do mathematics for the sake of doing mathematics and if it applies somewhere, well that's good, but that wasn't the reason for investigating it.*
>
> **I read . . . that generally mathematicians do their best theoretical work when they're young.**
>
> *I've heard that too and it scares me. I'm in trouble.*
>
> **You have heard it?**
>
> *Yeah.*
>
> **What do we do with mathematicians after they're forty years of age?**
>
> *I don't like that one.*
>
> (Mathematics, November 12, 1999)

It is clear, however, that the interviews generally engendered a comfort level that allowed for humor and other forms of fruitful diversion to take place. As we had hoped, there were some moments when a need for mutual assistance appeared and was taken up, particularly among faculty with whom we had less contact before the development of our project. As we have seen, the elementary education professor wished to explore further the possibility of her department's majors taking their own children's literature course simultaneously with the English Department's interpreting literature course, required of all students pursuing an undergraduate degree (November 18, 1999). The mathematics professor recognized the value of more writing experience for his majors, and promised to steer advisees toward our introductory technical and scientific writing course. Following our interviews, the sport management professor decided to include one of our department's professional writing courses in his undergraduate program. Part of this decision may have been based on an exchange during one interview that fruitfully departed from our progress through the set schedule of questions.

I know that, with today's high-tech society the way it is, . . . there ought to be more computer classes you can take to satisfy the Liberal Studies requirements, and right now there's only one class you can take . . . that's a computer course.

Another thing you might want to do . . . is find out the courses in the other areas . . . that actually do use computers. For instance, our technical writing course, we've got them in a computer lab every class.

Really?

They're doing things with PowerPoint; they're doing things with web pages, that's . . .

Thank you for bringing that to my attention.

There are probably some other departments that are doing that sort of thing. I remember I had a student in tech writing last semester who was putting together a web page. She goes, "Do you know how many classes I'm doing web pages in this semester?" One of them was . . . a History class. . .

That's great. What English is that, the tech writing?

That's 205.

. . . You're not computer science, exactly.

But we're using computers all the time.

(Sport Management, July 27, 1998)

We embarked on these interviews to alter and expand on our preconceptions of what various disciplines entailed. We see the same thing happening here with our sport management professor, who, naturally enough, wouldn't associate increasing computer familiarity with traditional areas of general studies. Can you master commonly used software programs while learning history or practicing particular kinds of writing? What a concept! As the enrollment in his program was growing rapidly, the sport management professor thought he could strengthen his students' abilities by including more offerings from other departments in the degree requirements, while simultaneously helping those departments with enrollment figures not as healthy as his own (July 27, 1998). The emphasis on specialization within our schools and our culture often creates an impression in students that only one type of learning might be gained from taking courses in particular disciplines. Seeing their teachers interact across disciplines, and use what they learn from those interactions, may be the most effective way to demonstrate the interconnectedness, where it exists, of what our system of scholarship has wrought.

INTERDISCIPLINARY STUDY THROUGH CONVERSATION

In the undergraduate curriculum, and at a teaching university such as our own, interdisciplinary study can be so very hard to do, as Stanley Fish cleverly put it. But we do not share his conclusion that it is impossible (237). We choose, instead, to reject a notion of "study" as strictly linear, as a process of inquiry represented primarily by intradisciplinary publication, and by a sense of argument as assertion of a singular perspective that illuminates objects other perspectives cannot see. We will not deny the value of such inquiry, nor diminish the physical, social, economic, or even cultural benefits that its practice has provided. But at our level of learning, among students who are not yet "disciplined" and whose strength is often found in their cognitive and sentient diversity, and who mostly prepare for quotidian gardens of activity where academic practice seems to function more as gateway than as landscape, such inquiry may not always be the most appropriate mode of operation (see Chapter 6). Among undergraduates we must teach the knowledge discipline has provided, but for use alongside the knowledge of myriad disciplines, in worlds where such knowledge functions interchangeably, and inseparably, as an instrument of rhetoric and action.

To discover how to prepare students for life in these worlds we need to recognize and live within the worlds of our own institutions, and ask if they are really so different in the character of their practice and their knowledge from the worlds our undergraduates may soon enter, or to which they already belong. To recognize the institutional worlds in which we carry on our professional lives, it may be that we need to practice a different form of inquiry than the one that serves, or at least has served, our specific disciplines well. Cross-disciplinary conversation is our method of choice for engendering the recognition of which we speak. Each of the miscues we have identified within our interviews—the piling on of questions, the anticipation of particular answers, the interruptions—seem to us born out of a desire to occupy another's point of view, when what we really need to do is recognize, acknowledge, and perhaps assimilate that point of view. Each of the moves we see ourselves and our colleagues making in order to perpetuate our discourse—the mutual moldings of common meaning, the affirmations, the restatements, the discoveries or sharings of common experience or knowledge—seem born out of a desire to stretch, rather than eliminate, the confines of the knowledge and language bequeathed to us by our disciplines.

For us, interdisciplinary study seems necessary, but more likely to happen when each of us realizes, along with Fish, that distancing one's self from the disciplinary ground on which we stand is not within our power (235), not without the unlikely acquisition of wings. Our approach has not been based on a belief that we can each transcend our disciplinary perspectives, but on a conviction that we can expand those perspectives through talk. The limitations of our perspectives are continuously recognized through the sobering work of conversation. At the same time, if our "ground" includes an acknowledgment of written discourse as inherent in the formation and enactment of disciplinary practice, if it includes the possibility that both our disciplinary practice and that of others can inform effective teaching, then interdisciplinary conversation holds great importance for us. We have gained much from our educations so far, but we need more, because we are all, like Cicero's orators, in search of both eloquence and knowledge.

All but the last of the remaining chapters of this book (4–7) are an exploration of issues involving composition and discipline-specific courses raised by our colleagues and ourselves. Within their pages we offer up a tentative, limited but infinitely expandable, localized but by no means unfamiliar, set of observations, opinions, and speculations concerning how we and our colleagues can more consciously use written language to prepare our students for their postgraduate lives. The following chapters are meant to serve as reportage and provocation, especially for faculty in institutions with missions similar to our own, and not as unique discoveries of the realities of our instructional contexts, nor as resolutions of the difficulties that exist within those contexts.

Because we are conversing with faculty who are not compositionists we revisit some issues specialists within our field probably consider to be long settled, such as the appropriate relationship between questions of correct usage and writing pedagogy. (Recent work by Hillocks and others suggest these issues have not been resolved for large numbers of writing teachers as well, who may or may not be regarded as adequately schooled in our field's knowledge.) But if we are prepared to engage in cross-disciplinary conversations similar to those we have described so far, then we must also prepare to address perspectives reflective of how others see us, rather than of how we think we see ourselves. Each cross-disciplinary conversation, as we've noted earlier in this chapter, will occasionally find itself reinventing meanings that some more tightly organized conversations may safely take for granted. As intended, the conversations either revealed or recalled to us the perspectives of colleagues with whom we share an institution, not a set of disciplinary assumptions, and stimulated our thinking about our own places and roles in undergraduate education. They represent initial experimentation with a practice that may help us change for the better the curricular structure and the teaching encountered by our students.

4

What Should Students Write?

Distances and Proximities Among Classroom, Disciplinary, and Workplace Genres

> Piaget brings the child to a mature outlook as if the thoughts of the adult were self-sufficient and disposed of all contradictions. But, in reality it must be the case that the child's outlook is in some way vindicated against the adult's and against Piaget, and that the unsophisticated thinking of our earliest years remains as an indispensable acquisition underlying that of maturity . . .
>
> —Maurice Merleau-Ponty
> (*The Phenomenology of Perception*, 355)

DEFINING GENRE

One of the first motives we had for our conversations with colleagues in other disciplines was a curiosity about the kinds of writing taking place within the professional practice related to those disciplines, and the kinds of writing that our colleagues thought might prepare their students for professional practice. Our curiosity about the relationship between professional and classroom practices first manifested itself in our introductory course in technical and scientific writing, when one of us devised the following assignment:

> The second [paper] will discuss communication practices within a particular field—their purposes, processes, conventions, and or genres. The student may review and categorize several kinds of writing within an academic or professional field, analyze one piece of representative writing in the field, or interview a professional as to the role of writing in the acquisition or application of knowledge in the field.

The assignment was an admission that our course could not, on its own, duplicate the distinct writing activities students might encounter in their major courses or in the professional practice that might follow their graduation. The possibilities were too diverse, and so the best alternative seemed to be to encourage student thinking about disciplinary writing as a professional task, rather than as a mere conduit for content knowledge acquired in their courses, a task they might begin to master now and apply in some near but still indistinct future.

Just *how* to encourage productive student thinking about their field's writing has been an ongoing challenge since the assignment was first devised. We were asking them to ponder the form or function of acts and artifacts they had seldom been encouraged to consider worthy of their focused attention. (Even among English professionals, close textual analysis of writing not identified as "literary" was rare until the last quarter century.) We only hoped to initiate thinking about writing tasks imitative of those actually performed in disciplinary and professional contexts, or at least discussed by those actually inhabiting such spaces. But recent studies of, and theorizing about, scientific persuasion, genre, and the role of writing in "communities of practice" have demonstrated just how theoretically naïve we were. We did not fully understand what we had asked students to do.

The complications can be encapsulated by the word *genre*, a word that may only seem safe when confined to discussions of popular film and fiction within English departments, where it is commonly used to classify cinematic varieties or types of creative writing. During our second interviews, we asked our colleagues for examples of "major genres" in their fields and the "genres" students produced in their courses, mistakenly assuming the meaning of the word would be easily understood within those contexts.

> **. . . what are examples of the major genres of writing in this field?**
>
> Yeah, genre.
>
> **Meaning what types of writing do a health education practitioner do? I realize there are probably academic and nonacademic practitioners, but what type of writing do they do?**

Well, writing is, usually what, how a community health ed program actually, how effective it was in practice. Here was the target group; here was the literature that fed this. These are the biggest health problems of this particular group, here's how people were recruited from the indigenous population to serve as paraprofessionals in this, here are the measures to determine whether or not we were successful. Here's what we found; here's what we think it means. Here's our implications for future practice.

Those . . . are types of writing that will appear in professional literature, right?

We get a lot of practice literature type.

There are descriptions of programs and their success.

Or a lack of.

Is there a name for that type of article?

I'm sure there is; I just can't think of it right now. Some people might call that case study. Some people might call that, the phrase I've seen is "practice wisdom." One thing we try to do in this profession is give a lot more opportunity to the people out there actually doing health education in non-university settings to get the word out.

(Health Education, July 16, 1998)

. . . We just talked basically about the structure of a typical article, right? But can you think of other genres in your field? You've got the research article, the published article . . .

Give me a definition of genre.

. . . Genre in fiction would be like a novel. It's a form, it's a way that . . .

I always pictured genre as a kind of, there's mysteries and there's romances . . .

Yeah, that's getting a little bit more specific. You can go deeper. Then say genre is like, for instance, a movie genre is horror films. It usually follows a particular form, has a particular purpose or reason for being, and so . . . in mathematics there are certain forms of writing that fit certain purposes.

Yeah, I think . . . off the top of my head I would identify three genres. There's the research article, which is meant to be, like Hemingwayesque. There are articles for students, which are the college and recreational journals. Where it's meant to be professional and conversational at the same time. The third ones are the classroom type articles. These are things for you, the teacher, to bring into the classroom, but not in the form in which they are written...

(Mathematics, November 12, 1999)

As these two exchanges suggest, "genre" can be defined, even during a relatively casual conversation, in terms of content ("practice wisdom," classroom activities), form or arrangement of material (target group, then literature, then health problems, then recruitment, measures, findings, and implications), purposes (describe a health program and its level of success), authors (health education practitioner), intended audiences (students, teachers, researchers), and prose styles (Hemingwayesque, "professional and conversational at the same time"). Moreover, as our conversation with a mathematics professor suggests, a genre can be defined at different levels of abstraction, so that both a novel and a particular kind of novel can be discussed as distinct "genres" (Miller, Carolyn R. 37). Another variation in the identification of a "genre" involves the intent of someone who is critically analyzing a piece of written discourse (Devitt 703), such as a peer reviewer looking to justify acceptance or rejection of an article submitted to a journal.

...when you try to publish in sport management yourself, is there a very definite idea if you're writing for a specific journal how you're going to write it?

Yes. I know for the Journal of Sport Management, if I don't have...

Have you tried to submit something to them?

Twice. And got turned down twice.

Would the reviewers talk about why they didn't...?

One of the reviewers... said they thought it was too practitioner oriented and it needed to be put in something in athletic business or something like that. It was not theoretical enough....

(Sport Management, June 12, 1998)

Here genre is a quality ("theoretical") recognized by author, editorial staff and peer reviewers. It is learned, sometimes by trial and error, by authors.

The dominant trend in recent theorizing about genre has complicated the matter even further, by moving away from examination of specific textual features and considering genre more in terms of "typified communicative practices that arise under the demands of recurrent socio-rhetorical situations" (Prior 64). In other words, genres happen because activities carried on under certain social, economic, political, and/or epistemic circumstances engender their existence, as well as their ongoing modification and transformation. An academic discipline or a profession can be perceived as an "activity system" whose communicative needs are met by genres unique to the activity (Russell, "Rethinking Genre" 510). But it is also important to remember that these genres are dynamic and evolving, rather than stable in their features (Devitt 713). As recent attention to the work of Russian critic and linguist Mikhail Bakhtin suggests, the concept of genre is no longer applied to just the preservable discursive record, but instead encompasses both speech and writing as "typified" communicative actions.

> The wealth and diversity of speech genres are boundless because the various possibilities of human activity are inexhaustible, and because each sphere of activity contains an entire repertoire of speech genres that differentiate and grow as the particular sphere develops and becomes more complex. Special emphasis should be placed on the extreme *hetero-geneity* of speech genres (oral and written). (Bakhtin, *Speech Genres* 60)

The highly contextualized notion of genre that emerges from Bakhtin's dialogism, Russian activity theory, and North American genre theory heightens the importance of "genre knowledge" (Berkenkotter and Huckin ix) for our students while problematizing the teaching of such knowledge. For our students to function successfully in whatever "activity system" they find themselves, they need to be able to recognize, participate in, and possibly modify or transform the genres that propel the activity forward. Otherwise, as professionals they will too readily rely on preexisting templates uncritically, in ways that actually impede the efficiency these bureaucratic genres were meant to enhance. Asking students to "practice" or replicate only a selection of genres ignores the heterogeneity and dynamism of the genres they may encounter. Helping them to develop heuristics that could be applied to any "socio-rhetorical" enterprise may seem more appropriate, although we must be careful that general ized pedagogical approaches don't minimize the generic differences writing teachers and writing center tutors should more consciously help students to identify (Pemberton 118).

As students respond to the "field-related" assignment previously mentioned with acceptance, curiosity, or bewilderment, and sometimes with all three reactions simultaneously, we have kept devising teaching aids we think may help them along: for example, a lecture on the historical development of the scientific paper that emphasizes how shifting social, epistemological, and rhetorical circumstances might form or alter discipline-specific genres; a hand-out and powerpoint presentation describing the conventions and functions of an experimental paper's highly regularized parts; a sheet of questions students can pose about samples of disciplinary writing that allow for rhetorical analysis of the answers to those questions, rather than promote simple descriptions of the content of various kinds of documents; and a sheet of questions from which students can draw for interviews with practitioners. These aids have certainly helped students analyze or classify typical documents, but we are less sure our analytical task has helped them know how to effectively assess the communicative needs inherent in the situations in which they will eventually find themselves. Genres have functions as well as features, and so defining them requires more than definitions. They are seemingly inexhaustible in their variety.

Explaining the concept of genre to our colleagues, therefore, has proven as challenging as assisting students in identifying the features and functions of those genres to be found in their own majors. After reading a draft of this chapter, their comments reflected the ongoing difficulties created by theorists seeking more accurate descriptions of how "types" of communication closely connect to the activities that engender them.

I still don't know what genre means.

(Sport Management)

For me, the concept of genre remains a difficult concept. The chapter helps in terms of the authors' explanations, but also those of the interviewees . . . . The discussion on genre was useful but I thought got into the technical language of English writing, which again I find very, very useful but I just didn't warm up to it as much as the other two chapters [6 and 7].

(Health Services Administration)

It's interesting that genre needed a definition, reminding me that Elementary Education, or Literacy Education, and English have something in common, that we take terms for granted—genres etc. A lot of dissonance as I read this, that indeed people across the campus probably should focus more on how to teach writing. But what do we want, to go train these people? Certainly not a model that I'll buy into.

(Elementary Education)

Here the constraints of the already full teaching commitments of those at institutions such as ours became apparent. But once we had made the concept of genre familiar, our colleagues identified a number of them rather easily.

IDENTIFYING GENRES

We are acutely aware of the localized nature of our study, and hesitate to make any statement that could be construed as universally or even generally applicable. This book is about dialogue, not data or the inferences that might be drawn from data. Nevertheless, this chapter on "types" or "genres" of writing is one point where simply reporting data culled from the interviews might prove useful to our readers, with the disclaimer that none of our data should be inferred as "true" of entire disciplines or of the educational institution known as a public comprehensive university. Our colleagues mentioned a large number of "types" of writing taking place in their courses, in their disciplinary publications, and in their professional practice. Sharing those genres with our readers would seem to satisfy a basic curiosity, or to use the phrasing of our health education professor, such information would be "nice to know" (July 16, 1998).

Our colleagues used dozens of labels to identify particular types or genres of writing found in the field. It is easy to categorize some of them as "classroom" or "practitioner" writing, with the former defined as writing assigned within the context of a course of study and the latter as writing performed as part of the day-to-day practice of a profession. Several classroom "types" were mentioned more than once: research or term papers; journals or logs; executive summaries; summaries, commentaries, or critiques of professional articles; powerpoint presentations. Of these, the first two seem most familiar to us as composition instructors. English students are frequently asked to keep reading or writing journals, and the second semester of a two-semester composition sequence most often tackles the challenge of teaching the argumentation associated with developing a thesis in a researched paper (see Chapter 5). Some professors assign empirical research projects involving a research question, a review of the literature, a survey producing data and a discussion of results. Others assign field studies or reading-based critical essays citing a series of sources. Most classroom genres seem clearly related to student learning and the development of critical thinking, although the executive summary mentioned by our nursing professor as part of her students' term papers implies a particular kind of summary for a managerial audience. The practitioner writing was understandably even more diverse, although five "types" were mentioned more than once: memos, grant applications, executive summaries, e-mails, and lesson plans (cited by the professors involved in education).

Naming a third category that would encompass the remainder of the identified genres was more difficult. Calling them "academic" would be misleading, because the "classroom" genres should also be considered academic, even when they seemed primarily concerned with some clearly vocational practice. Calling them "knowledge-producing" would exclude a great deal of material that seemed to be more about "knowledge distribution." We've settled on "published," meaning all that discipline-specific writing consciously distributed to students and to fellow academic and nonacademic professionals through the media of books, Web sites, journals, newsletters, and the like. Within this category, theoretical articles, research articles, and textbooks were cited more than once.

The tables of genres identified within our interviews, beginning with the classroom variety, were generally appreciated by our respondents as giving them a sense of the range and the functions of discipline-specific writing. Our health education and sport management professors, after reading a chapter draft, mentioned the usefulness of these tables in seeing the range of writing available across disciplines.

> *The tables . . . were very helpful in showing how trying to get at certain things, certain concepts, whatever, this is how this discipline does it; this is how this discipline does it; this is how this discipline does it. So these disciplines must have some kind of knowledge base that somebody's trying to follow somewhere.*
>
> (Health Education, Draft Response Interview)

> *The Classroom Genre Table helped to explain a lot, as did the other tables to a lesser extent.*
>
> (Sport Management, Draft Response Interview)

In compiling these tables, we have attempted to use as much of our interviewees' descriptive language as we can, although we have altered some labels for compression's sake. Many of the listed genres are discussed in this and other chapters; it may be useful to explain a few items in each of the tables. For instance, the "filling in the gap" papers under mathematics appear to be the result of an improvised assignment in a seminar course, meant to encourage students to follow the logic of a proof closely.

> *. . . I have given them articles and asked them to either present results or synopsize it. This third shelf down with the nice colorful journals on it. Those are all at the college level, recreational journals. . . . I'm teaching math seminar right now and so the past few weeks the . . . students who are in there have been presenting a paper. I've been giving them . . . different papers. So they've been presenting it by filling in some of the gaps that . . . one usually*

TABLE 4.1 Classroom Genres

Computer Science	Elementary Education	Health Services Administration	Health Education
Computer programs;	Research papers;	Future-based scenarios;	Professional portfolio (coursework and cover letter);
Code documentation;	Article critiques;	Case studies;	Article reviews;
Research papers;	Lesson plans;	Credo;	Goals and objectives;
Article commentaries;	Auto-biographies	Power-point presentations;	Health promotion program evaluation
Executive summaries		Vision, mission, and value statements	

Mathematics	Nursing	Physics	Sport Management
Writing proofs;	Research or term papers;	Term papers;	Small and large research projects;
"Filling in the gap" papers;	Article critiques;	Lab instructions;	Essay tests;
Operations research paper & presentation;	Abstract summaries;	Free writes;	Internship logs;
Translating word problems to math	Community health assessments;	Chapter summaries;	Personal evaluations;
	Agency reports;	Biographies;	Speeches;
	Executive summaries;	Journals;	Power-point presentations
	Graduate research projects or theses	Relating journalistic articles to class topics	

> *reads when writing something up. You kind of assume that the person jumps from point A and point B; well, I'm asking the students to fill that in.*
>
> (Mathematics, November 12, 1999)

Such a method is akin to the technique of "progressive disclosure" found in the "interrupted case-study method" one of the authors encountered through a case study on the hypothesis of parental favorites, posted on the Web site for the National Center for Case Study Teaching in Science. Students are given sections of a journal article and asked to fill in the gaps, such as predicting a methodology to solve a problem. They then see the actual methods section that appears in the article. In this way, students practice the critical thinking or "logic" of experimental design as a kind of apprentice practitioner (Herreid).

Likewise, the sport management professor's "essay questions" are motivated by a concern for active student learning—actually reading textbooks, retaining the information they contain, and recognizing their applicability in professional practice. He thought professors too often ignore required textbooks and are consequently "shooting ourselves in the foot" (July 27, 1998). But he also recognizes the limitations of simply memorizing information.

> *... Both of my undergraduate classes that I teach are intensive writing courses and so ... a majority of my tests are essays. I will throw some true/false, fill in the blank, multiple choice type of things in there to kind of round out. But there are always three or four questions, 8 to 10 points each, where they are responsible to be able to read, to write. Plus the other thing I try to do with my tests. I try to make them as job specific or as case study oriented as I can. In other words, give them a real life scenario. Because I think it's real easy ... for us to come into a class, you and me, we know, "Okay, well, he's going to ask this information." So we memorize the information and we spit it back out on the test and then 3 weeks after we walk out of the door at the end of the semester, we can't remember what ... it was.*
>
> (Sport Management, July 27, 1998)

This acknowledgment of the importance of more than "covering content" is one of the chief differences Herreid identifies between many science faculty, who feel the pressure of content so strongly, and humanities faculty accustomed to asking more open-ended, interpretive questions, a penchant also noted by our interviewees (personal interview).

> *They [the interviews] weren't just simple answers. They were all open-ended questions. And they made me think.*
>
> (Computer Science, Draft Response Interview)

Thus, the sport management professor's remarks regarding the drawbacks of teaching content more than application illustrate the way in which conversation could allow professionals across disciplines to think cogently about alternative pedagogy. In English studies content-based questions are sometimes methods of testing for reading, as a prelude to literary analysis or application of a particular theoretical framework to a situation or work of literature. Nonetheless, such essay questions, regardless of discipline, are clearly classroom genres serving an educational purpose and generally do not take the form of "published" genres addressed to other professionals, which we describe here.

In compiling the table of "published" genres, we have recognized that many of the labels used by our colleagues simply reflect the common "knowledge-generating" and "knowledge-distributing" apparatus of academic life, including refereed articles, professional books and book chapters, and textbooks. However, some colleagues took pains to differentiate between "theoretical" or "empirical" articles and those directly focused on daily practice and the "how-to" of their disciplines, in educational and professional settings. The significance of these distinctions will be discussed at some length in Chapters 5 and 6.

We want to emphasize that these tables do not reflect our sense of the number and variety of actual written genres that exist within a given discipline or profession; they are merely a listing of the genres that were mentioned or discussed during our interviews. The number of distinct published genres that exist within computer science, for instance, may be considerable. But, for whatever reason, only three were mentioned specifically during the interviews with the computer science professor. Our nursing professor pointed out the lack of opportunities for publication among practicing nurses, and the relative anonymity of their efforts in an area like patient education pamphlets.

> *. . . They will be producing documents but not, except for those students who go on into academic settings, there won't be a lot of opportunity of publication. What they will produce more for, some of the stuff we were talking about incorporating in our course; it's not unusual at all for a nurse to write patient ed materials, things like that. What's interesting to do is pick up patient ed material. I do this; nurses, they read obituaries and they read things in the lobby like patient ed materials (laughing). I look and see if it's credited or not. Some places are very good about crediting the actual employee that wrote the document. Sometime they are very poor about doing that.*

TABLE 4.2 Published Genres

Computer Science	Elementary Education	Health Services Administration	Health Education
Scholarly articles;	Experimental articles;	Trend articles;	Empirical research articles;
Trade articles;	"How-to" articles derived from research;	Case studies;	Theoretical articles;
Web pages	Reviews or digests;	Statistical research articles;	Case studies;
	"Political" or "reform" writing;	Simulations;	Articles on practice for professors, school and community teachers
	Autobiographies	Textbooks	

Mathematics	Nursing	Physics	Sport Management
Articles on proofs;	Patient education materials;	Original research articles	Refereed articles;
Articles showing problem solutions;	Web sites;	Review articles;	"How-to" articles;
Teaching articles;	Research articles;	Popular articles;	Books and book chapters;
Articles for students;	Articles on nursing management	Scientific encyclopedias;	Press releases
Articles on games;		Textbooks	
Synopses of articles;			
Textbooks;			
Popularization			

> ***Now, is it likely to be the health professional . . . who does that rather than a technical writer working with the health profession?***
>
> *The content will come usually from a health care provider. What support they get varies from someone to type it, someone to print it. For them to get support in quality of the writing and someone . . . editing is not real common. A major medical center may provide some of that.*
>
> (Nursing, June 17, 1998)

In the published category, a few of our colleagues mentioned genres within their fields that appeared to resemble the kind of "public" expository and persuasive writing often featured in first-year composition courses. Our health services administration professor spoke of a trade magazine entitled *Health Care Executive*, formatted in a fashion similar to that of a weekly newsmagazine and featuring material that "kind of captures current trends" (July 1, 1999). In elementary education, our colleague mentioned "political writing" that would appear in both professional journals and more general venues. "The idea of how education ought to just . . . start from scratch. Let's just do it again. The idea of big time reforms" (November 18, 1999). Apart from the usual academic genres, like term papers that synthesize information and article reviews that summarize recent research, the connections between discipline-specific published writing and English classroom genres often seem hard to make. The public expository and persuasive writing in health services administration and elementary education just mentioned were exceptions, although we must not forget the significance of context when confronted with what might be superficial generic similarities. First-year composition professors often ask students to analyze the rhetoric of popular, issue-oriented writing, or to take a position on an issue themselves, but it is another matter to actually obtain submission requirements for a particular magazine and contemplate the reaction of its editorial staff and readers if the article were published. English faculty find it as difficult as other faculty to decide whether to accept the additional challenge of taking extra time to contextualize an assignment in this way. Often, they are as likely as faculty outside English to limit themselves to teaching critical thinking about the issue more than about the document to be produced.

In mathematics, the variety of published genres spawned through specialization may have been more apparent than in some other interviews. There was queuing theory and operations research, which generally appeared to involve much problem solving for commercial and production purposes, and game theory, which seemed more speculative and, of course, more playful, in spite of the deadly implications of some of its subject matter.

> ... We were looking at two-person competitive situations. An article came out on something called truels, which is a made-up word for a duel involving three people instead of two. It was rather interesting because, depending on how the rules go, there are different strategies. If everybody is supposed to shoot at once, there's one strategy, but you're supposed to take turns shooting, there's a different strategy. If you have three people in a duel and person A shoots first, then person B, then person C, the only winning strategy is to shoot into the ground. If you're person A and you shoot person B, well, then it becomes person C's turn and he only has one person left to shoot so he's going to shoot you, which means you shouldn't shoot person B. Same thing if you shoot person C; then it's going to be B's turn and he's going to kill you. The only way to win is not to do it. That's counterintuitive and I think that makes things interesting.
>
> (Mathematics, August 6, 1999)

Our final table illustrates what we call "practitioner genres"; that is, the writing performed each day during the carrying out of a practitioner's professional duties. This kind of writing has received considerable scholarly scrutiny in recent years (Odell and Goswami, Bazerman and Paradis, Spilka). But we sometimes found ourselves having to pose more than one direct question about this kind of writing before interviewees opened up on the subject. One possible explanation is that it may be easy for academic professionals to differentiate this kind of writing from the published academic varieties required for promotion and tenure, and to think of it as not really "writing" at all, due to its obvious functionality. Much has been written about how graduate programs fail to prepare graduate students for undergraduate teaching, but they may also fail to adequately prepare graduate students for the often invisible, pragmatic work of university service as well. Many practitioner genres are similar in and outside academe, as can easily be seen below.

One reason for the detailed list of genres under sport management is that one interview explored the specific documents student interns were being asked to write while gaining experience at various arenas, athletic organizations, and sports teams. For example, one intern wrote a "spill log" categorizing and describing all incidents when a beverage was spilled at a particular form of professional sporting event, and tracking possible ensuing litigation. "So, in other words, somebody dumps a beer in section 142 . . . was there anything that occurred because of that" (Sport Management, July 27, 1998). A "sponsorship proposal" was a seemingly more common genre because at least two current interns reported working on such a document.

TABLE 4.3 Practitioner Genres

Computer Science	Elementary Education	Health Services Administration	Health Education
Computer programs;	Lesson plans;	Fact sheets;	Lesson plans;
Technical documentation;	Individualized education plans;	Financial statements;	Program evaluations;
User documentation	Letters to parents;	Letters;	Grant applications;
	Responses to student work	Strategic planning documents;	Chat rooms and listservs
		Decision briefings; Advertising, marketing, and fund-raising documents	

Mathematics	Nursing	Physics	Sport Management
Conference papers, including those of students;	Memos, policies, and guidelines;	Grant applications;	Program descriptions;
Operations research documents	Executive memos;	Business correspondence	E-mail;
	Patient charting and record-keeping;		Interoffice memos;
	E-mail		Sponsorship proposals;
			Employee manuals;
			Spill logs;
			Sexual harassment policies

What is a sponsorship proposal?

A sponsorship proposal; well, this is a student . . . working for the . . . _____ _____ National Soccer Organization and they do not have sponsors right now. For example, AT&T, IBM, these different things that will actually put in a lot of money . . . helping the organization and team out and in return they're getting their name used in advertising. . . . [A]nother student . . . he's doing it at a high school level. _____ High School doesn't have any advertising in their stadium. So what he's doing, he's gone to a sign company and they made up . . . different size signs . . . he's going around to local businesses in the Pittsburgh area and saying, "Okay, for a hundred dollars you can get a sign this size and we can have it here on top of the press box. For a thousand dollars you can have a sign on the scoreboard." So what that's doing is it's a sponsorship proposal, an example of a sponsorship proposal. . . .

(Sport Management, July 27, 1998)

The practitioner writing that the sport management professor describes during internships are often the first opportunity for students to put their school-based expertise to actual use. Internships increase a student's sense of "belonging" to a profession and make the production of discipline-specific genres "real" (Dias et al. 211); presumably, the "spill log," the sexual harassment policy, and the employee manual will be put to actual use by the enterprise once the intern has completed them. In education, a student's "supervised teaching" is the equivalent of an internship and, therefore, the place where "authentic" writing situations might take place, such as letters to parents or responses to student work.

My students write lesson plans. They're abstract. This is what I might do; lesson plans were real different from . . . this is what I'm going to do with real kids and this is what I learned from it. Obviously, that's the best way to give them feedback. Let them work with kids.

(Elementary Education, November 18, 1999)

Aside from internships and their equivalents, there was sometimes a gnawing sense that actual participation in practitioner writing was simply out of reach for our students.

Do they have to do things like written assessments of students or things . . . for social agencies?

Probably, maybe, somebody would. But I would think that kind of writing, you would really look at IDEA, the Individuals with

Disability Education Act. Learning to write IEPs, ERs, all those letters. The IEP is the Individualized Education Plan for our student teachers.

So that is something that gets done in special ed, if they might enter in . . . special ed?

All my students take an Intro to Special Ed and I'll bet it's touched on, but the technical part of writing an IEP today, they're like an 18-page document. I would think that kind of training comes from when they're employed.

That's interesting.

I'll bet we don't do a lot. I'll show them the forms and we'll talk about it, but some of it is real specialized.

(Elementary Education, November 18, 1999)

The physics professor indicated that grant writing was also best learned on the job.

. . . I think at the bigger schools the heads of the groups spend a lot of their time writing grants and evaluations and their progress reports and maybe less at actually directing research.

Now, can you envision ever using those kinds of assignments as part of the writing assignment in classes at the undergraduate level?

Writing proposals?

Yeah—proposals, grants, progress reports, these kinds of things as a way to synthesize material and at the same time, perhaps imitate kinds of writing that they might ultimately have to . . .

I guess that if it was just an exercise then I think it would be very difficult. If somehow there could be a degree of authenticity to it, where you actually engage in the project that you're proposing, then it might be reasonable. . . . I imagine there are some schools that have emphasis on undergraduate research and so perhaps they have things in place to tie that into their curriculum.

So if you had a school that had a facility for undergraduates to actually be involved in research you would have that.

Yeah, but that doesn't necessarily mean that the students would then be emulating this grant writing procedure because some people might view that as a waste of time. Why not just let them do the research and get some experience, rather than . . . ? So, it's an interesting idea. I couldn't imagine it could happen here, just because of the way we're structured. I doubt if it's very common. But it sounds . . .

> **But it is the case of writing that apparently one might ultimately do in the field.**
> Yeah, it's very authentic and extremely challenging too.
> (Physics, November 16, 1998)

Although the physics professor finds it unlikely that such a pragmatic assignment could be used, it may not in fact be so difficult to include such practical genres in English department practice, particularly if assignments are presented as scenarios or case studies. One of the authors incorporated pragmatic scenarios similar to those used in technical and scientific writing courses into first-year composition. For instance, students read articles on advertising and learn to write analyses of them. Then they write letters in which they take the position of an advertiser or magazine editor, offering a rationale for an ad's suitability or lack of suitability for a particular publication, and basing their judgment on the product and the editorial copy that might be most appropriately placed along side the advertisement.

As noted earlier, the greatest impediment to such activities in courses in and outside the English department may not lie in conceiving the assignment itself, but in finding time to discuss the genres of writing appropriate for completing it. For instance, in the English assignment above, students look at examples of complementary copy, review business letter formats, examine magazines for content, audience, and existence of complementary copy, and so on. The physics professor is probably quite correct that some people teaching or studying physics might find grant writing a "waste of time" compared to getting research experience, the principal activity for which scientists are trained. One of the things that cross-disciplinary conversation can accomplish is to create dialogue about such matters. For clearly a binary opposition does not exist between research and grant acquisition. In fact they are quite interdependent research-oriented and practical professional activities that students will need to know. Can there be an interdependent relationship between classroom and professional (published or practitioner) genres as well?

CONNECTING CLASSROOM AND PROFESSIONAL GENRES

Although, as our physics professor indicates, it may be difficult to imagine the production of pragmatic documents outside of real contexts, our interviewees often mentioned assigning classroom genres clearly meant to both imitate genres found in professional practice and to prepare students for related, if not identical, writing tasks. The health services administration professor asks students in one course to write what would be components of a "strategic planning document" for a health care facility, including "a statement of mission, vision, values, strategic objectives and a personal credo" (November 23, 1999).

> *Most of the documents we generate are descriptive for the courses I teach. The exception is, if you're going to talk about a strategic plan for a facility and what you're doing in fact is establishing mission, vision, values and strategic objectives . . .*
>
> (Health Services Administration, July 1, 1999)

Of interest in this teacher's approach from the point of view of rhetoric and composition teachers is that he emphasizes "appropriate format" and content—"transferring data into information and that sort of thing"—when teaching these genres, rather than the collaborative nature of strategic plans or how format and content create "a persuasive document." Even though these socio-rhetorical issues are recognized, they appear to exist outside the document.

> *Well, the Health Service Administrator or essentially the executive team really, has to sell the strategic plan to the members of the organization, and if there's no buy off in mission, vision, values, and strategic objectives, then the strategic plan would not be implemented across the 5 or 10 year period of time you're trying to do it.*
>
> (Health Services Administration, July 1, 1999)

His approach remains descriptive, rather than addressing audience, purpose, and situation, which could suggest context-specific alterations in the content, organization, and stylistic features of the document itself.

The health education professor, on the other hand, emphasizes the similarities between himself as a reader of a student's portfolio cover letter and a future workplace reader of the same document. Each part of the portfolio has not only a content but an arrangement, an audience, and purpose.

> **They have to write . . . an evaluated cover letter?**
>
> *Yes they do. "In folder one under this, this and this, I've placed this document. Here's why I have it here. Here's what I think it means. Here's why I have this here. Here's what I think it means." Somebody just says here's what it is, and they don't tell me what they think it stands for, they don't do too well in the portfolio assignment, because if they can't tell me what it means, then*

> they're not going to be able to tell a potential employer what it means. One of the reasons they do this is to build up their sense of, this is what I know and what I can do. Here's what I can share with somebody in the course of an interview or somebody that doesn't know what a health educator is all about.
>
> (Health Education, July 16, 1998)

He sees a direct correlation between the format of classroom assigned "article reviews" and the grant proposals health education practitioners are frequently writing.

> One reason we stress the article review. The IMRAD [Introduction, Methodology, Results, and Discussion] model is still the template used for grant acquisition. You still have to identify the problem, what you produced supporting that observation, what you think you could bring to bear on the problem, and how much money you think it's going to cost, and also put together an evaluation protocol. Since a lot more RFPs [Request for Proposals] want more than just lip service in terms of how you are going to evaluate what you accomplished, what you think you've achieved.
>
> (Health Education, July 16, 1998)

In both these instances, the content of the writing appears to be inseparable from the effect the writer hopes to have on a reader.

In the disciplines of physics and elementary education, the professors could see perhaps even more direct similarities between classroom and professional genres. In physics, upper division term papers synthesizing recent discoveries were seen as potentially imitative of a range of professional writing, from scholarly review articles to popularizations of such discoveries as might appear in magazines like *Scientific American*.

> I mean, even in junior and senior level classes where I've had students do term papers, if I was going to analyze what they are producing, I would call it more a synthesis than a generation of new knowledge. If they're going to write on the Heisenberg Uncertainty relation, which is something in quantum mechanics, that they would use sources to synthesize information into some kind of concise whole, but they wouldn't actually be developing any new knowledge.
>
> So . . . would you perceive it as a way to summarize and the purpose of it would be for their own understanding, to make sure they understood the arguments rather than to add something.

. . . But I think that when I ask students to write papers, one of the purposes is to be persuasive like you wrote in your question, so they're not going to generate any new knowledge, but they need to assimilate it enough that they can write about it in a coherent way that is appropriate for the reader of whatever level we decide, whether, usually I ask them to write for their peers. So in Concepts of Science, they would have to write it at a level where a nontechnical person, just the man on the street, could pick up the paper to understand it, and in a junior level class so another junior who didn't do all of the background reading could read this paper and learn something from it, so there's no conceptual gaps and no big holes.

. . . You're talking about them understanding the material enough that they could write it for a peer who would also then understand, but this might not be that sort of activity a "practitioner" of physics would ever engage in on the job.

Well, that's not exactly true. There is a need for practitioners to synthesize knowledge for an audience. There are in the scholarly journals, there are review articles that are actually quite variable in terms of their length and their comprehensiveness. And there are encyclopedias that need to be written, technical encyclopedias, scientific. There's articles for popular magazines that are sometimes written by practitioners, sometimes written by science writers.

(Physics, June 22, 1998)

One of the authors recalls an instance of the latter when she was employed at another institution. A colleague in the English Department, a creative writer, had been employed to synthesize medical information for governmental agencies making policy decisions. Another connection between classroom and professional genres is evident among elementary education professionals.

Autobiographies reflective of the changes that could be wrought through education are an increasingly common genre within elementary education, as our colleague within that field observed. One reason for the genre's emergence as both a classroom and professional "type" of writing appears to be its motivational power when either read or written by future elementary teachers. In other words, classroom writing was both similar to published professional writing and perceived as in some way influential when it came to future professional practice.

Like narratives?

What I learned from this. How I changed. That type of thing. A lot of people in our department recently have been doing reading or writing or learning autobiographies.

> *... I do know in teacher research that some have moved towards these kind of extensive, either oral histories of somebody's career as a teacher, or Columbia Teachers College is doing a lot of that.*
>
> *Right, and I can see why that's appealing to a lot of people. I think my students like to read really inspirational stories about how a teacher changed a child's life or when they read something that kind of, how wonderful teaching could be, it kind of speaks to them. I think I see a reflection of that in some of the papers they write for my class, when they start to talk about their own learning. You hear their voice. You know this person. ...*
>
> (Elementary Education, November 18, 1999)

Like the physics and health education professors, our colleagues in nursing and computer science sought to assign classroom genres that would make students aware of how the audience influences the type of writing they will do as professionals. As mentioned earlier, the nursing professor required an executive summary as part of student "term papers" because managerial personnel often read such summaries rather than entire documents, and many nurses now hold managerial-level positions. This part of her assignment serves an academic purpose as well, because it requires a meta-cognitive approach to the document in the same way that the cover letter does for the portfolio assignment of the health educator described above.

> *... in my Informatics courses, students who are in Informatics must be able to communicate with people who are not directly in clinical settings. They have to communicate with administrators, they have to communicate with vendors, with a whole range of people, and they also have to do that very clearly and very concisely so I include assignments. I include group term papers, because they have to learn to write together, to agree on proposals that go in from groups and they also, I include an Executive Summary on the front of those because they have to be able to condense and clearly state their main points and then be able to write a more full proposal that supports that. ...*
>
> (Nursing, June 17, 1998)

The nursing faculty member expects students to be able to adapt the information-gathering activities of a term paper to proposal writing in the workplace. She has created a kind of border genre, a term paper that includes an executive summary and that is collaboratively written. This genre will require attentiveness to stylistic differences among writers and the best expression to choose for the purpose and audience, whether or not these issues are actively addressed in the classroom.

The computer science professor differentiated between audiences when she distinguished "technical" documentation of programming code, intended for fellow programmers, from "user" documentation, appearing to emphasize the latter more than the former in her own classroom.

> **Do they get into . . . the difference between writing for different audiences, for instance, a user as opposed to . . . another practitioner?**
>
> . . . Somewhat, but not, I would think that . . . would be where the English department and the scientific and technical writing would get more involved in that. Although when I did, I have in the past taught systems analysis and when I taught that course we did talk quite a bit about the difference between writing documentation for users as opposed to tech use. Most of what . . . I do now is have people, whether they're writing . . . programs, in whatever code it is, . . . Cobol or Basic or whatever, or writing executive summaries, that's more for the manager or the supervisor or the user as opposed . . . to a technician.
>
> (Computer Science, August 12, 1999)

Clearly, professors at our institution are making connections between classroom and professional genres. However, all of these instances raise a question that has long intrigued us, one that has sparked debates over the last dozen years or so concerning the implications for teaching of recent theorizing about genre. Will a student be more prepared for their professional writing, regardless of possible variances in circumstances, because of their exposure to the above classroom genres?

CONSIDERING DOUBTS AND POSSIBILITIES

We want students to learn disciplinary knowledge and to learn a field's communicative practices. (Characterizing these aims as writing to learn and writing in the discipline may create a false dichotomy for some. Doesn't learning a discipline involve learning its discourse? Is knowledge separable from practice? See Chapter 6.) At the same time, we suspect that classroom genres will always only partially fulfill our aims as instructors, and only in certain ways. For they can assist in the learning of disciplinary knowledge, primarily by encouraging students to link pieces of studied material together or to apply the material in problem-solving activities and case studies, but several studies have also found that writing won't necessarily help students recall various particulars, or improve comprehension of concepts. Students can avoid as well as engage in critical reflection while writing, and writing tasks need to be carefully structured to insure that the material teachers want to be addressed is addressed, and in useful ways (cited in Geisler 44-50). This step-by-step and conceptual approach in the classroom is one difference Dias et al. find between classroom and professional contexts.

Some classroom genres can provide students the opportunity to perform various cognitive functions, such as summarizing, synthesizing, analyzing, and reflecting, but students may also tend to emphasize those functions that best fit their own personal agendas of the moment, less than a classroom or professional context. Classroom genres can give students the experience of producing disciplinary writing similar to that found in actual practice. But distinctions in context mean that students will not replicate that writing in the workplace; instead, this "generic" writing may be best regarded as a way to learn and reflect upon the influence of not just audience, but also of individual and institutional purposes, as well as other circumstances, and their influence on content, arrangement, format, style, and tone.

As mentioned earlier, composition teachers often seek to encourage such meta-reflection and learning through the use of journals or logs focused on the student's own reading and writing. Two of our interviewees mentioned trying such genres with their students and then abandoning them: the sport management professor had students write them while engaged in internships and the physics professor assigned journals during his regular courses.

> . . . I used journals a little bit, but I didn't have much success with it. Science majors were not very familiar with writing in journals, and it was hard to get them to do anything more than just recopy the notes or rehash what we had already done in class. It was hard to get them to go beyond that, so I dropped that after a couple of tries and never reintroduced it again.
>
> (Physics, November 16, 1998)

> . . . *do your students in your internships produce writing?*
>
> Yes. They have to; well, right now there's one thing that they do that we're going to stop doing. They have to do logs. I was real hesitant about eliminating the logs, but after the student's been there three to four weeks, a lot of the interns are doing the same things they were doing the first three to four weeks so it becomes very repetitive and very redundant. So I feel that is an exercise in . . . futility and so we're going to eliminate that.
>
> (Sport Management, July 27, 1998)

It seems, in both these cases, that the journal or log was primarily used for recording or reporting information and events. Such composing can be a useful function for writers, but we suspect it is only so when the writers see how the recording or reporting might be leading to a pay-off of some kind, in terms of a project or piece of writing that could not be completed quite as well without the material so accumulated. Journals or "notebooks" are a time-honored form of scientific writing, of course, although even Leonardo da Vinci might have been less motivated to write and draw in his if he had not felt that the helicopters and anatomical studies were leading him some place gratifying. And another thing we teachers may tend to forget is that a "personal" record could be more attractive to students the more truly personal it is; that is, when the writing of it is less an obligation than a preference.

Our own experience as writing teachers suggests that a journal or log assignment, made popular when "writing to learn" was ascendant in the WAC movement during the 1970s and 1980s, works best if its aims are communicated in a quite specific manner, and it functions as an almost unavoidable "step along the way" to some desirable end. A journal could be a venue for "trying out" or "drafting" that is informed by reflection on needs or purposes for writing, and not just the needs and purposes of individual students but of peers and teachers and employers as well. A journal could be a vehicle for matching those reflections with "generic" decisions regarding content, tone, format and appropriate usage. Getting a journal to function this way is an admittedly tricky business, refined through trial and error, and a business many of our colleagues might feel is best left to compositionists such as ourselves.

Of course, a journal need not be personal at all. Journals intended to reflect solely on a student's learning have a value of their own. Journals in other disciplines can be useful to learning when they serve as a record of observations. At our university, unfortunately, organized and institutionally sponsored WAC activities have been nonexistent for several years, and the kind of guidance that could assist faculty in formulating journal assignments not doomed to failure has been absent (see Chapter 2). One thing is clear, however; their form and function are dynamic and easily adaptable. After reading a draft of this chapter we're hoping our colleagues in physics and sport management will try logs or journals again, but only after giving further thought to how such assignments will function for their students, as an aid in completing actual professional or academic tasks.

You make an excellent point about students' difficulty in understanding the purpose of journals.

(Physics, Draft Response Interview)

The journal information was interesting and useful.
>(Sport Management, Draft Response Interview)

Beyond journals, logs, and other recognizable classroom genres, Dias et al., when studying writing in both academic and workplace settings, appeared to cast doubt on the efficacy of teaching professional genres in college courses. Along with our physics professor, they see classroom attempts to duplicate certain professional writing tasks as "contrived" (November 16, 1998) because the contexts in which such writing gets done cannot be duplicated (202). Not only are the contexts of workplace writing too varied to be anticipated but school and work settings also "constitute two very different activities" (223). Their aims, and the social processes those aims trigger, are supposedly too far apart to warrant the learning of workplace writing through simulation. Dias et al. identify two distinguishing characteristics of university writing that set it apart from workplace writing; an "epistemic" quality that enables "students to see the world, and to categorize reality in new ways and ways characteristic of specific disciplines" (48), and an evaluative quality that allows for the "sorting and ranking" of students (44).

The evaluative quality influences what is expected of the writing, how the writing is used, and how the writer views his primary reader. In the workplace, "the institutional goal is to elicit the best possible product from each employee each time writing is undertaken" (Dias et al. 62), whereas university writing aims to supply evidence of differences in ability among students. Moreover, university writing is generally destroyed or buried once a grade has been given, whereas completed workplace writing serves "an ongoing role in the institutional conversation and memory" (62). As experienced writing teachers know, it is difficult for students to separate the evaluative function of school writing from whatever other aims we assign to it. Dias et al. argue that students may keep "a partial eye on the announced goals of a task," but "are much more concerned by what it is the teacher really expects of them" (73-74).

Dias et al. think school writing tasks are "abstracted" from the specific contexts in which professional writing takes place in order to facilitate the "epistemic" function just cited. Because the aim of the writing is to help students learn the disciplinary perspective, the tasks are "carefully sequenced," whereas workplace writing is generally "improvisatory"; the school context is "simplified and facilitated," whereas workplace contexts are "messy" (Dias et al. 190-91).

All of the above would appear to suggest that no matter how well classroom genres assist learning and evaluation, they are unlikely to prepare students for the writing they will perform following graduation. Highly contextualized notions of writing, and the sense of genres as inherently "unstable," seem to imply that serious attempts to simulate professional writing are exercises in futility. Instinctively, however, we back away from such an "either–or" or dualistic conclusion. Although other studies have also claimed that "on-the-job experience" is the "major source" of learning workplace writing ability (Mackinnon 51), do those conclusions preclude schooling as a "preliminary" source of learning such writing? Even practical activities performed by experts are performed sequentially, and if there is less need for reflection it may be precisely because earlier learning has been internalized rather than because distinct contexts make it so.

What assumptions are held about the kinds of assignments made and the kinds of contexts created within classrooms? Don't workplace writers write not only to carry out tasks but also to get a promotion based on differentiation, just as grading systems differentiate and promote? In businesses, the quality of the product and the timeliness and seamlessness of project implementation run parallel to half-year or yearly review processes that determine salaries, promotions, and even retention. Evaluation is tied to successful completion of assigned tasks by stated deadlines in both venues. Even when teams have worked on projects together, salaries and reviews are individual. Supervisors make judgments about the relative contributions of team members and adjust ratings and salaries accordingly.

As our own interviewees show, students are increasingly asked to prepare portfolios of work that facilitate their transition between school and work environments, because the portfolio itself is increasingly an employment document in a variety of fields. Portfolios present final copies of writing as evidence of meeting course goals. If such goals are shaped with workplaces in mind, the assignments and portfolio speak to this context, whether orally in an interview with an instructor standing in for an employer (as in the case of our health educator), or in a written memo in which the student explains how the documents demonstrate mastery of not just subject matter, but practice. Some schools have cooperative and internship programs that can help students envision assignments as workplace tasks. Collaborative assignments and portfolio assessment can diffuse emphasis on not only individual student performance but also on the grades of individual papers. Portfolios can be presented on CD-ROMs with evidence of multimedia capabilities and used in program assessments by outside evaluators from business, government, or industry. To this way of thinking, the possibilities for preparing students for professional writing while they are still in academic contexts seem real and attainable.

The search for "authentic" writing situations, for situations in which students write for audiences other than teachers and while participating in some palpable "community of practice," is familiar to English teachers at both the secondary and post-secondary levels. School newspapers, literary magazines, and in-class publications such as newsletters, chapbooks, or magazines, all have been developed to create a sense of authenticity and participation. One outlet for writing that represents direct participation in disciplinary discourse has been student research papers or faculty–student presentations at conferences. Undergraduate conferences or sections of conferences, organized at the department, university, regional, or national level, have become increasingly common.

> . . . the MAA [Mathematical Association of America] is devoted more to undergraduates than to just professionals and have 3-hour-session student talks, running as parallel sessions. . . . To see the look on their face when they realize that student research is not outside their grasp. A lot of students tend to think research is this big, high and mighty thing. I can't do it. I have other classes to take. I don't know enough. Because there are always other things to take. There are always other subjects to know, so there's no way I could know enough to do research. And they go to this meeting and they see what student research is all about and they go, wow, I could do this. . . . I saw a student give a talk on baseball playoffs. That the wildcard series was a couple years ago; the Cleveland/Baltimore series is five games, three in Cleveland and two in Baltimore. And this person's study was, is there an arrangement: home-away-home-away-home or home-home-home-away-away; what is the best arrangement to give the team who's hosting, the team that's supposed to have a better record, the better chance? And he admitted the . . .
>
> **Looking for an excuse. (Laughing.)**
>
> That was a great presentation. It had a huge impact on people because it was a subject they could readily understand; mathematics was interesting. It was not just a cheesy little slap-together thing, but again it was accessible. It really kind of lit the fire . . .
>
> (Mathematics, August 6, 1999)

In a way, the existence of internships and student-friendly conferences can be taken as an admission of the distance between classroom activity and actual professional practice, just as our conversations are something of an admission of the distance between English composition courses and discipline-specific writing experiences. But for us, these distances are not necessarily a reason to be discouraged. First of all, awareness of these distances can be useful in dissipating the illusion of direct transferability (the notion that a student can easily apply the ability to perform writing in one discipline to that of another without considering the socio-rhetorical implications of such a move), and in realizing the potential for school writing as practice in the recognition of context as significant to composition. Scholes recommends that students in English learn to read "a range of texts . . . Good reading involves reading every text sympathetically, trying to get inside it, to understand the intentionality behind its composition" (168-69). For us, to understand "intentionality" is to understand the context in which a document has been written, and the best way we know of for increasing such "sympathy" is for writers to attempt to write themselves, when the context in which the writing takes place is richly descriptive and the task is clearly articulated as part of this context.

TRANSLATING, PLAYING, AND ADAPTING

Genres are creatures of context, and Janus-like in their shifting natures and shapes, depending on the interests, the situations, and capabilities of those considering them from a variety of possible vantage points. How people create them, assimilate them, adapt them to new circumstances, and put them to use is difficult to assess and still more difficult to predict. One way to value classroom genres might also be to ask which ones could offer the most diverse possible benefits, as opposed to, let's say, the narrowly conceived benefit of duplicating some anticipated type of professional writing document or context. What we may be looking for is the ability to "translate" rather than the ability to "transfer."

Translation involves a sensitivity to context, to tone, and to idiom; attempting to create one-to-one correspondences between various elements usually results in failure. The ability we are attempting to imagine here may be analogous to what our mathematics professor is hoping for when he asks students to begin converting "word problems" into mathematical procedures. The resistance he encounters may be the result of students' realization that there are no easily recognizable one-to-one correspondences between the mathematical symbols and equations that have been the working tools of their previous, and commonly successful, encounters with math and the words and sentences of the problems that now need to be translated into mathematics. And yet, without this ability to move between linguistic and mathematical symbol systems, students are incapable of using their math knowledge in the worlds outside the classroom. Student writers must learn to use the genre knowledge developed in school and to translate it for professional contexts, where the genres are seemingly more fluid and the contexts that spawn them more complex and variable.

> ... When you finally admit, yes, we're going to start doing word problems, and that groan kind of rises from all over the room, my reaction is always, "Life is a word problem; get used to it." No one ever says, "Here's something, what's the answer?" They say, "Here's little situations."
>
> **But then you said earlier, of course, that when we're doing math we actually model situations.**
>
> Yeah, that's my point. You're given a situation; no one is going to say, "Here's a bunch of equations, find the solution." They say, "We have 5 different distributors and 10 different bottling plants. What's the most efficient way to get this to the market?" Then you're the one that has to figure out what the shipping problem is and how to model a shipping problem and what the technique is to find out minimum cost.
>
> **It's where language hits mathematics.**
>
> Yeah.
>
> **It's the place where if you're going to do mathematics you've got to do language.**
>
> Yeah.
>
> (Mathematics, November 12, 1999)

Many ways of finding connections between classroom and professional genres may exist if we adopt this flexible mentality. For instance, although word problems are a classroom genre used as a jumping off point for mathematical activity, they are admittedly simulations, "fake little situations." The situations confronted daily by a mathematically trained operations researcher may not duplicate or even closely resemble word problems because the context is more fully embodied and visceral. The researcher may have to perform several levels of translation, moving from a variety of data and observations to problem statement to mathematical procedure, and then back again to an explanation of the solution comprehensible to nonexperts. Nevertheless, our mathematics professor believes that extensive experience in moving back and forth between verbal language and mathematics is an important way for his students to become familiar with a professional operation they will have to continuously execute while practicing their discipline.

> ... when they take these kinds of jobs, do they do much writing, and probably we're going to have to entail getting into what writing means in mathematics, but do they do much writing and what kind of writing do they do?

> I'm not sure about the actuaries, but I do know the operations research people who have taken OR classes, and I teach the OR class here, it entails a fair amount of not just writing but of reading, because you have to be able to assess the situation and change that into a mathematical problem. So that's basically, in the classroom basically it's reading a bunch of word problems and learning how to translate the words into mathematical language. In operations research there's a lot of writing in terms of presenting your results. When you give your results out, you're not talking to a bunch of mathematicians. You have to be able to convert things into a language they can understand. Where your solution comes from, why your solution works and what your solution needs doing.
>
> (Mathematics, August 6, 1999)

Translation, as we've said, cannot be a matter of one-to-one correspondence between elements in distinct languages or symbol systems. Successful translation occurs through the capture of tone, intent, and meaning, not through slavish replication of word denotations or phrasing. In the same sense, when thinking of how humans successfully move from genres engendered by one set of activities to those engendered by another we must characterize this movement as creative and adaptive, not repetitive. Carolyn Miller argued that genres, as "recurrences," cannot be considered as material entities because every "material configuration of objects, events and people" has to be unique (29). Genres, therefore, are "interpreted," rather than "duplicated"; you simply cannot transport whole specimens from one setting to another.

> Because human action is based on and guided by meaning, not by material causes, at the centre [sic] of action is a process of interpretation. Before we can act, we must interpret the indeterminate material environment; we define or "determine" a situation. (Miller, Carolyn 29)

Rather than hoping students can duplicate classroom productions of a genre in the workplace, in other words, we must help them recognize what may be necessary to effectively communicate in a particular setting. What students would learn is not a reusable genre but a "habit of thought" importable to other settings, with each importation accompanied by a gradually increasing sense of familiarity and self-confidence.

Indeed, it may be better to think of classroom writing not in terms of "simulated work" but of artful "play," the kind of play in which we place ourselves within imagined contexts that produce particular "types" of action. This is one effective way children learn and that creative, open adults continue to learn. Because such play can involve imagination, and was for Piaget a step between concrete and purely formal mathematical and scientific operations, we tend to emphasize it as a kind of rarified mental activity. In this sense, imagination is also at work in conceiving one context as similar to another, as when a child "plays" being an adult by actually dressing up in a parent's clothing. But it is instructive to notice that here simulated activity takes on a concrete, not just imagined form, just as it does early in development when a child imitates adult activity as on going, in full view (Baldwin 64ff), before the capacity for conscious memory and representation is well developed. We need to be wary of making the same mistake Piaget did, in associating play too strongly with symbolic representation.

Mainstream psychologists distinguished imaginative from imitative activity and emphasized imitation in the absence of models (which they termed true imitation) in order to clearly distinguish human from nonhuman behavior, notably in the capacity for symbolic activity and innovation (Russon et al. 104). As a result, investigations in comparative biology stagnated, although Darwin's belief in evolutionary continuity would have had us value shared characteristics across a much broader range of qualities, qualities that span the gap between humans and animals, just as we are trying to establish a continuity between classroom and workplace practices. An attitude favoring discontinuity discourages exploration of the possibilities for applied classroom activities.

Ironically, mainstream psychology prized the capacity for symbolic activity precisely because, as symbolic, they thought that it allowed for imitation across contexts. New aspects of the environment would then produce opportunities for creative adaptations. Perhaps playful imitation of workplace writing, however dynamically portrayed, can begin in one context and take on a more fluid form in another. To this way of thinking, translating genres across contexts seems possible. Casebook methods such as those developed in Harvard's MBA program, or in law schools where ready supplies of real-world legal briefs are available for analysis, are only beginning to be implemented in undergraduate teaching. Therefore, the death of classrooms as a preparation for the workplace seems greatly exaggerated.

New contexts acted as catalysts to further intellectual development for Piaget, ensuring the progressive character of that development. In the case of disciplinary writing, such a fact would imply that actually inhabiting the workplace continues the development of writing skills already underway in the academic setting. Maybe some recent researchers into disciplinary writing would not so readily discover discontinuity between contexts, when discussing genre as activity rather than form, if they would only grant to students and classrooms the dynamic contextual characteristics they so readily grant to workplaces. If the physical models of behavior and form present in dynamic workplace contexts do not yield slavish repetition but innovation, there is no reason to conclude dynamic classrooms yield only repetition and not innovation. We can recover the value of playful imitation in classrooms, where teachers and students seek to create writing experiences that imaginatively connect to disciplinary and professional practice in more or less concrete ways, depending on how assignments and classrooms are designed to simulate actual workplaces.

We tend to forget that the "true imitation" prized by developmental psychologists begins in the presence of models that serve a very serious instructive purpose in growth and development. Merleau-Ponty, as the epigraph asserts, warns us not to assume that the outcome of development is an adult who has surpassed "childish things," but to acknowledge instead that development is a palimpsest upon which successive layers of experience are etched. Perhaps various academic settings can serve as particularly fertile layers, with professors and others already acting as mentors or models to student apprentices. Carter discusses a five-stage continuum of cognitive learning for developing writers, from "global," "process-based," and "problem-solving strategies" for novices to "hierarchical and case-dependent strategies" for intermediate and advanced students (cited in Shamoon and Burns 139). Within academe, the mentoring mentioned previously could help move students beyond the global and process-based stages in "master classes," "studio seminars," "clinicals," and other "directive tutoring," as well as in writing centers usually run by English departments (143).

Some writing center scholars have recently challenged the orthodoxy of a generic, process-oriented approach to tutoring. Such an approach not only focuses on the useful areas of tone, audience awareness, coherence and correctness but also ignores discipline-specific discourse features (Pemberton 118) and the often directive, hierarchical help given by experienced mentors to advanced students who are on the verge of engaging in professional writing practices (Shamoon and Burns 135-37). Shamoon and Burns recall a series of anecdotes from faculty across the curriculum about the way dissertation advisors served as mentors by actually rewriting and editing student work, functioning as masters to their advisee apprentices and thus helping them bridge the gap between schooling and professional practice. At some colleges, writing center tutors serve as consultants in "writing-enriched courses" within their major, assisting students as they negotiate academic discourse in specific disciplines (Gill 169-70).

Such mentoring behavior reflects an attitude toward writing Dias et al would find compatible with workplace contexts, where "the best possible product from each employee" takes precedence over a need to discover which writer, left to her own devices, will display superior ability (62). The apprentice creates, and the mentor collaborates in the development of the creation. During this collaboration, the apprentice is free to artfully imitate the mentor, to borrow and emulate rather than merely replicate. In another case, first reported by writing center scholar Muriel Harris, a student spontaneously generated writing assignments during writing center sessions, and observed the tutor's process in responding to them. Then the student attempted a similar assignment (cited in Shamoon and Burns 144). Performing such imitative activities, the students can gradually identify with appropriate discourse communities, seeing themselves as participants, thinking like insiders, not just by learning the epistemic point of view, values and assumptions of a field, but by applying them through pragmatic decision making during document production (145).

Academic sites and their genres are not necessarily more fixed in form than workplaces and their genres. Pew grants and National Science Foundation grants are currently funding Internet sites devoted to case-based, problem-solving learning activities across disciplines. One sponsored by the State University of New York at Buffalo is of particular note (http://ublib.buffalo.edu/libraries/projects/cases/case.html). Can we incorporate and adapt such sites more consciously to the passage of writers from novice to discipline adept? Can we do so through both artful play and an unashamedly directive master–apprentice model? Workplace writing may be "messy" and "improvisational" because experts rely intuitively on "knowledge base, pattern recognition and recognition of holistic similarity" (Shamoon and Burns 139). Is such improvisation different in kind from the play and case-dependent strategies that can occur in academic learning?

Scenario-based cases, collaborative assignments, and even improvisation seem possible to us with appropriate pedagogical moves. One of us requires students to work collaboratively on scenarios that include both personal and contextual data about personalities in the workplaces. Students work in groups on "in-box" projects and keep a work log. One of these projects, connected to a course in community-based health in the Nursing Department, resulted in a brochure on heart health that was actually adopted by one of the health facilities with which the nurses were working. Another project asks students to gather as a group briefly in the classroom to receive a time-contingent assignment and then return to their computers to work on preparing the documents, which have to be on the CEO's desk by a designated time directly after class. Students are to respond to their supervisor in writing regarding an explanation for a missed deadline and present a work plan for eliminating such occurrences in the future.

After their initial meeting, students must work exclusively through e-mail, in the classroom at distant workstations, as if they were communicating from their cubicles at a workplace. They must devise the best form for the assignment themselves, based on their audience and purpose.

Classrooms may not be able to replicate workplace writing situations, but we are not convinced that replication is necessary for preparing students to write as professionals. Inculcating habitual literate responses to particular writing challenges may be of greater use. Anne Freadman argues that "If writing—or speech—involves discovering the practical difficulties likely to arise each time that kind of job is to be done, and acquiring an arsenal of tricks to deal with them, then 'reading' is part of the apprenticeship" (121). Using a genre is "recognizing it, certainly, but also reading its tactics, its strategies, and its ceremonial place. Learning to write, equally, is learning to appropriate and occupy a place in relation to other texts, . . . learning the rules for playing, the rules of play, and the tricks of the trade" (121-22). We think there is much that can be done to create such places in the classroom. When a study draws conclusions about the differences between classrooms and workplaces, are they also certain as to the specific abilities that can be attributed to work experience, as opposed to school experiences with writing? Do they envision only a narrow range of classroom genres?

Given Bakhtin's sense of any "utterance," including school writing, as connected to other utterances past, present, and future (*Speech Genres* 91), it seems easy to argue that classroom genres, including those found in English composition courses, can only exist in relationship to either disciplinary or quotidian practices and discourses, and as socio-historical responses to those practices and discourses. In other words, classroom genres cannot be anything but related to the practices and discourses that occur outside classrooms. The question moves then from whether a genre can help prepare students for future practices to how it may do so, and whether the outcome justifies the execution of a particular act of writing.

Freadman gingerly steps back from this task, not wanting to explore the complexities of "curriculum design and classroom practice" (121). But, as professors in a teaching university, such complexities are an unavoidable part of our workday. Nevertheless, since she mentions an apprenticeship model, that we don't learn to write until we learn to "read" writing situations, and that reading is what an apprenticeship supplies, the key may lie in creating apprentice situations, as noted earlier. Without contact with practicing professionals outside academe, teachers may feel uneasy about such a move, but such unease is not irremediable. Much can be done by using scenarios, by instructors becoming active in professional organizations of other disciplines and professions and inviting professionals outside academe to present to students, by hiring professors with experience outside academe, and by creating program assessments that involve practicing professionals who examine student writing portfolios and offer suggestions for curricular change. Although Freadman declines to suggest how to create apprenticeship models in the classroom, she ends her essay implying that it is up to her readers to make this commitment (121-22).

VALUING CLASSROOM GENRES, CONTEXTS, AND COLLABORATIONS

We don't want to be too linear, or literal-minded, in our thinking about the possible correspondences between classroom and professional genres. "The notion of using a genre as an operational tool, even when embedded within activity theory as Russell and others do so well," remarks Amy Devitt, "seems far too simple to encapsulate the complex interactions of multiple genres within a given activity system" (714). Just how students both create and use classroom genres may be more diverse than current theory has anticipated. If, for instance, students draw from "other genres of academic and nonacademic writing" to create something as supposedly mundane and stabilized as a research paper (Devitt 713), then they may just as likely draw from a variety of previously experienced genres when first seeking to master workplace genres. Who knows, at that point, which previously encountered genres will prove most useful to a newly minted professional? Both explicit and contextual teaching of genres may create avenues of recognition for new professionals that help them adapt to workplace environments, just as they may help the transfer from one workplace to another.

Even regarding the assignment of research papers, a notably academic genre, there could be room for adaptation. We can't be sure, when referring to the term *research papers* in the tables of genres provided earlier in this chapter, just how many distinct subspecies we may be encompassing. Five of our eight interviewees said that "research projects," "research papers," or "term papers" were classroom genres they and their colleagues within their disciplines assigned. But it was hardly certain that these assignments were similar in terms of their goals, their forms, their styles, or their composing processes. We have already indicated the variety of research projects assigned in first-year composition. The physics professor emphasizes synthesizing in his research assignment, whereas the elementary education professor wants students to explore both sides of a pedagogical question, to force them to look at a broader range of resources than might otherwise be the case (August 3, 1999). The sport management professor assigns both smaller, individual research projects and "one major research project in every class . . . I have" (July 27, 1998). Students produce the major projects with a partner. The nursing professor also gives collaborative research assignments and sees "term papers" as differing in style, intent, and putative audiences, depending on the course in which they are written.

> **When students write term papers, is that a kind of academic writing, would you say, or is it in some way preparing them for executive management, or . . .**
>
> *I think it depends on what they're writing the term paper for. If they're writing the term paper . . . , for example, for a technical writing course, then it would clearly prepare them for writing those kinds of term papers. If they're writing the term paper for nursing faculty, it would probably look more towards preparing them for writing journal articles or writing, yeah, I would say writing more toward the academic . . . unless it's a course that is specifically . . . geared to teach them that executive writing style.*
>
> (Nursing, June 17, 1998)

Other factors that make predicting the value of particular classroom genres for each student problematic are the motives, interests, and viewpoints of the students themselves. David Russell noted how easily students can become conflicted when confronted by the demands of their lives and their various courses of study:

> The activity theory of genre I am developing suggests that individual students feel the contradictions between and among activity systems of school and society as double binds about whether to involve themselves primarily as consumers of a discipline's or profession's commodified tools (knowledge) in distant genres, to place themselves on the periphery of its activity system, or to become involved actively in its life through deeper participation. . . . Of course, students cannot become deeply involved in all the disciplines of their courses unless they are pursuing an extremely narrow professional curriculum. Hence, they must make difficult choices for and about themselves when they write. ("Rethinking Genre" 533-34)

Prior urges those investigating writing in any situation to regard "activity as laminated and perspectival" (24), while defining "lamination" as "the multiple trajectories of personal, interpersonal, institutional, and sociocultural histories being relatively foregrounded or backgrounded by participants" (64).

On a more concrete level, our elementary education professor described some students using their exposure to disciplinary genres to simply accumulate practical teaching applications, whereas two others would "question," "disagree," and "play devil's advocate," and yet another made "connections" and "thought new ideas." "I have one student now, she has basically told me that once she finishes this, she's going to get married and have children, but even she is hedging, 'or I might get a job'" (Elementary Education, November 18, 1999).

Just accepting the idea of formal models and dynamic contexts may not be enough, however. There is more argumentative work to be done here, because it is our behaviorist-influenced equation of imitation with repetition that still hampers our ability to see how imitation of workplace or classroom genres can be imaginative, creative, and adaptive. A wooden sense of imitation posits that the original stimulus must be present to elicit an appropriate reaction. Given this sense, in order for imitation to succeed, the model imitated—person, place and/or thing—must be in place and accessible for rigorous duplication, even though many claim that genres are dynamic activities. But isn't the point of an activity theory of genre that imitation is more than either slavishly reacting to a present model or a merely mental representation carried imaginatively into new environments? Merleau-Ponty's phenomenology of embodiment offers an alternative. Must the student become wooden just because genres and contexts are now seen to have the fluidity and dynamism Piaget formerly asserted only for mature, individual imagination?

A more fruitful way to think of the learning in both classrooms and workplaces may be to consider, along with Piaget, that the goal of imitation is always adaptation, not repetition, but also to recognize that concrete practice in both similar and different contexts, not just "true imitation" (imaginative representations), can allow for such adaptation. We don't need the exact context, nor an exact mental or classroom representation of that context to effectively adapt new forms to new situations. A young child improvises with whatever instruments are at hand, and in the presence of the model. Our students and we can also. One is constantly adapting in imitation, not merely copying, and this process of imitation is written in our neural networks as well as represented imaginatively. Recent interdisciplinary research among psychologists and philosophers indicates that "cognitive schemata often begin their development as meaningful structures at the level of our bodily movements through space, in an interaction between an organism and its environment" (Gallagher 225). The mind is first in the body as a kind of kinetic representation. The content of our propositions arises through "nonpropositional schematic structures" emerging from embodied experience (225). If this model of imitation is fully comprehended, need we be concerned that classroom simulations are exact, as if what is needed is a mental representation or physical replication of duplicate circumstances in order to cross between academic and workplace environments? Even workplace situations would seem inadequate sources of exact imitation under such rules, because situations can change not only day to day, but minute to minute. It may be best to speak of a continuum of genre activities that bridge the gap between classrooms and sites of literate professional practice.

If collaborative activity is also desired as part of those professional contexts, much may be done to create opportunities for physical interaction among students in both traditional and computerized classroom environments. We don't have to be caught between two theories of imitation, as reflex stimulus–response mechanism or purely symbolic representation, and not fully realize the implications of what it means to learn by an apprenticeship model. Learning in the classroom need not be only abstract and epistemic. Neither classroom nor professional activities are mechanically carried out as the inevitable product of particular circumstances.

In *The Phenomenology of Perception,* Merleau-Ponty, like Freadman, realized that we can "read" behavior and situations through the flesh, as it were, and "pick up" many contextual clues in an environment (230). Because his desire was to investigate perception, Merleau-Ponty was less concerned than Piaget with the adaptive shift—that imitation be "deferred" to new environments. But his work clearly suggests that wherever the "apprentice" relationship exists, imitation will take place on both conscious and nonconscious levels, and that even adaptation to new circumstances is a kind of imitation since it suggests molding behavior in synchrony with circumstance. Appropriately, Freadman puts the ball in the teacher's court in "Anyone for Tennis." Teachers can arrange classrooms to provide for practice. Project and scenario-based classrooms could prepare students to recognize how work circumstances might impact the aims, the forms, and the styles of their writing—how translation, not simple transfer from classroom to professional context, is possible. What may be necessary is to more richly describe and create contexts surrounding assignments rather than to lament separate spheres.

Aviva Freadman observed how we have a habit of talking of classrooms as decontextualized (201). In contrast, she was impressed with the "richness and thickness of the texture of the context" in law classrooms and how "this enabling context was established through the lectures, through the readings assigned, through the questions posed in the seminars to the students, and through the talk and social interaction in general in the lecture hall and seminar room" (201). Law classrooms are, of course, deeply involved in problem-solving approaches to learning, using real legal cases full of contextual detail. Although the vividness of lived experiences in workplaces might be lessened by reading about them, and by working in simulated environments instead of being present in them, we believe teachers can prepare students if they begin conceptualizing "assignments" as Freadman suggests:

> The teaching must always be done either in the context of, or in very close proximity to, authentic tasks involving the relevant discourse. . . . Of course, the success of even such contextualized teaching depends upon the accuracy of the teacher's explicit knowledge and the congeniality of the student's learning style. (205)

The latter two comments are particularly interesting because Freedman mentions the importance of the accuracy of the teacher's knowledge several times, and spends most of her article criticizing the teaching of genres as forms with explicit features rather than as the product of places and activities. She may be suggesting, as Segal et al. do for different reasons, that English writing professors need to have more contact with professionals and their organizations outside their discipline, just what our conversations have tried to create. When she ultimately admits that some students' learning styles can benefit from "explicit discussions of the formal features of genre" (205) because they can then recognize them more readily and apply them in their own work, she validates a combination of reflective and problem-solving approaches. In other words, an activity theory approach to genre need not imply either a mentalist view, where all activity must be representable symbolically before imitation is possible, or a materialist view that thinks actions are reflex reactions to explicit environments required to produce them. A phenomenological approach, especially one drawing on Merleau-Ponty, may help us discover something in between (*Phenomenology of Perception* 355).

We can have perceptual clues to workplaces in the classroom, such as students functioning as the staff for class magazines, as creators of Web sites devoted to selected subject areas, or as work groups tackling knotty communication problems. We can have activities with richly described contextual details, involving circumstances, constraints, and carefully delineated personalities. Where an effort is made to create activity-based classrooms that simulate professional or more advanced academic environments, students may be able to "pick up" on similar cues in real workplaces to ease their transition. Where such cues are absent, their own bodily schemas may carry forward the residue of activities to bring them safely from classrooms into new contexts, while adapting to new contingencies. At teaching universities like our own, activity-based classrooms can be implemented as part of the same thinking that draws genre studies into reconsidering genre as something more than form, and as part of programmatic assessment and educational reforms. To say that genres are not just forms, and to say that genres are activity-based, is not to say that classrooms cannot prepare students for the reading and writing of genres they will encounter in the future. Much depends on all of us across disciplines, in and outside academe, working together.

5

Writing as Inquiry, Argument and Persuasion

> The truth is . . . that rhetoric is a combination of the science of logic and of the ethical branch of politics; and it is partly like dialectic, partly like sophistical reasoning. But the more we try to make either dialectic or rhetoric not, what they really are, practical faculties, but sciences, the more we shall inadvertently be destroying their true nature . . .
>
> Aristotle (*Rhetoric*, Book I, 4)

Scanning the genre tables that appear in Chapter 4, it is easy to see the numerous occasions when students, faculty, and practitioners within a variety of disciplines will write to question, to dispute, and to persuade. Some classroom genres seem quite similar in form to those found in composition courses, such as "article critiques" and "research papers." Some published and practitioner writing demands attention to the elements of effective argument within particular disciplines—refereed articles, professional books, grant applications—whereas other writing under the same headings needs to be equally convincing while addressing nonexpert audiences—teaching materials, popularizations of scientific inquiry, policy and planning documents. In and out of academe, students will have to draw conclusions, to assert or question claims, to use or judge evidence, and to make choices regarding various arguments and their applicability to current learning and future practice.

Given such evidence, and much, much more that can be found in the professional literature devoted to workplace and disciplinary writing, it would seem a serious dereliction of duty to *not* teach argumentation in both composition and majors courses. "A person who can argue coherently and cogently commands a considerable amount of authority in our culture," Christopher Schroeder observes, "and such a person is considered to be educated, to have power, and to be capable of taking his or her requisite place in society" (95). The relationship between the exercise of power and authority and the ability to critically grasp and effectively generate arguments, arguments convincing to both narrowly disciplinary and broadly cross-disciplinary audiences, seems so obvious as to be somewhat trite. Dias et al., in tracing the development of monetary policy within the Bank of Canada, take note of the gradual decrease in straightforward technical data and the increase in "interpretation, synthesis and evaluation" in documents produced by increasingly senior-level staff, until the final document produced by the institution's board of governors, a press release, is "almost entirely prose," announcing and justifying actual decisions made by the bank (143-46). The obvious implication is that written argument is often the prerogative of power and the means of exercising that power, whatever the work setting in which students will find themselves.

Students' need for an introduction to the language of power poses some difficult questions for composition teachers. Traditional first-year writing courses, with their emphasis on eliminating "improper" and "nonstandard" written English, have frequently been seen as anti-democratic screening instruments aimed at the linguistically inept mob, as "punishment for failure to master a highly idealized version of the written dialect of a dominant class" and "as a border checkpoint, the institutional site wherein students either provide proper identification or retreat to wherever they came from" (Crowley 231). Others have challenged its alleged role as a molder of classless managerial automatons in the service of corporate America, introducing students to the instrumentality of argument without heightening their awareness of argument's ethical implications (Ohmann 205-06). On the other hand, to deprive students who represent the first generation in their families to experience higher education, commonly a majority in universities such as ours, of the ability to employ and to recognize the language of the powerful strikes many of us as equally base and demeaning. Somehow, we want our students to be able to sway others while maintaining the ability to reflect on and choose the appropriateness of the means of persuasion in each particular instance.

We also wonder about just what it means to learn argumentation. Is it simply a matter of becoming familiar with particular approaches to inquiry, such as the rules of evidence and modes of proof available to one when seeking to discover the likeliest conclusion or the most preferable action? Is argumentation *all* about dialectic? And is dialectic all about logical paths to the least refutable hypotheses, within either public or discipline-specific professional arenas? Or is there a dialectic that exists "off the page," in simple observation and first-hand experience? Are there other forces of suasion involved? Which ones? And in what settings should students learn of them?

We have long assumed that one of those settings must be a first-year composition course. However, since the 1980s, many compositionists, and other academics involved in the writing across the curriculum movement, have embraced "a social theory of knowledge that maintains that because a community creates its knowledge through language, its language is embedded in its context and its context is implicit in its language" (Blair 384). One reason we wished to dialogue with colleagues outside of composition was our uneasiness concerning our capacity to teach written inquiry, argument, or persuasion in the second semester of a 1-year writing sequence. We knew that our students would move on to majors courses where knowledge formulations and the disputes those formulations engendered simply could not be anticipated by whatever activities took place in our classrooms. Just how could we connect what we did with what our colleagues would do in those upper division courses?

Complicating that question is the understandable perception of ourselves as the people who "do" writing, as opposed to, let's say, mathematics or nursing. When we showed a draft of this chapter to our interviewees in October 2000, it was difficult for some colleagues to see how our concerns related directly to their own. The mathematics professor thought the forthcoming material, such as our discussion of the possible uses of the Toulmin Model, were "more oriented to the writing professional." And if our manuscript might function as a "cookbook" for "academics who teach writing courses," the sport management professor wondered, then why were we spending so much time discussing something like "emotions in argumentative writing." Was it that these colleagues could not connect Toulmin or emotions to their own concerns about how students might understand disputation, proof, and persuasion in their disciplines? Or was it that disputation, proof, and persuasion, as purposes of writing, could not be disconnected from the professional responsibilities of composition teachers, clearly seen as distinct from their own? Has composition become trapped in an historical cul-de-sac, constructed through the persuasiveness of past arguments for removing writing from the disciplinary locations in which it commonly takes place? Even now, when many of us seem ready to return writing to appropriate disciplinary contexts, it will be difficult for some to see our moves as altruistic, or even necessary.

Perception, experience, training, and disciplinary orientation may all have something to do with the reception our desire to "share" the burden of teaching inquiry, argument, and persuasion will receive, of course.

"You really brought up a lot of good questions obviously not just relative to the teaching of English," the health education professor said after reading a draft of this chapter. "I just let myself be carried along." And the physics professor, after a decade of reading and discussing WAC material, and thinking of how he should use writing in his own teaching, thought this chapter "the easiest to read, the most accessible." Accessible or discipline exclusive? We are still not sure just how a reader will react to what follows, as we explore what emerged in our interviews regarding inquiry, argument, and persuasion in writing, as well as where such writing should be taught, and by whom.

LOGIC, EMOTION, AND AESTHETICS IN INQUIRY AND ARGUMENT

I guess when I talk about . . . arguments in the field, some of the present health care debates, . . . whether people should carry a private burden for paying for health care or whether it ought to be supported by the federal government . . . the current argument about things like abortion, euthanasia, and things like that, what I find is that when we address these issues, students are more likely—in fact, not just students, the general population—are likely to respond emotionally, . . . rather than systematically gathering facts and figures and presenting them, allowing . . . the logic of the argument to carry to conclusion, as opposed to the emotional positions taken on prior to, in many cases, the presentation of information.

(Health Services Administration, November 23, 1999)

It is common within our culture to think of the best argument as an argument free of emotion or other elements distinct from "pure reason." Rationality and objectivity are seen as the true paths to a satisfying conclusion. In the past, composition and rhetoric textbooks have reflected that thinking, often drawing on a tradition of formal logic derived primarily from Aristotle. (See Corbett and Connors as a prominent, and unusually thorough, example of this approach.) Sections would be devoted to definitions of deductive and inductive reasoning, and to lists of formal and informal fallacies. Somewhat less often the segment on deduction would explore the details of syllogistic reasoning, explaining how to determine formal validity and possibly including the square of opposition, Venn diagrams, and that persistent example regarding Socrates as human and mortal. (Socrates may have willingly gulped the hemlock, but his syllogism lives on, guiltless and obtuse.) Unfortunately, both classroom experience and critical scrutiny have raised questions about the appropriateness of instruction in formal logic for students learning written argumentation.

Formal logic can help us identify and explain what may be troubling about an argument we or others have constructed; the problem is that formal logic, as James Crosswhite points out, "posits" a "universal audience" of "perfectly logical minds . . . not limited by memory, attention, or time" and therefore capable of making the "calculations" necessary to either create or determine a "valid proof" (161). Flesh and blood human beings, on the other hand, habitually draw inferences "in an instant," even when subsequent calculation demonstrates our results are just as logically sound as if we did painstakingly follow the rules (Toulmin 5-6). So although the "science of logic" (Toulmin 2) may succeed in providing a clear and accurate description of a tightly knit, convincing argument, it fails to represent how arguments are commonly constructed, commonly written, or commonly evaluated.

Formal logic, or as Walter Fisher termed it, "Technical Logic" (cited in Fulkerson 436), also tends to hide the distinctness of arguments made under different circumstances or in different fields (Toulmin 113). Even within what might be called "public discourse," formal logic's focus on a "proof" as "either valid or invalid, sound or unsound" ignores the fact that the acceptance by audiences of most arguments is usually "a matter of degree" (Crosswhite 169), and that the arguments themselves are generally "comprised of probabilities" (Schroeder 96). Crosswhite contrasts the "universal" audience of logic with the "paragon" audience posited by rhetoric. Unlike the paragon audience, the universal audience "lacks any sense of the importance or meaning of what is being argued" and is "oblivious to the ambiguities and resonances and moods of natural language." The paragon audience, on the other hand, is capable of contradiction and of change, making "what counts as reasonable" actually unpredictable (162-63).

Composition teachers, by temperament and professional preparation, are generally oriented toward viewing written text as persuasion, but not persuasion reduced to strictly logical arguments; we ask "how convincing is this?" of even aesthetically self-conscious work like poems and stories and personal essays. English majors are trained in literature courses to look for the structures, the tropes, the perspectives, and the diction marshaled by writers intent on getting readers to accept the vividness or verisimilitude of a setting, the motives of a character, the truth of a theme. To us, language does not necessarily sway others because it accurately represents tightly connected objects and concepts, but may just as effectively do so because of its ability to move and delight.

Nevertheless, in courses devoted to argumentation and to technical and scientific writing, we have often gone against the grain of our own professional instincts and training. For example, the emotional or pathetic appeal is one we have tended to de-emphasize. Our bias obviously reflects the more general cultural bias against this appeal, found in the customary preference of professional and technical writing for transparency in prose, and in a fear that emotion distracts an audience from the rational arguments that, we assume, will lead us to the wisest or most effective conclusion or action. An emotional appeal is the element in rhetorical discourse that seems most distant from the rigors and hyper-rationalism of the dialectic; such appeals smack of the manipulation for which rhetoricians have been vilified since before the days of Plato. Humans need to be "moved" to do the right or best thing, of course, but even that ameliorative comment seems more applicable to public discourse directed toward less educated audiences than to the discourse of scholars and professionals. As composition teachers we sometimes regard ourselves as a counterweight to all the overtly emotional, aggressively irrational persuasion to which our students have been subjected all their lives, particularly in the form of commercial advertisements.

We assumed, before embarking on our conversations, that colleagues in various disciplines would reinforce our emphasis on tight reasoning, while telling us something of the form and substance such reasoning manifested within their fields. Possibly, we could relate that form and substance to our forays into reasoned inquiry and argument within our first-year composition courses, discovering along the way what global strategies for such writing might ease the transition of our students into the discourse of their disciplinary locales (see Chapter 1 and Carter).

Such assumptions probably deserve whatever slap from the hand of reality that they will inevitably receive. What we encountered during our interviews, instead of "formal logic," were frequent descriptions of emotional and aesthetic appeals, descriptions that were not necessarily pejorative in tone. Maybe, as immersed in a scientific methodology as most of our colleagues were during their education, they saw an occasional nod to such appeals as of little threat to the dominance of that methodology. Or maybe it was because, in their professions as in others, people do need to be "moved," whether to get up in the morning with a sense of energy and purpose, or to work hard for common goals, or to commit money and influence toward valued causes or positions. The health education professor seemed to see such appeals as necessary if balanced with arguments based on hard evidence.

> . . . We can show that there's going to be less smoking, or people taking up a certain habit, and we can put a . . . different type of cost on this, cost . . . benefit analysis, cost effectiveness, two or three others. So we've got some material arguments. I think there are some things that we can tie into regarding children's health that give us a lot of positive visibility. We are able to get a lot of

people interested in our message when we make it a childhood or teenager or young person's health concern. In fact, this may not always be the most accurate way to portray a health problem, but it is certainly an effective way. One of the reasons that the tobacco companies are . . . having so much trouble right now is that former FDA commissioner Dr. Kessler re-framed tobacco, and tobacco addiction, as a pediatric disease. Cigarette companies knew they couldn't argue against that. Once you can kidify something, even if it's not really a kid's disease, but if you can do that and if it's true, and a lot of things we do in health education definitely have a focus on children and youth. . . .

(Health Education, July 16, 1998)

Closely related to such an emotive strategy is what we have chosen, after Richard Weaver, to call the *sermonic appeal*. The elementary education professor mentioned that such appeals are a common form of persuasion in her field, which hardly seems surprising. School children are in frequent need of motivation, we know, and in recent years, society seems to be gradually arriving at the realization that teachers could do with a little motivation as well, of the positive more than of the negative kind. On reflection, we may realize that sermonic appeals can be found throughout people's professional lives, thus explaining the presence of such well-known motivators as college football coaches and erstwhile preachers on the corporate lecture and workshop circuit.

. . . I think another popular person my students like is Regie Routman. . . . I can't think of any research she's done, but she's very, very popular because I think she's inspirational. . . . And she speaks with conviction. She's been a teacher so she has practical voice, and I guess because teachers have tried her ideas and think they work well. Students will read anything Regie Routman writes and be glad to read it.

But there's almost still in elementary education kind of that ministerial or conversion motif.

There is. I think so. It is.

That's been there a long time, obviously, and it's still there.

I've been asked a couple of times to give in-services or other presentations and told just to be motivational, be inspirational. Doesn't matter what you say, just . . .

Sermonic.

That's right. Come in; get us ready to go back in the classroom. Surely that's her function. I guess that's okay. . . .

(Elementary Education, November 18, 1999)

Another form of persuasive appeal our colleagues mentioned could be characterized as "stylistic" or "aesthetic," meaning having to do with the form of the language used or the structure imposed on the argument being made. The mathematics professor mentioned his appreciation of "well-written" or "elegant" proofs, an appreciation he thought was generally beyond an undergraduate's reach, because it had developed over time and through the experience of examining many different proofs. So what we have here is an appeal that has gone beyond the rational, but that appeals to the initiated rather than to the naïve.

> *. . . The other thing is a well-written proof. Something that is a really neat twist. I don't think students find either one of these persuasive because they don't have an appreciation. I remember being an undergraduate and having the professor talk about an elegant proof. And I'm sitting there thinking, "How can you use the word elegant to describe any of this?" Now I understand it and I can use that word also. Still, I don't think the students have the experience of having seen lots of bad proofs to understand the particular beauty in a good proof.*
>
> (Mathematics, August 6, 1999)

The health services administration professor spoke, on the other hand, of accommodating the structure of arguments to a preference ingrained in both students and the larger culture for receiving information in "short bursts." This appeal was seen as *sadly* necessary, rather than one which gained in strength with the sophistication of an intended audience.

> *Well, again, I think if you're going to persuade students, . . . the narrative format is not particularly effective. The kind of format I find effective are real short bursts—a picture, maybe with bullet type of information. And I do think anecdotes are persuasive, but again . . . because of the attention spans we're dealing with. Again, this isn't a criticism of just the students. I think the entire TV generation my age are not used to examining arguments of any length, of information packaged of any length . . . it's much more effective if it's in sound bytes, the kind of thing that we're seeing now in the political process, . . . seeing in advertisements, seeing in TV shows.*
>
> (Health Services Administration, November 23, 1999)

The above passage begins to move us back toward that sense of emotion and "style" as rationally suspect, as making appeals that distract an audience from the "logic," or lack thereof, in an argument. But such thinking also returns us to the conception of audience as both completely logical and universal; an audience, in other words, not to be found in nature. In helping our students master the language of persuasion, will we really succeed by positing such an audience? As Weaver argued, not one of us is a "merely rationalistic being," and we are all in need of having our "sensitivity" and "imagination" primed if we are to understand and reflect on some set of circumstances (220). Instead, we must realize that there are "degrees of objectivity" in human discourse (Weaver 222), a concept that was also reinforced for us by our colleagues.

For example, the concept of *reproducibility* is one we have strongly emphasized when discussing scientific discourse with our technical writing students; that is, the notion that observations or results must be repeated by others conducting the same experiment before consensus can emerge within a disciplinary community, validating the discovery of a commonly applicable theory or, in rare cases, even a law. The comments of our physics professor helped us see how scientists might retain a healthy skepticism regarding what has to be a key element in the persuasiveness of scientific inquiry, without rejecting the value of the concept itself. In short, he was simply recognizing that having "degrees of objectivity" does not eliminate the possibility of a level of disinterest that can create useful science.

> *Even if you could imagine taking the exact same apparatus and transporting it to another laboratory, that apparatus was used by different people. It's not the same experiment. Because it's not like . . . the information you're getting is just reading off of some dial. You have to set the thing up; there's a prelude to the experiment.*
>
> **There's a new environment.**
>
> *And there's a new environment too, physical environment. So that's where some reputation might come in too and even a theory that is accepted doesn't have to be universally accepted, because a scientific theory has the potential to be falsified or it's not a theory. So the persuasion may not be universally persuasive and that sometimes happens; not too often, but I guess that depends on how high the stakes are. . . . You can't, and it might not be even appropriate to call it a bias because the word kind of gives you this connotation that it's premeditated. But some biases, I don't know what the plural is, they can be inherent, and I mean not articulated . . . you can be operating under a bias and not aware of it. So there is no true objectivity, if there are people involved.*
>
> (Physics, November 16, 1998)

What our colleagues kept telling us, we have concluded, is not that the logic found in their disciplinary knowledge generation and professional practice lacked validity because contaminated by bias or emotion or a sense of style, but that argumentation in their fields was always an historical event governed by particular contingencies. Even in mathematics, where "proofs" dominated by symbols and numbers seemingly execute a clear one-to-one correspondence between the thing to be proved and the formal means of proving it, historical circumstances could influence argumentation. As with physics, there are "high stakes" moments of disciplinary inquiry, when proposed solutions to particularly difficult or long-standing problems would receive extraordinary scrutiny before they could be accepted.

> *In 1994, Andrew Wiles announced he had a proof to Fermat's Last Theorem. People more or less thought he had it. People believed he had it, but they weren't going to crown him king until it had been through the whole process. When it went through the process a hole was found. A couple of years later they were able to close it up, but there was that gap. Another example is the four-color problem. Say any map in the plane, any two-dimensional map, can be colored using just four colors so that no adjacent areas have the same color. Five colors have been proved, a long time ago. Four colors were still unknown. Then in the late 1970s or early 1980s two people in Minnesota claimed to have proof, but the proof came down to reducing this to some special cases and having the computer actually color in the special cases. Some people still don't accept that as a method of proof because, just because you've done the special cases doesn't mean the computer found all the cases. So there is still some skepticism about that.*
>
> (Mathematics, November 12, 1999)

The interviews have given us examples of not just contested knowledge but also of attempts to expand the range of methods operative within disciplines, in order to gain knowledge that may not be general in nature, but still useful for practice. Our elementary education professor discussed a movement in reading research, particularly on the part of the American Educational Research Association (AERA) and the National Council of Teachers of English (NCTE), toward "qualitative" inquiry, research featuring such methods as direct classroom observations, note-taking, interviews, and case studies, that would allow for "naturalistic generalization" concerning instructional strategies or techniques teachers might find useful (August 3, 1999). The health education professor took care to explain that research methodologies were not simply adapted without reflection and debate, but that the kinds of "qualitative" techniques mentioned above did provide information that would be otherwise unavailable.

> . . . there are some ethnographic techniques we can borrow, but it has to go through a process. We think we have something to say about that process. We borrow, but we borrow selectively. . . .
>
> **So to a certain extent what you are saying is that the things like rules of evidence and the modes of proof in health education have been undergoing a shift or change.**
>
> I say we've become more eclectic . . . we understand now that the complexity of what happens when communities or small groups or individuals change, [you] just can't capture that totally in a quantitative fashion. You've got to look at the qualitative to give meaning and interpretation to the numbers.
>
> (Health Education, June 16, 1998)

In that same interview, the health education professor explained that their majors learn about statistical inference in three required courses. "So there is a fair degree of empiricism there, more than I got when I was their age." But when asked what he found most persuasive when reading the professional literature he admitted that he was more enthralled by "pieces on how to advocate for certain things" than by traditional experimental studies in education. His preference seemed a verification of Weaver's dictum that "people listen instinctively to the man [sic] whose speech betrays inclination. It does not matter what the inclination is toward, but we may say that the greater the degree of inclination, the greater the curiosity or response" (64). Our professor could articulate clearly how experimental studies serve as persuasive arguments that may inform and improve professional practice, but he also recognized the power of advocacy, of emotional investment in the matter at hand, to attract and hold readers.

> **You're not excited by . . . those traditionally empirical educational studies where you have control groups, experimental groups and so on.**
>
> I'll normally skip to the discussion. I'll look directly to the implications, "What does this mean?" I will pull from those what I can use in my methods class. I will say, "Okay, after the study is done, what have we learned?" We've learned that in this case fear tactics; scare tactics are only going to work once with a certain population. For the most people, for the most health promotion bang for the buck, we're going to have to do these three things and not these three things.
>
> (Health Education, June 16, 1998)

In nursing also there was discussion of moving beyond the "numbers" when performing on-the-spot diagnoses, or even evaluations of professional literature. When charting a patient's condition, nurses must relate documentation, such as reports from sources as diverse as labs and social workers, to their own firsthand perceptions of the patient, and recollections of what the patient had displayed in the recent past (June 17, 1998).

> *The reputation of the journal, and just the sixth sense that says let me hear this story completely through before I believe you.*
>
> **Okay.**
>
> *And nurses, I think, are a little easier to bring that out in. Nurses are used to the stories that people tell them and they do develop over time a pretty good sense of if the story fits together. Or something's missing from this story.*
>
> **Okay.**
>
> *You've raised four kids; you know what I'm talking about. (Laughing.)*
>
> **Right. (Laughing.) There's a crucial moment here where you remain silent.**
>
> *Yeah, and I think that same skill can be learned if we start out with the assumption that everything written is not accurate. And tell our students, and then start to develop that sixth sense. Is this article accurate? And yes, it becomes . . . just like; this kid never lied to you before. Then you're less likely to be suspicious than if this kid's always got something going on.*
>
> (Nursing, June 17, 1998)

In judging the credibility of professional literature, nurses will check citations, consider the reputation of a journal, and stay alert for factual inaccuracies. But in the nurse's clinical situation, the certainty ostensibly required by scientific "proof" is simply inappropriate. We must turn instead to something like the phenomenology of Merleau-Ponty, in which there is a perception beneath self-consciousness, in contact with the world and sure of itself. This "perceptual logic" appears to be called on by nurses, or anyone else for that matter, who must make judgments without the crutch of elaborate dialectical arguments (Merleau-Ponty, *Notes* 158).

In general, we discuss "logic" during our department's second semester of the first-year composition sequence. This course (entitled College Writing II) commonly seeks to prepare students for future academic writing through the use of evidence, documentation, and reasoning that supports some position vis-à-vis a question or issue. One important implication extracted from our interview experiences, therefore, is that when we speak of "logic" in the future, it may be important to remember the term encompasses far more than the "formal" or Aristotelian variety. People reach conclusions from evidence derived from enumeration and calculation, but also from direct observation, note-taking, transcribing, interviewing, listening, and so on. They connect data to claims by the familiar warrants of inferential statistics, but also in less formulaic or repeatable ways that range from protocols to tacit instinctive leaps. Such lessons may also have value for any course intended to strengthen "academic" writing, including so-called writing-intensive courses in major programs.

Both education and clinical medicine may be fields where decisions must be made based on warrants providing less certainty or probability than those usually applied in what Toulmin, Rieke, and Janik label *theoretical science* (50). Tight mathematical inferences do not provide practitioners in certain fields with enough to literally "go on," so we are more likely to find warrants such as the following: "If Dr. Bernard has a hunch that this is the virus kind of pallor rather than the overwork kind, then you can take it that it's probably a virus" (Toulmin, Rieke and Janik 51).

Indeed, in reviewing what our colleagues told us about their disciplinary inquiry and argumentation we often found it difficult to determine whether the persuasive appeals they mentioned could be classified as "logical," rather than something else. For instance, a form of argument we've decided to call functional appeals persuades by pointing to the success or failure of a particular procedure or action. The warrant is the outcome of the practice itself. In computer programming, as one example of such appeals, the value of a program is first determined by whether it runs, and runs "with not only the test data, but the data that's supplied by a user" (Computer Science, August 12, 1999). At a further stage of evaluation, three questions are asked of the program's output: Is it relevant to the user's needs? Is it timely? Is it accurate? The functional appeal, according to our computer science colleague, seemed prevalent in her professional milieu.

> *... if you design a system and nobody uses it. ... That would pretty much tell you that you failed. I mean, if you design a system and it runs, that's great and it produces accurate data, but what if nobody uses it? Something is wrong.*
>
> **Okay, that's very good. Are there any other examples?**
>
> *If you were ... charged with constructing, let's say, a web page for a corporation and no one ever visited it or people visited it and never ordered any of the products ... one of the workshops I went to at the ... Sig Chi Conference (the Computer–Human Interface Conference) was ... a 3-hour workshop on web design in ... commerce and it was the people that worked for _____ and they*

> said that they found that lately people . . . have gotten . . . so sophisticated that if they . . . can't intuitively figure out when going to the very first page of a web site how to order something they just move on to some other page and some other site and order it from some other company, if it's too difficult to use, or it takes too long to load; that's the other thing. It could be a real sophisticated . . . design with all kinds of jazzy animations but if it takes too long to load, most people won't wait for it.
>
> **Okay.**
>
> And they were talking in terms of seconds, not minutes. [Laughing]
>
> (Computer Science August 12, 1999)

The health services administration professor also discussed the functional persuasive appeal, implying it might be applied in his field to anything from mistaken amputations to patient morbidity to an institution's marketing strategies.

> . . . More recently, JCAHO [Joint Commission on the Accreditation of Health Care Organizations] has taken the position that if you have a "sentinel event" in your hospital; for example, you cut off the wrong leg; that would raise sufficient quality concerns that your institution could be subject to an on-site visit in addition to submitting a root cause analysis and action plan. Failure to convince JCAHO that the institution has identified the basic causal factors and has identified strategies to reduce future risk may result in the institution being placed on Accreditation Watch or having their accreditation status changed to Provisional Accreditation.
>
> . . . If you're going to make a marketing investment, the rule of evidence that you ought to take a look at is the return of investment. You know, will we get a $2 return on every $1 invested. What are our chances of success and that sort of thing? That's a rule of evidence and mode of proof that . . . most executives will want to look at before embarking on a new invention, you know, or new venture.
>
> (Health Services Administration, July 1, 1999)

In surveying all the forms of evidence, modalities of proof, and variety of appeals—sermonic, pathetic, or aesthetic—that were described during our interviews, the one thing that seems most rare is a "formal logic" consciously aimed at an audience undifferentiated by any cultural, historical, experiential, or intellectual bias. Can positing such an audience while composing College Writing II papers truly contribute to our students' abilities to inquire and argue when confronted with the more specifically characterized audiences of their chosen disciplines? Because we have read what we have read and done what we have done in terms of cross-disciplinary conversations, we could share with our students a variety of persuasive moves found in professional discourse, moves that some might find fascinating, or at least of passing interest. But will such sharing allow them to anticipate the kind of firsthand, experience-based perceptions that can sway the judgments of health professionals? Or the historical and material contingencies that will influence the "degree of objectivity" with which mathematicians or physicists may view a research problem? Can a kind of "global" awareness of discipline-determined persuasive strategies translate into greater success for our students when they themselves enter into a profession's discourse? And if so, then just when should such an awareness be imparted, by whom and in what manner? In composition courses offered by English departments? In upper division writing-intensive courses within a major program? During both instances, or when courses are team-taught by compositionists and content-area professors?

THE SHIFTING CIRCUMSTANCES OF ETHOS IN ACADEME

To the variety and the contingent nature of the "appeals to reason" described by our colleagues, not to mention the emotional and aesthetic appeals they identified, we must add one final appeal to our list of disciplinary and professional means of persuasion, that of professional or ethical credibility. The issue of a writer's or speaker's "ethos" came up so often in the interviews as to warrant special attention. In June 1998, when we heard it discussed with some frequency while listening to the first interviews we attempted, we decided to address credibility directly in the schedule of questions for the second interviews with each of our chosen faculty. We asked, "How important is researcher credibility to the persuasiveness of arguments made within your field?" (see Appendix B). As we listened to our colleagues talk about "credibility," two important considerations kept recurring to us. One is that, for academics, professional credibility and ethical credibility seldom seem to be mutually exclusive terms; instead, they often appear to blend with each other. Aristotle said that "good sense, good moral character, and good will" were the three traits that "inspire confidence" in someone who is seeking to persuade ("Rhetoric" 623). Within academic disciplines, "character" and "good will" are demonstrated by one's "good sense," by the thoroughness of one's scholarship, the circumspect nature of one's hypotheses, the courtesy of one's attributions. It is hard to think of someone who does not have a clear and thoroughgoing grasp of a discipline's subject matter as possessing "good will" when speaking of issues of concern to us. And for that reason, the "logic" of one's arguments seems inseparable from one's "credentials" or position within a particular field.

The second consideration is derived directly from this sense of good character as inextricably bound up with knowledge and erudition. Academics whose positions require more teaching than scholarship will—frequently or occasionally, depending on an individual's temperament—perceive themselves as less credible when arguing on points of disciplinary concern. Howard Tinberg of Bristol Community College has written that "our relatively low status (and low pay) as teaching faculty (in sharp contrast with the profile and pay of our privileged colleagues at research institutions) has marked us off as nonspecialists and nonexperts" (68). Institutional status appears to strongly influence our faculty members' scholarly self-images, more so than, for instance, personal income. SRU's salary scales are quite competitive, but a sense of professional inferiority lingers because of our status as a primarily teaching institution.

> *Researcher credibility is a huge thing, especially when you talk about new and breakthrough results or something like that. If someone really claims to have solved what was considered an unsolvable problem, if it's the guy at Princeton, you're going to be wild; he solved it. If it's the guy from _____, you're going to roll up your sleeves and say okay, where can we tear this apart? Basically you think that somebody from a small university wouldn't be able to do it or they wouldn't be at a small university.*
>
> **Unless they wanted to teach.**
>
> *Right. I was talking over with somebody in the department, about 6 or 7 months ago, finally getting over that hump of saying, you're at a meeting and you meet somebody from the University of Michigan, is to realize that you're no better or worse than this guy. It doesn't really matter that he's at a big time, big name research place. That has no effect on the work that you've done. We were talking about finally getting over that. Not being intimidated.*
>
> (Mathematics, November 12, 1999)

Besides institutional affiliation, professional credibility accrues to traits such as perceived expertise and frequency of publication, although there is a clear link between all three. In physics, for instance, research in certain areas tends to cluster at a handful of institutions, places where the expensive equipment is present or a particular research leader has been hired.

> . . . In the field that I did my research in, there was [sic] only maybe twenty or thirty people in the whole world that researched that same area, so there were certain groups, like three or four different places, and so essentially you studied everything that came out from these three or four places. Every single article they wrote, you read, because there wasn't [sic] that many people doing the research.
>
> (Physics, June 22, 1998)

Our sport management professor cited prior publication in combination with institutional and departmental affiliation as giving a member of his field credibility. Affiliations may enhance or decrease chances for publication or the possibility of being read when published.

> . . . A lot of these people you've never heard of before; you don't know. It's somebody that just started writing. Have you been around a long time? Maybe they're one of the gurus in . . . marketing, but you just never heard of them. So you sort of get a jaded view of what you're reading and determine if it's from someone who knows what the heck they're talking about. Now for sport management people that you know about, there are obviously those that are more credible, those that write often in . . . [Here the interviewee cited an article in a particular professional journal.] Now this ____ ____ is a brand new guy at _____ _____, . . . obviously they put him on, start giving him things to get his name up and give him a couple of publications. . . . There are others that . . . if they were to write an article and get it accepted some people wouldn't even read it because they would consider them "non-researchers" or non, I don't want to call them "non-academics," but they're coming from weaker programs and, you know, people would not tend to . . . read their article with as much depth or whatever as some of these other individuals.
>
> (Sport Management, July 27, 1998)

As academics who spend most of their time reading student work, preparing classes, and meeting with students in classrooms and offices, our interviewees were also well aware that credibility as researchers was not the only type of believability they had to possess, and that their journal-reading colleagues in other institutions were not necessarily the primary audience they needed to impress. In short, just as the logic you used was dependent on the audience for your arguments, so was the form of credibility that made you most persuasive. Degrees and publications help academics obtain jobs, but at an institution like SRU tenure and sometimes even promotion decisions can be dependent on how well a professor does with his students. So our colleagues seemed very much aware of what gave them credibility in their teaching. Not surprisingly, some in less text-oriented professions than ours, like the sport management and health services administration professors, believed the greatest source of such credibility was their "real-world" experience as managers.

> ... I've been out in the business world for four to five years and so I had done it and I knew what to do and it's not the same thing as coming in and, nothing against professors, but I think one of the knocks on professors is, a lot of times ... you're talking about what to do and how to do things and yet students say, "When was the last time you did it?" "Well, fifteen to twenty years ago I did, or maybe I'm reading about it. I'm staying current in my readings, but I've never done it myself."
>
> (Sport Management, June 12, 1998)

> ... The first part: "How important is research credibility to the persuasiveness of arguments made within your field?" ... I interpret that to be how important is it for me to be a researcher in terms of me being credible for my students. ... I think not very. I do think doing research is important in terms of informing me, but in terms of how my students reflect on the research I may have done in the past, I think very little. I think what gives me credibility is my ability to take what's in a textbook and say, you know, I've had that experience professionally as a practicing health services administrator and this is how I dealt with that. ...
>
> (Health Services Administration, November 23, 1999)

Disciplines legitimize knowledge, while institutional affiliation—research university, smaller teaching university, liberal arts college, or community college—often influences the legitimacy of knowledge purveyors for particular audiences. But the carefully constructed, century-old, discipline-based apparatus for legitimizing knowledge and its purveyors—through the granting of degrees and the publication of scholarship—may now be threatened by the fastest growing medium for distributing knowledge, the Internet. The explosion of possibly erroneous, or at least unsanctioned, information on the World Wide Web was of particular concern to the nursing and health education professors. Because health issues are of high salience to people experiencing specific physical difficulties, Web sites devoted to distributing information on such issues have grown rapidly, and health professionals have been scrambling to keep up. The nursing professor sees patients exercising more choice in terms of the doctors they visit and the forms of treatment they seek out.

> *There's a problem with credibility. They are changing probably everything. They are changing the access to information not only for ourselves as professionals but for our patients, and that's changing our whole relationship. MEDLINE, which is the literature database in medicine developed by the National Library of Medicine, is a primary database . . . the largest database. It is now available free on the internet and when it became available, within the first 6 months of its availability, one-third of the people accessing it were consumers of health care, not professionals. . . . And in a field where the knowledge expands every 18 to 24 months this has changed who has the access and what is the access. . . .*
>
> **Now, in terms of the issue of credibility we were talking about . . . if the patient him or herself has access to information, is one of the things you're suggesting, is they come in as a patient sometimes more informed and it changes the relationship between patient and doctor or nurse for that reason?**
>
> *Uh huh. Or even where they go. As they are more informed they begin to say, "Well, Dr. so and so has done a lot of research in this area. I think I'm going there," or, you know, asking doctors for consults with. . . . So even where they elect to go to health care and what they see, uh, alternative medicine. . . .*
>
> (Nursing, November 21, 1998)

Such choice may seem attractive at first glance, but our colleagues were concerned about a loss of professional credibility, and about how both professionals and the general public might be educated to recognize the best information when a strict screening process like that employed by the refereed journals is no longer operative. "You can fool well-educated people if you haven't taught them how to evaluate the quality of information" (Nursing, November 21, 1998). In health education, our professor said he was assigning Web site evaluations in all his required courses for majors, presumably to help students judge information using disciplinary parameters and to subsequently pass on those judgments to those they will eventually encounter in schools and community health education programs.

> *Well, one thing that I've tried to get our Health Ed majors to become a lot more cognizant of is that, they are going to have to scrutinize more than ever before anything that is on the web regarding health information. They really have to get a handle on who the author is; what they've done before, and in fact . . . just about every required course I teach they have to do an evaluation of a health web site. The questions that they have are pretty similar to similar assignments that my colleagues do across the coun-*

try. You've got to identify the URL's site according to APA [American Psychological Association], find out when the last time this was updated. How accurate or up to date are the links. What has the author or authors done to have this published. In other words, who owns the web site; is it commercial, educational, or is it government or whatever? Would you recommend it to somebody for the purpose they are recommending it for, why or why not? We're trying to get them as professionals to become more critical about web sites, because one of the things you have to do as professionals is to help the average consumer become a very critical consumer of health information on the web site. We're talking about researcher credibility. . . .

That's a major issue right there.

The credibility issue is becoming a bigger issue, not a lesser issue, because there's no review process in terms of what's on the Internet.

Outside normal publication.

Yeah, it all looks good, and it's not until somebody clicks on or inside, scroll here and there, that you can find what is biased or what do you think bias is, or do you think this is; not that every dot-com is biased. There are some commercial sites out that have excellent health information. In fact, we know now by request you can get an e-d-u even though you have nothing to do with a formal education association. It's a matter of courtesy. You request an e-d-u; you'll get it. Doesn't mean you have any kind of legitimacy in terms of education or not, and the worse you're going to get is an o-r-g. Okay, but I thought only high schools and colleges could get an e-d-u. No, anyone can get an e-d-u; you've just got to ask for it. They'll never check.

(Health Education, July 16, 1998)

In training students to critically examine Web sites the focus here seems to be on questions that address the credibility of the individuals producing the research and the entities sponsoring or producing the sites themselves. Perhaps delving into the claims about health care found at a site, and the evidence and inferences supporting the claims, is too time consuming, more suited to close scrutiny of single pieces of research by people with more training in methods of inquiry than undergraduates usually have. Addressing individual and institutional credentials may be the more realistic approach to evaluating the huge chunks of material found at "health Web sites."

In any case, the educational task seems challenging, in ways we ourselves have encountered while teaching students writing based on documented research. To a certain extent the Web has been a noticeable asset, giving our students access to a range of source materials that was inconceivable not many years previous, when whatever they obtained came from the shelves of our own cash-strapped, space-limited library. At the same time, first-year college students need considerable introduction to just what that range of materials portends. And there doesn't seem anywhere near enough time within a semester to impart the tools they'll need for judging the credibility of the material. (Of course, there is also the previously mentioned problem of our own lack of expertise the deeper a student may delve into discipline-based sources.) Resistance frequently occurs when simply trying to encourage students to move beyond favorite or familiar search engines, which often yield a confusing array of narrowly focused, and sometimes hyperbolic, advocacy Web sites mounted by both organizations and individuals. Our library now offers students an impressive array of databases, which provide access to plentiful editor- and peer-reviewed publications on just about any subject capable of drawing in the curious. But both the variety and depth of these databases often seem daunting to our students, who frequently maintain their allegiance to the search-engines.

For undergraduate classroom instructors, the most significant change wrought by the Internet is that disciplines no longer necessarily control the flow of information about subjects that were always their clear focus. Instead, faculty must prepare undergraduates in their field to ask the same questions about researcher credibility once handled by such gatekeepers as journal editors and peer reviewers. Another very real fear, given the growing democratization of disciplinary knowledge distribution, is that other academic fields will have to endure the politicization of research methodologies and researcher credibility that schools of education have experienced in recent years.

> *I've thought of the group of presenters who are banned in California, who cannot go do anything but what the State Department of Ed sponsors. I don't know exactly how that works.*
>
> **Wreaking confusion among the teachers.**
>
> *We don't want to bring those people in. I thought of that immediately. I thought of our local school board and how they are just complaining to high heaven because some document they've gotten has John Dewey's name in and they don't want that in there.*
>
> **John Dewey is the devil.**
>
> *I guess, and so I'm shaking my head. He's the devil incarnate right now. . . . So, in thinking about that and how demonized certain researchers or scholars, theorists could be.*

> **That's interesting. Is what you're saying is that within certain elements of the political realm of education there are people who kind of have reverse credibility?**
> If they did it, you know it's suspect.
>
> (Elementary Education, November 18, 1999)

In thinking about modes of inquiry, the arguments that inquiry might lead to, the need to "move" and delight conversants, audiences, and readers, and the professional credibility of those making the arguments, the contingent nature of persuasion becomes increasingly real. Persuasion seems ever more accurately an "art," not a "science"; perhaps even a "liberal art," but if so then one that remains such an art even when taken out of the realm of composition and placed in any of the eight disciplines represented by our colleagues. We can develop student awareness of how to be credible for academic audiences, but what of learning to be credible within their professional practice, including those moments when groups may be hostile to that practice, and especially when professional identity no longer guarantees authority?

WHAT, THEN, SHOULD WE TEACH?

All of what we heard about inquiry, argument, and persuasion in a variety of fields contributes to the feeling, alluded to at the beginning of this book, of composition teachers being out of their depth in a world of discourse too diverse to be adequately absorbed, much less mastered, and still less taught. Whether viewed as persuasion (Aristotle's "sophistical reasoning") or as a seemingly more rigorous search for "truth" (dialectic), argumentation is often either exclusive and difficult to follow (discipline-specific) or democratic and difficult to analyze (advertising, political discourse). Can we universalize argumentation by teaching some form of logical thinking? In considering this alternative we need to recall what we've already suggested, that the customary preparations of composition teachers have left them both open to understanding argumentation in multiple forms and generally unfamiliar with the categories and "rules" of formal logic. We often find ourselves scrambling to fill in the gaps left by textbooks' cursory reviews of this material. Sometimes inexperience even leads us to futilely attempt a connection between the categories and rules and the complex argumentative texts our students read and write.

Sadly, we must admit agreement with Michael Halloran's conclusion that a "speaker" and an "audience" who "live in the same world" can no longer be assumed, as it may have been when classical rhetorical theory was developed. "Deprived of a given world, the modern author is likewise deprived of a given rhetoric" (cited in Miller, Susan 42). And with the loss of that assumption, Cicero's ideal of the polymath rhetor seems even more distant than when we first began our conversations. The question for compositionists then becomes: Should we abandon any notion that we can prepare students for the modes of argument and persuasion they will encounter in their major courses and professional lives? If the answer to that question is yes, then should we leave any rhetorical instruction related to whatever academic "worlds" that can be identified for student writers up to the faculty members responsible for their major programs?

Before we respond it may be best to consider just how the transfer of responsibility might take place. We have to concede the limits of our own disciplinary expertise, as well as the limits of the discursive practices of *any* discipline (Blair 386). But we must also acknowledge that it is this very recognition of rhetorical limits that constitutes the current expertise we bring into the conversations with our colleagues, a pale substitute for the "mastery" of all knowledge posited in *De Oratore* that will have to do for now. Acknowledging such limits opens us up to what our colleagues can tell us regarding their own discursive worlds, vis-à-vis our own. And our very acknowledgment gives them permission to place those worlds within a larger discursive universe, where difference and the necessity of translation and adaptation become quickly apparent.

This acknowledgment of rhetorical limits, culled from our teaching experiences, our endless perusals of student writing, and our scholarly reading, is one of our key contributions to cross-disciplinary conversation. Is it also the contribution we can make, at least for now, to the students of the university—an awareness of the multiplicity of limited discursive worlds, worlds that they will have to somehow discern and adapt to? Is this awareness necessary to their learning of inquiry, argument, and persuasion? Is it possible? Where can we begin? Can we begin with the very inadequacies of the aforementioned textbooks, and our own futile efforts to "plug holes" in their preferred "logics?"

For their part, composition textbooks characteristically reduce formal logic to what is deemed manageable for first-year undergraduates and consequently do violence to the subject matter of logicians in any case, a phenomenon succinctly described by Richard Fulkerson in a 1988 *College Composition and Communication* article. Induction, as explained by the textbooks, leaves out so much of what logicians mean by the term that it could be more clearly and usefully described as "*argument by generalization*" (439). Regarding deduction, Fulkerson concluded it might be better to just abandon the concept altogether, because most textbooks represent it solely through the categorical syllogism, a form of argument rarely used by writers. Such syllogisms require for validity something called a universal premise—that is, a statement that can be applied to all within a group and therefore yet another creature seldom found in nature. In seeking to imitate this form of argument, students are prone to create the kind of generalizations that are impossible to prove, such as "all freshmen at Berkeley are eager to succeed" (Fulkerson 440). These syllogisms also function as if the evidence presented makes the conclusion unavoidable (The evidence "entails" the conclusion, to use the logician's term), a trait that makes their application to most arguments, in which the conclusion may be acceptable because "probable" or "better than" others, highly problematic (Fulkerson 440). Finally, so many people find it so easy to confuse induction with deduction that the terms hardly seem to have the descriptive powers they are purported to have. Stephen Toulmin points out that Sherlock Holmes commonly equates the verb "deduce" with the verb "infer," an equation most people accept without comment. But a logician could very well argue that Sherlock's usual mode of reasoning is inductive rather than deductive (Toulmin 121).

Using lists of fallacies to demonstrate faulty logic poses additional problems. Formal fallacies aren't even relevant unless one is using valid syllogistic reasoning as the standard students' written arguments must meet. Most composition textbooks consequently ignore the formal kind, in our experience, and vary widely as to how many of the informal kind they will discuss. Within these lists the fallacies are often "not clearly defined and distinguished from each other" (Fulkerson 443). This failing of the textbooks may be symptomatic of a familiar, and more fundamental problem—that whether a fallacy is a fallacy depends on the argument being made and the audience to whom it is addressed (Crosswhite 173). When, for instance, does a generalization become convincing, as opposed to "hasty?" When the statistical "range of error" for a particular sample drops below a certain amount? When the anecdotal evidence reaches some predetermined "critical mass?" As composition teachers, we have had some students build quite forceful arguments on the basis of anecdotal evidence. At the same time, a few of our interviewed professors suggested that the "anecdotal" argument is hardly confined to the "public discourse" we may feature in a composition course.

> So I think . . . part of the whole notion of writing and the kind of arguments that I find persuasive again is this packaging of facts and figures so that logical conclusions follow. Within literature I see a mix of both anecdotal and inferential-type evidence. Sometimes a very powerful argument can be simply a presentation of what someone did, how it was received and the payoff, which is . . . anecdotal and would not fly in the professional journals. But from a practitioner point of view sometimes that's very effective.
>
> (Health Services Administration, July 1, 1999)

. . . there's [are] actually a certain degree of importance or validity when you actually take participants' words or reactions verbatim and report them out in a narrative fashion. . . . There's [are] actually ways to take those statements and look for common themes and say these are the themes we are teasing out from the narrative that point to program benefits and these tend to be pretty persuasive. . . . I would say that in this field, the qualitative types of comments are becoming more and more important. I'm not saying they're taking the place of quantitative. In fact, all our people are saying we use a judicious mix to find out what the real benefits of the program are. But I think if you try to capture, you try to use both types of evaluations to persuade people that what you're doing is working or not working, I think you're going to convince the researcher and you're going to convince the practitioner. I think you're going to convince the person who's providing the funding.

. . . One thing you said there is, . . . verbatim narratives can actually point to program outcomes. Can you think of anything else?

Well, I guess like a lot of other professions, at some point the anecdotal evidence in some areas becomes pretty hard to ignore. In fact, it's really from anecdotal. . .

It becomes something more than anecdotal?

Yeah, at some point you probably begin to quantify it. You begin to frame some kind of quantitative evaluation based on some of the things that we find anecdotally. How would I get a practitioner to accept a claim? I guess stories of shared experiences, shared successes or things that didn't go too well and why they think that happened.

(Health Education, July 16, 1998)

Because of the problems with "formal" or "technical" logic explained above, composition teachers during the last two decades have often turned to the Toulmin Model of Argument, primarily through the textbooks they have chosen to order for their courses. (Rottenberg, Crusius and Channell, and Barnet and Bedau are three argumentation textbooks that feature Toulmin's model prominently and that have gone through several editions.) Developed a little more than 40 years ago by British philosopher Stephen Toulmin, his model seems applicable to a much wider range of contemporary discourse than is the case with Aristotelian logic, and it avoids any mention of induction and deduction. It allows teachers and students to consider the substance of an argument as well as its form, and it "explicitly deals with the contingent nature of conclusions" (Fulkerson 445).

Toulmin's model provides a basic vocabulary of elements he claims "can be found in any wholly explicit argument" (Toulmin, Rieke and Janik 25). First of all, every argument begins with an assertion or *claim* to which the person making the argument is committed (Toulmin 97). The claim must have *grounds* that might consist of "experimental observations, matters of common knowledge, statistical data, personal testimony, previously established claims, or other comparable 'factual data'" (Toulmin, Rieke and Janik 25). The grounds might be developed or evaluated by students using the STAR system, which asks if examples supporting some generalization are Sufficient, Typical, Accurate and Relevant, given the generalization being made and the audience being asked to accept it (Fulkerson 439-40). In fact, the STAR system would generally function within this model as a *warrant*; that is, "rules, principles, inference-licences or what you will" (Toulmin 98) that somehow "justify" using the chosen grounds to support the claim (Toulmin, Rieke and Janik 26).

The remaining three elements in the model explain why Crosswhite believes it is useful for determining "the level of demand for justification an argument reaches," or the "intensity" of the conflict that may have spawned the argument (124). An audience may insist that the writer provide *backing* for a warrant, or "the *general* body of information . . . that is presupposed by the warrant appealed to in the argument" (Toulmin, Rieke and Janik 26). For example, if a reviewer for a sport management journal insists that articles will only be accepted when particular statistical techniques are employed to reach their conclusions, then a powerful member of that discipline is providing the backing for specific warrants. A particular audience may also lead a writer to anticipate *possible rebuttals* of the argument or to employ *modal qualifiers* such as "usually," "possibly," or "probably" to the claim (Toulmin, Rieke and Janik 26-27).

The attractions of the Toulmin model are obvious; it seems far more accessible than the complex rules (The middle term of a syllogism must be distributed at least once.) and arcane labels (What's the "middle term?" When is something "distributed?") that characterize formal logic. The elements seem relatively easy to define and to recognize within modern prose. But that doesn't mean the model is without flaws when it comes to its usefulness as a tool in the teaching of written argumentation. Critics tend to warn that Toulmin is most effective if instructors recognize its limitations as well as its strengths, knowing what will effectively supplement the model as well as what may contradict it. For instance, Fulkerson points out that textbook writers who place the Toulmin Model alongside explanations of induction and deduction present students with information that is "theoretically inconsistent" and potentially confusing (445-46).

Because Toulmin's model is grounded in philosophy and logic, rather than composition and rhetoric, it "does not account for the nonlogical aspects of arguments, such as affective and stylistic elements" (Schroeder 97). As we have clearly seen, those "nonlogical aspects," including ethos, play a large role in what our colleagues say makes discourse persuasive in their fields. Moreover, the model fits "any move from grounds to claim" but rarely helps students see how a full argumentative essay has been structured (Fulkerson 446), unless teachers guide their discovery of how each individual set of claim, grounds and warrants works with others to build a persuasive whole (Schroeder 103). Perhaps most troubling, as far as "critical thinking" is concerned, is that the model tends to encourage passive acceptance rather than active questioning of the "assumptions" or "rules that generate certain claims or that legitimize particular warrants" (Schroeder 97, 103). Crosswhite argues that the model "represents" a specific audience posing as a universal audience (125); teachers and students in composition courses, and perhaps in undergraduate majors courses as well, rarely have the moxie to critically examine the backing for a particular argument, even when they have gotten so far as to determine its warrants. Challenging the status quo, within disciplinary or "public" discourse, will always be daunting, but the Toulmin model simply identifies the existence of *backing* without helping to determine its value. It is not, as Schroeder points out, "a system of logic but rather an elaborate system of justification" (100). Such justification even occurs inside the peer review process.

> **Now in . . . a scholarly journal . . . peer review already acts as a kind of giving you some confidence in the results, if you rely on the fact that those articles to be . . . published would already have been peer reviewed in the field.**
>
> Yeah, but there becomes a problem with that. If what you're doing is so revolutionary or so novel, the peer reviewers only have . . . the kind of accepted body of information to go on to do their analysis. So if the work falls within that accepted norm and you've done everything logically correctly, you know, and there's not mathematical errors, then everything is going to be pretty much okay. But sometimes if you're in a novel area or something new, sometimes it's hard to get things through the peer review process because they haven't built the expertise to know whether it's right. And there are avenues for getting stuff like that published, but they're often not in . . . like the premier journals, because they are only going to accept stuff that is reliable, timely and important. There's some research that's more important than others in the eyes of the community. . . . The persuasive is not so much in terms of the writing style, but it's in terms of the methodology.
>
> (Physics, June 22, 1998)

The Toulmin model also shares a flaw with formal logic, a flaw that is crucial to composition courses. As constituted, it is essentially "a tool for analyzing existing arguments rather than a system for creating them" (Fulkerson 446). This limitation would also have to be considered by any professor thinking of using either Toulmin or Aristotle as a "tool-box" their students could employ in a writing-intensive course. Either logic could be employed when asking students to analyze, critique, or summarize published discourse in a field, although their shortcomings in implementing such analysis as that we've discussed would have to be kept in mind. But neither was necessarily intended as a way to generate argument, in either a composition or writing-intensive course.

Still, we feel, along with Richard Fulkerson, that this flaw in Toulmin may be more easily redeemable than those the model possesses as an analytical tool. It has potential as a heuristic for invention. Toulmin's scheme provides us with six clearly identifiable elements found in arguments. Those elements can be transformed into a heuristic by making them the key term in each of six questions:

1. "What is my claim?"
2. "What grounds do I have to support it?"
3. "What statement could warrant my move from the grounds to the claim?"
4. "How can I back up that warrant?"
5. "How much must I qualify my conclusion as contingent?"
6. "What counter-arguments that would weaken my conclusion do I need to acknowledge?" (Fulkerson 446)

Another approach to assist invention could be to incorporate Toulmin's elements into a handout identifying the traits that will be considered when awarding a grade to a completed student paper. Then the writer knows the demands of the prospective audience (without the fiction that the main audience is someone other than the teacher) and just how far the paper will have to go to persuade the audience. The handout could be distributed well before students are due to complete or submit drafts of their work, and need not slavishly follow Toulmin's specific terminology. For example, one of us distributes checklists to our students before they begin drafting argumentative essays, describing those traits the professor will look for when evaluating the submitted work (see Appendices E and F). One item on the list reads, "The writer's position regarding the issue is clearly stated," with the word "position" used to represent overall conclusions, as opposed to the various claims a student may make while building a particular case. Another reads, "The writer's evidence is substantial, effectively integrated into the reasoning, and relevant to both the issue and your conclusions," thus pulling together and expanding on the concepts of *grounds* and *warrants* discussed during the explication of the Toulmin model that appears above.

For us, any model that accurately describes what student writers can anticipate needing, or encountering, in arguments is better than none. But whether a teacher draws from elements of "formal logic," introduces the Toulmin model, lists and defines fallacies, or employs some other mode of instruction, assisting students in the development of argumentation contains an inherent challenge we must confront. That challenge is the realization that the form argument takes, and the overall persuasiveness of whatever someone writes, is dependent on the particular audiences for the writing and the disciplinary contexts or other cultural factors exerting influence over the whole of the activity. Toulmin may identify six elements that can be found in arguments, but the form those elements take will be context-dependent. Students may anticipate more potential for refutation from some teachers or peer groups than from others. Warrants and backings for warrants are often a matter of disciplinary expertise, as are the rules that determine whether a piece of evidence or data is permissible as grounds for a claim (Segal et al. 74). Moreover, if we are going to cover persuasion in a holistic way, then our interviews clearly suggest to us that we must move beyond Toulmin and consider the emotive and the stylistic as modes of engagement. We must discuss the ways writers establish receptivity within their readers, as well as believability and even authority for themselves. And to all of these considerations must be attached the caution that a writer's choices must attend to intent, to subject matter, and to audience. How easy it is to travel far from the mere consideration of "logic!"

Introducing Toulminian terms and other argumentation theory in first-year composition courses would probably have greater meaning to both teachers and students in those courses if they knew that forms of evidence, warrants, and backings for warrants would be explored in courses for majors as part of learning a discipline. Our interviews indicate that at our institution (and one may surmise at others) such exploration is far from guaranteed. One problem is that we can hardly expect our colleagues to be familiar with Toulmin or aspects of "technical logic" and "comp-logic," to use Fulkerson's terms (436). When we asked about "the rules of evidence and modes of proof commonly employed in your discipline" during the first interviews we received a variety of interesting and thoughtful responses, but not ones that would suggest our students are hearing of these matters in the kind of language composition teachers employed while discussing argumentation. When we asked the computer science professor what she found persuasive when reading professional writing she replied that she looked for authors' "credentials" and "agenda or bias," as well as "facts that support the person's opinion, or what research study . . . or studies on which the person has placed his/her conclusions and if the study was a large enough study and there was a random sample" (August 12, 1999). To use Toulmin's terms, this professor seems to us to be speaking of grounds, warrants and backings here (as well as ethos), but we can't be very sure the students will connect this language, as we have, to the language used in first-year composition. Continuing dialogue, such as that we have modeled in our study, or that Blair has advocated for WAC programs, could help our colleagues within various disciplines acquire awareness of Toulmin's language, employ that language in their instruction, or adapt it to fit the argumentative strategies of their field. Or composition teachers could closely consider how the model might lead students into more discipline-specific argument; although we must never forget that no rhetoric can be general enough to effectively persuade any number of disciplinary audiences.

Nor do we see our colleagues as necessarily committed to helping students view disciplinary material as open to question or as "contested," especially at the undergraduate level. The sport management professor sees his students as not strong enough in statistics to make judgments about the inferential techniques employed by researchers in his field (June 12, 1998). In health services administration, the professor said he primarily used professional writing to enhance "content delivery," rather than to explore how effectively the authors made the case for their conclusions.

> **. . . What is their experience as students in terms of, do they have to be taught to . . . recognize good evidence or . . . ?**
>
> *I'm not sure we even get at that level. I really think a lot of the recognition of evidence; if you're going to talk about, let's say, statistics, offering confirmation of clear hypotheses, I really do think that's at the graduate level. The kinds of things I refer to in terms of journal articles are things that extend to content delivery. For example, in information technology, I give them an article . . . out of Health Care Executive or some similar type of journal that talks about the things that CEO's look for in their Chief Information Officers. So what does a Chief Executive Officer look for and expect from their Chief Information Officer and that's what I'm talking about as anecdotal literature. I find that more useful at the undergraduate level.*
>
> (Health Services Administration, July 1, 1999)

For undergraduates, then, there will be no close examination of just how the authors of a journal article arrived at their conclusions regarding a CEO's expectations for a CIO; the professor merely intends for the student to learn what those expectations are. Our colleague in physics may have uttered the most comprehensive summary of how concerns for "content coverage" and adequate "background" may impact on undergraduate reading of disciplinary materials.

> **How do you train students to understand these matters? Do you think they find the same things automatically persuasive that you do, or is that part of that learning process, or do they just take it sort of on face?**
>
> ... so much of this stuff, I think it's transparent; you don't, you're not told this explicitly, as a student; what is persuasive writing and what kind of arguments are persuasive. You're just immersed in this culture where I guess you only respond or emulate things that are within that norm, and things that are outside of that are just, either you're not ever told that it's there in the first place or if you happen to do something in that style, you get immediately scolded by your mentor and so you're told never to do that again, maybe without even an explanation. It's not very overt and so I just have a feeling that we as teachers don't make this very overt either, because we weren't trained to make it that . . . the scholarly works are so dense in terms of the technical sophistication. . . . You know, I could bring in some physics papers for you that they will be 20 pages long and on each page there will be 20 equations. That's a lot of depth, and if you're trying to follow the mathematics of it and then interspersed between the mathematics is the text to try to guide you through; you know, sometimes it's hard to have that skepticism, because you're struggling so much with just trying to follow the arguments, and . . . if it was peer reviewed and it's in a reputable journal, you basically have this gut instinct that everything's on the up and up, and so you're trying to assimilate this and you're basically using. . . . Your basic mind set is that this is correct and I'm trying to just understand it, to gather, you know, where the writer, what their assumptions were and what their conclusions of this analysis were.
>
> (Physics, June 22, 1998)

Some Toulminian language, as a tool for invention, may assist both our cross-disciplinary colleagues and ourselves. But it may be in the areas other than "proofs" and "evidence" where we can most comfortably converse with our colleagues about argument and persuasion. Indeed, the thinking we heard on this matter leads us, as we've already suggested, to wonder if more time shouldn't be spent on such persuasive appeals as credibility and the emotionally evocative in our own composition courses. In any case, we are not dissuaded from our conviction that students should be made aware of knowledge as "contested." At the same time, given the burden professors in majors courses believe they must shoulder in regards to teaching disciplinary content and common professional practice, we are leaning toward the conclusion that such awareness may be most likely conveyed within our university's liberal studies courses, including courses within the liberal studies program offered by our conversants, rather than within the requirements of a student's major program (see Chapter 6).

Perhaps those major programs should each include a course that devotes itself to argumentation in the field. (The health education professor did mention the courses in statistical inference offered to those majors.) Students will need to know the types of grounding, warrants, and backings that will adequately support claims worth making in their workplace or academic setting. When to modify an assertion, when and how to anticipate possible refutations—those are judgments based on an awareness of disciplinary knowledge, disciplinary method, and a sense of appropriateness or kairos developed through instinct, experience, and instructive failure. Before, we were primarily operating on theory when guiding our technical writing students as to the questions they might ask or the documents they might examine when considering communication in particular fields. Now our colleagues have given us a multitude of examples to draw from, and a clearer idea of the variations to be found.

We sensed that our colleagues generally regard the learning of what is persuasive in their disciplines as no one's responsibility but their own, primarily through the discussions of the various "critiques" or "evaluations" they assign to their students. The nursing professor pointed out a journal in her field that sampled professional articles and found a 33% error rate in the citations, and a book that observed how inaccuracies often didn't prevent certain articles from being frequently cited by others. The findings of the journal and the book prompted her to suggest that "the students are naïve, but there are concrete ways to teach them that they don't need to be so naïve" (June 17, 1998). Somehow we have to make sure we keep talking about persuasion in both general and discipline-specific terms. (It's hard for us to grasp how claims can be made about teaching "critical thinking" unless argumentation is addressed with the complexity we have begun to show here.) Looking at our interviews so far, we can certainly see the use our colleagues' observations have for us. If nothing else, they have problematized the role of our second-semester, first-year composition course even more than we had on our own, leading us to ask questions about its purpose, its placement in the freshman year, and even its placement within the English Department. It is our very insight into the multifaceted nature of persuasion that makes their reliance on us to teach it so troubling. We must talk still more about it, because, while they may see their own discipline as "scientific" in its approach to knowledge, we ourselves still cannot accept that persuasion within their fields can be so characterized. It must be fluid enough, changeable enough, and context-bound enough to remain an art.

6

Expert Knowledge

Knowing That, Learning How, and Asking Why

> . . . we think that *knowledge* and *understanding* belong to art rather than to experience, and we suppose artists to be wiser than men of experience. . . ; and this because the former know the cause, but the latter do not. For men of experience know that the thing is so, but do not know why, while the others know the "why" and the cause.
>
> —Aristotle (*Metaphysics*, Book One, I, 11, lines 24-30)

Bill Readings argues in *The University in Ruins* that the university became modern "when its activities [were] organized in view of a single regulatory idea"—in this case, Kant's concept of reason. Reason is the "organizing principle" of all the disciplines and replaced the divine, revealed truth of the medieval university (14-15). But of course, rational discourse preexisted Kant. Dialectic (science) appears in Plato as a kind of "general art" connected to discovering nature and understanding the causes of things as they are in themselves, different than the literary arts (poesis) or rhetorical arts employed in political persuasion (Readings 71-72).

Beyond the idea of reason, Readings claims that the idea of culture tied the university to nation-building, and had the most resonance for literary culture, which was seen to preserve national culture. Anglo-American literature was something of an exception because it preserved republican culture—a canon of choice more than of national tradition (16). Most recently, to Readings, the idea of excellence has held sway, as national cultures wane in importance in the face of globalizing Americanization. Literacy no longer refers to national culture but to the general ability to process information and deliver goods and services efficiently in the corporate culture accompanying the expansion of consumerism.

Few of us who teach in the university can deny that, at least where the undergraduate or master's degree is concerned, most of our graduates will enter their professional lives not as seekers after truth within the intellectual culture of the university but as practitioners of utilitarian knowledge that supports corporate culture outside of academe. Moreover, the myriad contexts in which each of the disciplines is pursued within and outside the university cause standards of excellence, or ideas of expertise, to apply so variously that the simple hierarchy between theory (asking why) and practice (knowing that) Aristotle implies in the opening epigraph hardly seems workable.

For instance, as we discovered in Chapter 5, specialization in physics limits the objects of study over which researchers can claim fundamental causal understanding; nursing clinicians test research articles against the wisdom of their intuitions; managers see academicians as less qualified than practitioners. In the flood of data-gathering, even among researchers in academe, knowing that an author is widely published or that a journal is peer reviewed may substitute for knowing why experimental results are valid. The complex and varied responses received to our questions about writing as inquiry, argument, and persuasion illustrate the difficulty in defining who experts are, and what kinds of knowledge they should possess or learn. We can't pretend there is only one context, or none at all.

Although the causal inquiry of dialectic—asking nature why—still may have pride of place among some research faculty, others, including teaching faculty and those who have been practitioners outside of academe—may privilege practical savvy. What works? How can I persuade others it will? How can it be implemented? The sport management professor challenges the assumption that "what works" necessarily connects to the merits of a particular theory. Everything depends on the fit between a specific situation and the results of a method of inquiry.

> ... we try to show our students in class both at the undergraduate and more in depth at the graduate level where things such as surveys can come into play, how you can use that information. In other words, there are theories and then you go out and collect research on it, but then how can you apply that in a real world situation. In other words, by talking about different types of management policies, procedures, talking about what works and what doesn't work and I think that's what they need to understand, that

you can't become so theory-oriented that you lose track of, what are you going to do with it?

(Sport Management, June 12, 1998)

When Readings recognizes that universities had a role in nation-building, he acknowledges that academe itself is a political and politicized institution and is itself the repository of myriad subcultures. Knowledge-building, like state-building, involves arguments and persuasion about what disciplines are really sciences; what data is worth paying attention to; and what is anomalous, what assumed. In this sense, everyone is a practitioner and everything an art. For science is something scientists do, even though, at the undergraduate level, students are mostly expected to take the knowledge base for granted—"knowing that" particular scientific information is so, not why, as if the authoritative version of the "facts" within a discourse were there before one's eyes as surely as landmarks present within a physical environment. Most undergraduates study science as content. Only recently have some institutions begun to pair faculty and students in undergraduate research in ways that might reveal it as a practice.

To help our discussion along, we will reserve the term *science* or *dialectic* for theoretical understanding of arguments regarding foundational truth claims within a field (knowing why and the cause), while thinking of experiential knowledge both as a kind of practical "know how" and a kind of intuitive "knowing that" because knowledge "picked up" from lived experience is usually trusted but "latent" (unarticulated unless challenged in some way). We use the phrase "learning how" to describe both the way that practical know how can be picked up in real contexts and anticipated within academe through the practice of writing and exposure to the rhetorical practices within disciplines that produce their foundational knowledge. We conclude that liberal studies courses may provide a unique contribution to critical awareness through instruction of non-majors. Because most disciplines seem to delay discussion of the processes that create their foundational knowledge until their majors enter graduate programs beyond the master's level, required electives for non-majors can introduce students to the critical thinking necessary to make persuasive arguments and judge their credibility. Citizens must often make judgments about public policy that bear on the ability to understand the evolution of scientific understanding or judgments about the credibility of media-derived information that bear on their personal choices. If non-majors do not get this critical awareness as undergraduates, and do not go to graduate school, will they ever get it? And can it serve as a transitional form of "learning how" that paves the way for the "know how" they could acquire from practically inclined teachers in the undergraduate major, or from workplace practitioners who are invited into the classroom?

The various kinds of expertise we've just described lead to further discussion of still more issues raised in Chapter 5, including the following:

- How dialectic is itself contested, an art
- What the nature of various kinds of expertise might be
- How English requirements in a core curriculum relate to courses in a major regarding the teaching of argument
- Where the contested nature of disciplinary knowledge should be taught at the undergraduate level, if taught at all
- Whether the disciplines should teach research design or modes of inquiry in the undergraduate major
- What the role of first-year composition should be, especially a second-semester course in the teaching of argument

It is one of the ironies of rhetoric and composition as a field that its expertise has often been perceived as dealing narrowly with practical rules of grammar and usage, even though those now trained in the field at the graduate level are heavily influenced by work in the social construction of science. Now, a frequent topic of concern for writing faculty is the art surrounding dialectic, by which the most sophisticated judgments regarding the construction of various disciplinary knowledge bases are undertaken. Many rhetorical scholars believe that writing is vitally connected to this thinking—to the ability to plan and conduct experiments, to analyze patterns and regularities in data, to form hypotheses in every field. Research is not simply a transparent and grammatically correct "write-up" or record of results, for some results are discarded as anomalies, whereas others enter the written record of an experiment. If academic work were simply the transmission of current knowledge claims, how could mistakes be rectified? If science were not something we do, as well as know, something we do by writing, then how could science progress? Students in majors outside English often seem unaware of the quantity and the range of writing they will need to do as academic or nonacademic professionals in their fields. Our conversations have begun a dialogue regarding many of these questions and have raised others.

When we began to plan our interviews, the curiosity that drove us forward was admittedly governed by our own sense of what undergraduate and graduate education might mean in terms of disciplinary practice and expert knowledge. If written language is the essential medium by which knowledge generation is carried out and disseminated in every discipline, then how could students know a discipline without consciously learning the function of written discourse in their major field? To find out the answer, we attempted to "join" our colleagues' "conversations," rather than only our own, as Segal et al. suggest (85). Whatever the answers we discover they bear on our place in the university as well.

When academic areas of study are identified strictly as knowledge bases, and the "methods of inquiry" used to construct them, can English composition be easily contracted to sets of testable information and "skills?" As English faculty in rhetoric and composition, we have protested not only that writing includes expertise not easily crammed into a model of scholarship and specialization that has dominated American universities for the past century but also that this expertise is not easily reduced to questions of correctness. As is evident in Chapter 5, our colleagues seem to agree in part with the former, even though they have been reluctant to give up on the latter (see Chapter 7). One example of their openness to understanding science in rhetorical terms seems to be some skepticism regarding the value of quantitative versus qualitative studies, studies that might be more relevant, comprehensible and readily applied by students. That is the subject to which we now turn in thinking about how English faculty might teach their writing courses.

CONNECTING EXPERTISE TO PRACTICE

One interesting thread that ran through almost all of our conversations involved a question not raised by Aristotle in his consideration of metaphysics, even though he thought that practical knowledge enhanced theory—the degree of direct connection between disciplinary research (asking why) and practice. Presumably, within science, the most powerful theory is the most general claim. But does the content knowledge (knowing that) that professors perceive their majors to need at the undergraduate level help them to "learn how" to be expert practitioners, either inside or outside academe? For instance, the professors of sport management, health education, health services administration, and elementary education all took note of a desire for or a trend toward "qualitative" and "descriptive" research that could reflect the distinct, complex, and situated experiences awaiting practitioners once they graduate from SRU's programs in those fields. In reviewing our manuscript some perceived a new trend, at least among professors at institutions such as ours.

> The "moves away from strictly empirical, positivistic disciplinary knowledge bases" reminds me of Thomas Kuhn's Structures of Scientific Revolutions. Are we seeing an older system straining at the edges, fixing to reform, rebuild? Or would the picture seem different if faculty from research institutions were interviewed?
>
> (Elementary Education Draft Response)

With the exception of elementary education, these disciplines are relatively new. Health education and sport management were formerly subfields within the area of physical education. Health services administration recognizes the unique management demands made by health facilities and programs, for which traditional business models aimed at maximizing production and profits may be inadequate.

In general, these areas of professional practice have gained legitimacy as knowledge-generating disciplines by following a social science model, using inferential statistics to test hypotheses that could be applied universally to the activities of the field's practitioners. Ethnographies, narrated case studies, and focus group responses do not possess the generalizability of such controlled social science experiments but seem, to our interviewees, to more accurately reflect the practice and experience for which their students are being prepared. Most undergraduates at institutions like ours are not going to be researchers themselves; the expectation on receipt of their degrees may often be that they can function within a professional setting without the "depth" of understanding graduate school provides regarding the nature of disciplinary knowledge (asking why). Theoretical models and statistically inferred hypotheses may be accurate as far as they go, but they lack the definition and specificity that may adequately reflect the variable and ever-shifting circumstances in which practitioners live and work. In some sense, Aristotle recognized this fact when he acknowledged that a scientist with practical knowledge was wiser than one without it. Although it is customary to think of concrete situations as examples or applications of more general theory in academic contexts, the truth is that theoretical knowledge is a generalization from the data of experience. As a generalization, it leaves out anomalies and may even prevent effective functioning in particular situations.

Although, in *Metaphysics,* Aristotle does not make the distinction between art and science in the way we have been making it, he acknowledges that "art" and "science" develop from experience and that people with experience often have the advantage in actual practice over "those who have theory without experience . . . experience is knowledge of individuals, art of universals, and actions and productions are all concerned with the individual" (499). However, in expressing his theory of knowledge hierarchically, the "highest" and "best" knowledge was that of causal theory. For our interviewees, it seemed the hierarchy was inverted.

> . . . Some of the academics that I've seen . . . I don't think could operate very effectively in health care institutions. There are several that I've known that I feel were somewhat tentative or would be afraid to be around patients or would be afraid to be in that setting.
>
> (Health Services Administration, July 1, 1999)

"Qualitative" research generates accessible, richly descriptive narratives students can recall and perhaps apply to some appropriate degree when confronted by particular professional situations, with a sense of the appropriate derived from both their own experience and that of fellow practitioners. More recent theories of "situated learning" emphasize the importance of novices having "access to arenas of mature practice," hence the emphasis some of our colleagues placed on internship experiences (Lave and Wenger 110). For our physics professor, lab experience seemed as crucial to professionalization as the struggle to understand professional research articles and a new area of pragmatic research also appeared to have significance for our sport management professor.

> *So let's do our Chi-squares and let's do our multiple t-tests or ANOVA and ANCOVA, whatever, but the relevance of what they're doing escapes the majority of people that are in the field. And I think if you look at what our students are getting into, only, I don't know what percentage, I would imagine in single digits somewhere are gonna go on and get their doctorate and be interested in this area. But for the most part, they're going to become practitioners. Those theorists, those people that are doing a lot of the theoretical writing are saying, well this, we are adding to the body of knowledge. And there's this sort of trickle down effect, if you will, to practitioners. I don't know if I buy into that, because I think that the amount of time it's going to take for the information to be disseminated and to be sort of diluted down to where a nonacademic or a more of a clinical practitioner can understand it, you're talking 3 to 4 years. By that time the information is outdated . . . what we try to do, and I have this written down in our mission, is that there's theoretical research and then there's applied, go out and do it. . . . In other words, what we're trying to show students is how research can be used to benefit them in an applied or practical nature. . . . It's doing simple surveys, using maybe just means, mediums, and modes, frequency distributions, those types of things.*
>
> (Sport Management, July 27, 1998)

Research appeared to be a way to test the applicability of more general theoretical results to new situations, and to improve the function of particular programs, rather than to know "why and the cause." Apparently, the knowledge of proximate results is better for practical situations. In contrast, Aristotle implies that the highest level of knowledge is that of remote/first causes or the nature of things.

The academic community's preoccupation with fundamental knowledge, and the workplace's need for practical savvy, account for some of Dias et al.'s assessment of the differences between academic and nonacademic worlds. It appears, however, that professors, at least at teaching institutions, are aware of the problem and hoping to address it.

> ... a real criticism of academic research in general is many times it has very little application ... day-to-day or by the time it gets down to application the connection is no longer a fact.... Within operations research there's a variety of quantitative models.... Those are applied day-to-day in a health care setting but not so that the practitioner understands it. Usually what it's captured in is inventory management software or project management software where the algorithm is buried in a black box. So all the ... practitioner needs to know is various assumptions that have to be met and constraints to apply the model, but they really don't have to know the model at all.
>
> (Health Services Administration, July 1, 1999)

In the following passage from our first conversation with the health education professor, the voice of empiricism is first cited in the case of evaluating a health clinic's performance ("we follow a truly scientific way of sampling people") and then overruled by the voice of realism ("Well, you can't randomly sample a lot of groups because they're simply not going to be available.").

> ... some courses the students take in some aspects of the discipline are very empirical, very quantitative in the way you describe, but I would say there is a real movement, even within those courses, to look at what can't be so easily captured on a checklist or a "q" test or whatever.
>
> **Are those ... other ways of establishing or developing knowledge ... being more accepted within the profession itself?**
>
> In our profession, actually we've borrowed a lot of our qualitative evaluation techniques from sociology and anthropology, and those are pretty much the way to go in a lot of those other disciplines.
>
> **So we're getting things like ethnographic studies?**
>
> Exactly, that's exactly the word we use. Rapid assessment procedures, rapid anthropological assessment procedures. We want to find out how a health clinic is working and we follow a truly scientific way of sampling people. Well, you can't randomly sample a lot of groups because they're simply not going to be available. You have to use focus groups. You have to use smaller, more intensive semi-structured or structured interviews. You have to use more participant observer. In fact, people who are actually doing health education out in the real world have probably been doing a lot of

these but never knew exactly what to call them. Well, now we have . . . more of a systematic language.

(Health Education, June 16, 1998)

Another way to describe the difference between quantitative and qualitative methods of research in Health Education is to recognize that what is going on in the latter variety is program assessment. If quantitative research relies on random sampling, it produces a statistically probable result, but a given situation may, in fact, be one of the exceptions. In a general sense, these anomalies don't matter, but if you are the anomaly, they matter rather substantively.

I have to make it very clear to them that research writing and the tools of the researcher are sometimes counterproductive to evaluating the program, and I have to be very specific, in terms of here's what research and here's what program evaluation is about. Some of the things we do are similar. Some of the things we do are quite different. And the types of things that a researcher wants to know are often very, very different to what a program evaluator wants to know because there's knowledge production on one hand and there's decision making or decision facilitation on the other.

(Health Education, July 16, 1998)

Needless to say, these moves away from strictly empirical, positivistic disciplinary knowledge bases raise some interesting questions about how undergraduate schools might provide a connection between disciplinary foundations (knowing why and the cause) and lived contexts requiring "know how" outside the university. What if the "whys" that can be known in professions closely tied to human and institutional interactions are so detached from the quotidian "hows" as to seem almost meaningless to practitioners? Geisler concluded her recent study of "academic literacy" by suggesting that expertise entails "the ability to negotiate three distinct worlds of discourse: the *domain content world* of logically related truths . . . the *narrated world* of everyday experience . . . and the *rhetorical world* of abstract authorial conversation" (240). Such a formulation acknowledges that questions may be raised and decisions made fruitfully in experiential contexts as well as in the world of ideas. The "man of experience" can do more than describe and relate without explanation. Moreover, as we have seen, we ask students to describe and relate within the world of ideas when we ask them only to recall content. Perhaps Aristotle was too preoccupied in the opening epigraph with the conditions of leisure and the class structure necessary to support scientific inquiry, rather than with describing real distinctions between kinds of thinking operative across contexts. On the one hand, the professors cited here do not necessarily expect their undergraduate majors to think critically about the status of basic knowledge in the field but to accept it and use it. On the other hand, they know that using it raises other questions that will call for making different arguments than those involved in typical disciplinary research. On what basis might students engage in a critique of and reflection on practice during their undergraduate years?

Our nursing professor observes that with experience a practitioner might become aware of the dissonance between a theory or experimentally circumscribed finding and "what works." The experience or practice should inform the theory, not the other way around.

> . . . we talk about . . . intuitive knowledge as a basis for decision making. Now by intuitive, I'm not speaking of intuitive in women's intuition, but rather intuitive as it's used when one thinks of novice to expert in the evolution of a professional. Meaning that one has had an enormous amount of experience with a particular type of client and almost seems to know intuitively what the problems might be or how to approach such a patient. An experienced nurse working with a very anxious patient would intuitively use a number of skills.
>
> (Nursing, November 21, 1998)

It appears that just as a discipline passes down a tradition of theoretical knowledge in texts, it also passes down a tradition of experience or practice. To those working in practical situations, this experience itself is often the best teacher, since it provides not only effective practice, but a skepticism about theory and extrapolated conclusions, especially about their relevance to particular applications.

Still, our interviewees also seemed aware of lingering questions regarding the legitimacy of a contextualized, "practical" and "unverifiable" knowledge. Would knowledge derived from story and description have less persuasive power than that at least seemingly derived from the testing of hypotheses, using numerical data teased out of a structured experiment? (The elementary education professor seemed a little bewildered by the political firestorm that has greeted much "qualitative" research on reading, since, as she put it, the material is "descriptive" rather than "prescriptive" in nature.) And if such knowledge cannot be confidently applied to professional situations across the board, then how can practitioners educated in such knowledge claim a distinct professional status and the vocational benefits that commonly accrue to such status?

> ... there's intuition still, of course, there's personality, there's energy and so on ... and there's still the "x" factor; we're not quite sure why things work or why things don't work ... but there really is the way that a professional plans, carries out and evaluates a program as opposed to "well, I feel this or I think this or the man on the street knows how to do that." The man on the street does not know how to do that. We know. We've tried that and we've seen what doesn't happen when we use what some people would say is common sense ... obviously we have a scientific method and that's what everybody else used, but we have some other methods of inquiry as well.
>
> (Health Education, June 16, 1998)

It is here that the limitations of separating an expert's theoretical knowledge (knowledge of first principles or of "why") from experiential or practical knowledge (knowing that a thing is so or how a thing is done but not necessarily "why") most clearly appear. It is not the nature of things that practitioners seek to establish but good technique and results. The "x" factor to which the health education professor refers may in fact only represent a residual consciousness of Aristotle's and others' expectation that knowledge of first principles is the mark of all true experts—in other words, the modern day equivalent of saying persons of experience *merely* "know that." We haven't had the language to describe what our health educator senses practitioners know that is different from what the "man on the street" knows, but some of our colleagues clearly believe in such knowledge. They seek out opportunities within the undergraduate curriculum for context-dependent, goal-oriented tasks that will help their students "avoid ignorance" in a way perhaps even more effective than learning theory. What kinds of critical judgments are involved in accurately recognizing a situation as calling for a particular response, in knowing something has worked and so using it again, or in sensing something will work in a new context? How does one move others to act in such situations? Apparently a starting point for forming such judgments may be to introduce the tools used in the context and to create a set of expectations regarding the practical context necessary for such critical judgment.

> ... at the baccalaureate level, other than part-time jobs, we primarily have traditional students and so what we're really doing ... is developing a set of expectations of what real life will be like ... so that when they go in to the hospital they have some understanding of the setting and the requirements for performance and things like that. So we really ... aren't at a theoretical level and I don't think it would be appropriate for us to try and do that. I

> *think our program is very pragmatic in terms of our expectations and pragmatic . . . in terms of giving them some tools that will provide them with some distinctive competencies. For example, I think it would be heinous if anyone graduated, got out of my finance course, and could not use a spreadsheet. . . . I think it would be heinous if they graduated from the program and didn't have the sense that health care institutions are periodically surveyed and that there's an accreditation process. . . . We give them that preparation. I think our students are very well grounded in terms of what they would expect to face in the professional environment. I think it's one of the things we do absolutely best.*
>
> (Health Services Administration, July 1, 1999)

But the skills necessary for practice include not just the tools of business management, but broader communication skills that may sometimes be underestimated or even denied in the negotiations surrounding the construction of the discipline's knowledge base.

> *. . . we talk about culture, and then my own approach is different from some people, but I feel . . . a real responsibility at the undergraduate level to teach tools, that . . . to be successful you have to have a tool box. That includes some of the quantitative stuff like finance, operations management, but another set that includes just how you deal effectively with people. I see these being two separate sets of skills and I have met people that have not been successful because they could only do one or the other. Sometimes you can get away with not having the quantitative skills if you can handle people effectively, but I've rarely seen where someone could just have technical skills and have no people skills and be able to work effectively in health care.*
>
> (Health Services Administration, July 1, 1999)

The ideal would be to value all types of knowledge, not privileging those in one sector—in other words, not creating a hierarchy of knowledge but recognizing, in contrast, that it is not only the person with theoretical knowledge who can teach, or only those without it with something to learn, as Aristotle claims ("Metaphysics" 499).

> *. . . the academics are not just in the business of conveying information or training future professionals or at least initially training future professionals, but we're also supposed to be in the business of generating the knowledge base. And this is not to say that practitioners can not do research. This is not to say that practitioners*

can not do rigorous program evaluation. In fact, that's one of the things that health education is becoming more sensitive to, . . . that there's a lot of practiced wisdom out there in the field that we can use to advance, in many cases, the theoretical foundations of what we say and, in academe, what I say in the typical classroom in Slippery Rock. There is a sense . . . shared with the practitioners that I bring in to talk to my students . . . that there's an expectation we will provide leadership in certain areas and the practitioners will provide . . . leadership in certain areas.

(Health Education, June 16, 1998)

There are many areas of expertise as well as knowledge, each with their strengths and weaknesses.

What are those areas?

With the practitioners we rely on them more now than we used to for internship sites. Normally, that will be near the end of the student's professional preparation program. We rely on the practitioners as well to come in and sometimes guest lecture or actually teach various skills at the invitation of the professor. . .

(Health Education, June 16, 1998)

In fact, our computer science professor definitely thought that among those in her field it was the practitioner who held the privileged position. The use of the term cutting-edge to refer to those outside academe indicates the mind shift that has occurred in the valences of theory and practice.

. . . there probably is good reason for some cutting-edge groups to think that academicians are not as good as, because in a lot of schools there isn't the money to buy the latest, the hardware and software . . . especially in the field of web design and information technology. This field is moving so fast that I don't think there is that . . . distinction. It's very difficult to even find anybody who . . . has the traditional academic training in web commerce or web design, e-commerce, working in the field. Usually these people are not considered credentialed. They just have all kinds of experience.

(Computer Science, August 12, 1999)

This shift is also apparent in the differences between many masters level graduate programs and those granting the PhD.

ASKING WHY OR LEARNING HOW IN GRADUATE SCHOOL

Perhaps not surprisingly, three of the four professors whose disciplines were undergoing significant shifts in approaches to knowledge generation (sport management, health education, health services administration) strongly emphasized during their interviews that their majors would need to attend graduate school if they wished to advance to positions that both demanded greater responsibility and also commanded increased prestige and higher salaries. "They [holders of master's degrees] are more likely to get higher paid management positions, yes," said the sport management professor. "The undergraduates will get management positions but . . . you're looking at somewhere in the high teens or low 20s" (June 12, 1998).

All three professors also made it quite explicit that graduate school would be the place where students could explore the research techniques and theoretical frameworks that made disciplinary knowledge, as our health services administration professor notes:

> . . . I really think a lot of the recognition of evidence; if you're going to talk about, let's say, statistics, offering confirmation of a clear hypothesis, I really do think that's at the graduate level. The kinds of things I refer to in terms of journal articles are things that extend to content delivery. For example, in information technology I give them an article . . . out of Health Care Executive or some similar type of journal that talks about the things that CEO's look for in their chief information officers. So what does a chief executive officer look for and expect from their chief information officer and that's what I'm talking about as anecdotal literature. I find that more useful at the undergraduate level.
>
> (Health Services Administration, July 1, 1999)

It was not always quite so clear just how deeper exploration of the "why" behind disciplinary knowledge would qualify people for the higher paying, more responsible positions, however.

> . . . If you expect to reach mid-level management . . . or beyond; if you expect to lead a hospital or lead an ambulatory facility or lead a home health agency, frankly, you should expect to have a master's degree . . . you can't be just a graduate of the school of hard knocks. The profession used to be that way. It used to be if you had a bachelor's degree, you had 20 years of experience you could expect to lead a hospital. I don't think any more. And I think part of that's driven by other professions in the field, but it's also driven

> by the fact that having a degree is a discriminator. And so they [students] know that if you're going to be a player in health services administration you're going to have to go out there and get a master's degree.
>
> (Health Services Administration, Nov. 23, 1999)

For the health services administration professor, the graduate degree seems to function as a kind of credential more than proof the holder has knowledge necessary to administer a position with major responsibilities. To the health education professor the master's allows practitioners to specialize, and "to specialize" is seemingly equated with "to professionalize."

> ... for our field the baccalaureate degree is still in many settings considered the entry level certificate. Now, one thing we're always very, very careful to tell our students is that this is one of those areas where a graduate degree is going to happen sooner or later; you will have to professionalize. So you have to look very, very carefully at what you want to get your masters degree in. Now, if a health educator wants to work for, let's say, for the Center for Disease Control in Atlanta, many times the entry level for that organization will be a master's degree and maybe one or two years experience, but for a lot of nonprofits, for the state, for most county positions, the baccalaureate is still considered, "hey, you're a beginning practitioner."
>
> (Health Education, June 16, 1998)

In sport management, knowledge of "theories and content" function as something of a supplement to specific business and management experiences. Here a starker difference between graduate and undergraduate knowledge, between "asking why" and "knowing that," exists.

> ... at the undergraduate level our students are going to come out and they are going to be at the lowest level, they are going to be entry-level positions in these different facilities, in these different teams and things like that. They are going to have the basics. Someone that has a master's degree is going to come out and it's going to be a lot more in depth. It's going to be, for example, we were talking about basic risk management plans or basic any type of marketing; when they are an undergraduate they are just going to get the high points, the peaks if you will, so they have a basic comprehension of what we're talking about. At the master's degree level, it's going to be way down. It's going to be in depth. We're going to actually pull out other ... business plans. For example, I have two copies of different business plans from different facilities across the United States and we can tear them apart

literally and see what makes them good or makes them bad and discuss them. We go a lot more into case study situations at the graduate level. This is an actual scenario. This is what really happened. What would you do in this situation? What we're trying to use is, we're trying to use normally the maturity of the individual plus some of the previous experiences to allow them to see how they can use that and then plus with the theories and content that we teach them, how they can apply it in a real world situation.

(Sport Management, June 12, 1998)

Graduate work was also obviously important in physics, although that professor seemed to suggest that the scope of his discipline precluded the possibility of most graduate students ever coming close to an encyclopedic knowledge, breadth being sacrificed for depth. Instead, graduate students in physics could count on the development and refinement of their theoretical and experimental knowledge within a particular area. On the other hand, graduate school did not figure prominently in our conversations with the elementary education professor. One possible reason is that students can generally land an initial teaching position on the strength of their undergraduate program, which features extensive field experience as well as course work. The second reason may be that beginning teachers have been required for the past generation or so to accumulate graduate credits both to obtain permanent certification and to increase their salary level. Apparently graduate school has a different goal and objective for practitioners.

In this sense, it may be that the emergence of the MBA model of graduate education makes it important to distinguish between doctoral programs and other graduate education. Within doctoral programs, master's degrees are sometimes conferred on those not wishing to seek, or those not approved to pursue, doctoral candidate status. Case-based graduate education in business does not presuppose that graduate students will find academic jobs. It credentials managers for ever increasing responsibilities and salaries outside academe. Many pragmatic disciplines appear to have increasingly developed such master's degrees as an opportunity for professionalization.

Graduate school was also less emphasized by the nursing, computer science, and mathematics professors. Undergraduates in nursing at SRU have already successfully completed hospital-affiliated registered nurse programs; the baccalaureate might even be considered an advanced degree for those students. Just what this degree, or the course work within the baccalaureate program, provides in terms of the ability to practice nursing is unclear. Is it, in a way, an initial managerial certification process? Beyond the baccalaureate, graduate work in nursing is focused on specialization in a medical area or on management, informatics, and finance skills, since increasingly nurses manage a considerable number of staff and have responsibility for very large budgets. Hands-on nursing is performed by personnel with a wide range of nursing degrees, and a wide range of titles, depending on the length of the nursing program and on the kind of institution granting the degree.

The computer science professor observed that the newness of her field has created a great deal of fluidity when it comes to the credentials of its practitioners:

What kind of degrees would they have?

Any degrees.

Any kind of degree?

Not necessarily. Some . . . folks working in web design today have no traditional degrees in anything related to what they're doing.

Would they be likely to have a college degree though?

Some of them would, but just as often you will find some of them not. One of the best books in web design that I read for doing research for this new Information Technology program was written by a 16-year-old high school student.

(Computer Science, August 12, 1999)

Undergraduates in mathematics, according to that professor, appeared to have quick access to jobs in areas such as actuarial science and operations research. In reading our manuscript, the computer science professor noted that students in her field find equally lucrative positions even before graduation.

More and more we have some students, and this is a nationwide trend, a lot of students don't even finish their undergraduate degree because they find that they can make more money just right now using the skills that they have and they'll say, "I can always go back to school and get a degree. I can't always make x amount of dollars."

(Computer Science)

As with physics, the math professor considered undergraduate work to be quite rigorous already. Again, graduate work was different in degree (depth) more than in kind:

Some of our students have gone on to graduate programs and, trying to explain to them what graduate programs are like, they're not really that different than what we do as undergraduates. The difference really is the depth. When you're a freshman, you take the calculus sequence. When you're a junior or senior, you take the advanced calculus sequence and it is the exact same subject, except this time you're going into the nuts and bolts of proofs, why things work, but it is the exact same subject. When you are a graduate student, you would take a real analysis course. You're going to repeat the same exact things, except more generalization and deeper proofs.

(Mathematics, August 6, 1999)

In mathematics, writing functions as a clear marker of growing expertise within the field, since the writing of proofs becomes a more and more prominent feature of advanced course work. Mathematicians in industry and government positions are frequently called on to explain their proofs to nonexpert audiences. One of the most difficult transitions for undergraduate majors involves letting go of an image of mathematician as calculator, and accepting a seemingly conflicting image of mathematician as thinker and writer of proofs. Once again, the distinction between practical and theoretical knowledge is made; however, the falseness of such a rigid distinction is also apparent. One wonders whether an actuary, who calculates insurance and annuity premiums, would think that proofs are "what math is all about," or that he or she is simply a "calculator."

As much as we do use writing within the discipline, I think it's something that the majors themselves tend to fight. The world seems to love to divide itself and so either you're good . . . at math or at English. Nobody is supposed to be good at both and when they get into Modern Concepts and to 300- and 400-level courses beyond that, and they learn we expect them to write because you have to write proofs, they rebel a little bit. I don't see why I should have to do this. First off, they tend not to have an idea of what math is all about. I will admit I was one of these people also, that a lot of time the reason we get math majors is they can get the right answers. I took algebra in high school and I took calculus and I tended to get the right answers.

Right, they like precision and exactitude.

But what they don't know is that that's not what a mathematician does. They don't see proofs in high school. You don't prove in a calculus class too much. You don't do it at all in an algebra class. So their vision of what a mathematician is and does and the reality are in conflict. That's why, I'm guessing at the number here, I'd say about one third to one half of people who start out as math

> *majors as freshmen aren't a math major by their junior year because their vision of what it was and what it really is were at odds.*
>
> (Mathematics, August 6, 1999)

Thus, it is clear that expertise includes many kinds of knowledge—of causal theories about the nature of things, of how to achieve and measure effective results in typical situations (a more positive rendition of a practical "know how" than knowing that a thing is so rather than why), of the tools and techniques used in a field, of firsthand intuitive knowledge rarely articulated. It is usually associated with a kind of authority within a specific realm and enough critical capacity to make appropriate decisions and do whatever it takes to convince others to follow through. Often those with one kind of expertise are perceived as lacking expertise in another. Where a degree appears to act as a credential, it is because the degree acts as a sign for the possession of expertise, no matter how defined or where the knowledge is learned—whether in school, on the job, or through a combination of the two. In this sense, the credential can operate much like an honorary degree that signifies expertise acquired, and demonstrated, outside academic institutions. Expertise is knowing why, knowing that, knowing how, and just knowing that I know. Moreover, the analytical mindset that characterizes those who "do theory" can be exercised almost anywhere and it frequently involves writing.

WRITING TO LEARN, REFLECT, AND CRITIQUE IN THE UNDERGRADUATE MAJOR

For the mathematics professor, the writing of proofs is integral to the practice of the discipline, and therefore such writing is inevitable once students begin to approach the level of actual disciplinary practice. But writing also serves many other functions during a student's undergraduate years. Moreover, these functions are not limited to "knowledge delivery," or the accurate restatement of "content" during exams. Undergraduates write to learn, reflect, and critique.

Our colleagues commonly regarded writing as an alternative to lecture and reading for student absorption of what is perceived to be important or necessary material. During the so-called "first-wave" of the contemporary WAC movement much emphasis was placed on "writing to learn"; the notion that writing might be a more effective way to understand and retain disciplinary content through pre- or post-lecture free-writes, responses to open-ended or clearly focused questions, brief papers connecting lectures or text chapters to material recently made public, and journal-keeping. This fact does not mean that writing-to-learn techniques are the same as rote memorization, however. Such techniques produce engagement with material, possibly increasing understanding and thus the ability to apply knowledge, just as other forms of reflection and critique we discuss below do. The writing to learn approach is evident, as we've said, in the teaching of many of our interviewed colleagues.

For the sport management professor, research papers were a way to implement what students had learned in their courses about "descriptive statistics" derived from surveys and other means. The writing would also serve to help students read, understand, and judge the utility of articles in both academic and trade journals related to the field.

> . . . right now . . . there's [are] two types of journals out there. There's the very rigorous, theoretical type of journals and there's the more applied Athletic Business Journal and things like that. What I would like to see, and I believe there's a need for a more middle of the road, something in between. That's what I'm trying to prepare our students for. I guess I'm identifying that as a trend and I'm trying to prepare our students so that if it does happen, . . . they are prepared not only to understand what they read there, but . . . could actually put some information into it in written form themselves.
>
> (Sport Management July 27, 1998)

The most aware and thorough user of the "writing to learn" (WTL) approach was the physics professor. His orientation was hardly a surprise, because he had for years participated in campus workshops and reading groups devoted to WAC, in addition to editing some issues of a newsletter, aptly titled *Writing to Learn,* that was distributed to faculty and administrators in the 14 universities of the Pennsylvania State System of Higher Education. He is not as keen on students "learning to write" discipline-specific genres because, as he explained, "if a person is going to be a researcher . . . they're going to learn that genre or research writing in the discipline once they're engaged in that research. Since we don't do original research as undergraduates it's kind of contrived, so they don't really learn that" (November 16, 1998).

The physics professor's criticism of the writing-in-the-disciplines (WID) approach echoes Dias et al.'s observation that schools can only offer pale simulations of the highly variable contexts in which college graduates will eventually find themselves writing, many of which lie outside academe and even outside research (202). The gap between actual professional practice and the various conditions seemingly inherent in undergraduate instruction appears to make any embrace of a WID approach problematic for professors teaching on that level. Although Chapter 4 indicates we disagree, at least in part, with such conclusions, critics like Harriet Malinowitz have come to see other reasons for preferring WTL to WID. WID, she argues, tends to encourage student's unreflective acceptance of "the mystique of dominant knowledge systems" (293). Focusing on the discovery of what is accepted and commonplace within disciplinary discourse will not give undergraduates the ability to both use and question such discourse, or to consider the social, economic, or ethical effects of such discourse. WTL at least attempts, by encouraging writing in a variety of reflective forms, "to disrupt learning as usual. . . ." (Malinowitz 294)

> I don't doubt that writing in the disciplines may be helpful to students as they seek entrance to particular intellectual or professional communities and learn to write and speak in ways that will identify them as credible members of those communities. Yet . . . it doesn't help students critically assess how forms of knowledge and method are hierarchically structured in disciplines so that some achieve canonical or hegemonic status whereas others are effectively fenced out. (Malinowitz 293)

WTL, in other words, can function as both a tool in an undergraduate's acquisition of disciplinary knowledge, and as a bridge to greater reflection on what the knowledge implies for practice.

When teachers want students to reflect on their learning, their career paths, or their potential practice, then writing is frequently the instrument of choice. Writing allows students to connect with, rather that simply restate material. Professors try to fit the form reflective writing may take to some specific goals of the major program. For instance, health education requires a portfolio and cover letter that students can use when going out on job interviews.

> *. . . the reason they even do portfolios is to try to see that . . . one, that a lot of their course work assignments, the majority of their course work assignments are occupation-related, if not vocationally focused. . . . It's also an attempt to, because of the letter to the reader they have to construct, that describes the papers they've collected . . . give the way they foster reflection, give the way to foster some degree of self assessment in terms of, here's where I think I'm strong, here's where I think I'm not so strong and here's some things I think I need to do to strengthen those weak areas, those deficiencies. There is some critical thinking that's going on*

with the construction of a portfolio, not just an accumulation of stuff. It could be, but that's not a portfolio. That's just a file cabinet.

(Health Education, July 16, 1998)

In elementary education, reflective writing includes self-discovery and pragmatic planning. Our professor has students involved in field experience compose autobiographies as well as lesson plans.

The idea of lesson plans reflecting on their teaching is very common, not necessarily my methods class, but once they are in field practicum.

Like narratives?

What I learned from this. How I changed. That type of thing. A lot of people in our department recently have been doing reading or writing or learning autobiographies.

. . . They do a lot of lesson planning?

Yes they do. The hardest part that I've discovered is, when you ask students to write about purposes, they're good at developing goals, but if you also ask them to . . . develop purposes, reasons why you do this, it's a stumble. They stumble. They can't do that without lots and lots of thinking about it.

Well, perhaps that goes back to what we were talking about earlier. In other words, the purposes are why they do it, the goals are learning what to do with the students.

What the student will do or demonstrate. The student will read a book. It was interesting, because . . . I just read a bunch of them. The students will read a book. Why should they read a book?

(Elementary Education, November 18, 1999)

The health services administration professor assigns the writing of timelines, strategic objectives, professional credos, and mission, vision, and value statements in a course entitled *Health Services Planning and Evaluation,* to encourage students "to think more broadly about what the field is about." Additionally, the writing of scenarios invites students to imagine various paths their careers might take, along with the motives that will keep them engaged with that career.

I ask them to write an optimistic scenario, a dark side scenario. I ask them to offer a . . . paradigm shift scenario and then a paradigm shift scenario that's enabled by technology. One of the things I ask them is: What will each of these particular scenarios do in terms of how will it affect your current preparation for the profession, how will it affect the first job that you have within the profession, how will it affect your opportunities for advancement and your opportunities for continuing education. So I challenge them to consider four different scenarios and then to write . . . their reflections on how those particular scenarios will affect what's happening to them right now as a student and what will happen to them in the near future. . . . Many of my students have some difficulty, particularly in the dark side scenario. I'll ask them how do you respond to this dark side scenario and they say, well, the dark side scenario is economically we're doing very poorly across our country. There are not many health care jobs; as a result, after four years at Slippery Rock I'm a clerk at _____ and so things are going poorly for me. . . . What I tell them is, if that's the dark side you're facing, are you going to live with that or what are you going to do to adapt to the fact that the environment has changed and job prospects or promotion prospects, or even prospects within the discipline aren't as rosy as you thought they were. What are you going to do? Are you just going to say, gosh, things are tough so I'm having a miserable life or are you going to try to influence your environment so you have a better life . . . many of my students aren't used to thinking that way . . . they're not used to articulating what their motives are. . . .

(Health Services Administration, November 23, 1999)

Regarding critique, our respondents generally believe that a knowledge of various disciplinary methods, or of what is considered mainstream or marginal in a field, including representative publications, is best left until graduate school and sometimes the higher levels of graduate study. Undergraduates are instead encouraged to be "consumers" of a usually controlled flow of disciplinary materials, even among those faculty who, as we've seen, might be critical themselves of some knowledge generated within their fields. At the same time, applying knowledge necessitates some form of critique. Rather than characterizing a practitioner as lacking the academician's theoretical knowledge, it may be important to recognize the kind of critical thought called for in practice. Those in managerial positions make decisions and use critical judgment in regard to "what works," not the veracity of causal theories. Perhaps as a consequence, it is clear from our interviews that when teachers want students to critically examine discipline-specific information, or to apply such information to particular instances of practice, or to connect or synthesize various concepts or research results, undergraduates engage in written critique.

Our nursing professor noted that "The emphasis in nursing has been on the practitioner at this level being a research consumer . . . we see them as needing to look at research and see that it applies or is useful in the particular group of patients they have" (Nursing, June 17, 1998). However, another aspect of critique was exhibited when the Nursing professor perceived that experience, rather than any specific knowledge of disciplinary theory, enabled her undergraduates to effectively criticize the professional literature.

> *... students are more naïve. If it's printed, they are less critical. If you prompt them and suggest that maybe there's something wrong with this article, they're more likely to come up with it. Now, my more mature students are the ones with a wider range of thought. They tend to be quicker to say, "You know, I didn't quite buy what this article says," in areas, especially, where they've had experience.*
>
> **Do you think this differs in nursing from, in general, your experience of how people ... ?**
>
> *I think probably the adult learner has had enough experience that they don't accept things printed so quickly as the younger students. I've seen some of my students who, some of it comes from a real life experience. Like it might say in an article that good adolescents need an opportunity to explore all aspects of their being, and you get some of these people who are raising adolescents. [Laughs.] And they say within the rules that I set down, they can explore. Then they start dealing with practical realities and start saying that this author doesn't really have a good feel for the confrontations you might have with an adolescent. The dangers if you don't stand firm in those confrontations.*
>
> **I see, okay.**
>
> *They'll say, you know, I've taken care of these kinds of patients and they don't act like that.*
>
> **So it's really experience more than anything else.**
>
> *Yeah.*
>
> (Nursing, June 17, 1998)

Mathematics may serve as another exception to the model of undergraduates as "consumers learning that" without "asking why" because graduates who take positions as actuaries or in operations research may very well be called on to employ their predictive and speculative abilities without benefit of further schooling at the graduate level. The math professor we interviewed encourages undergraduates to attend and present papers at regional conferences, and regrets the lack of a final writing project within his program. As was noted earlier, he also did not see much difference between upper division undergraduate mathematics and graduate school—both were theoretical, one just "deeper." This perception may be more frequent in highly theoretical fields like mathematics and physics. But his perceptions may also more closely represent those of someone trained at the doctoral level and working inside academe rather than outside it.

> *. . . a lot of schools with master's degrees have a thesis. That's writing you don't see, especially in a program here. We don't require student projects. There are undergraduate schools that do require that.*
>
> **How do you feel about that requirement?**
>
> *For the record, it's tough not to have a writing requirement. This again . . . goes back to the MAA [Mathematical Association of America] meeting because students see they can do the research and then they talk themselves out of it. It's sometimes for their own good to have to force somebody to do something. And I think having a requirement like this forces students first off to look at the different things they've studied, to decide what they do and don't like. And then in doing the project they would learn a little bit more about how to work on your own, because you're not going to be in a classroom setting; you can't discuss this with other students. . . . It would force them to read on their own and then, in putting all the results together, force them to write on their own.*
>
> (Mathematics, August 6, 1999)

Critiques or summaries of journal articles related to the discipline appear to be a particularly common classroom genre, mentioned specifically by the health education, nursing, elementary education, and computer science professors. Such assignments seek to match a variety of instructional goals related to the development of disciplinary expertise: introducing students to the professional literature, introducing students to concepts or information not covered by other means, encouraging students to connect concepts or information derived from various sources to each other and to instances of disciplinary practice, helping students identify bias and poorly substantiated claims.

> *In the undergraduate [program] there is much . . . emphasis on critiquing articles, reviewing articles or looking at how articles can be implemented into the practice.*
>
> (Nursing, November 21, 1998)

Returning graduates have assured the Health Education professor that frequent writing of this genre "helped them in some of their grant writing skills."

> *Article reviews typically will start off with, they have to tell me . . . what the authors found, what the authors concluded. The scenario is, if I haven't read the article, I would pretty much know what the author said by their initial summary. Then in the second part . . . they have to answer a series of questions. They have to relate the article to something we talked about in class, relate it to something in the text, relate it to something that has to do with their career as a health education specialist.*
>
> (Health Education, July 16, 1998)

The elementary education professor also received positive feedback.

> **. . . Students do read these genres a little bit, right, in particular courses?**
>
> *Yes.*
>
> **Do you think it informs or affects how they write, then?**
>
> *You know, . . . I saw that question, and a student, just yesterday we were talking. I have them do critiques of professional articles. I was asking them how they like that assignment, should I change it, what did you all think about it? There was one very staunch defender; she said that it was so great to read all these articles and then when you tried to write it, to try to pull together from all of them and you just thought new ideas. She apparently really liked the paper she wrote. The articles she chose all related to her paper, and for her, reading those helped her make connections. Helped her see things that maybe had been isolated before.*
>
> (Elementary Education, November 18, 1999)

In the following exchange, a sense emerges that English faculty could collaborate with those outside of English to help students think critically, because of the maturation that often occurs after first-year composition and through applying critical judgment in upper division major courses.

> *Usually what I have them do is summarize what the person said and then combine it with their own commentary, their own critical analysis of the article. I joke with them. I want to know if it's good, bad, or ugly and why, what was good about it? I don't want to just say this was a good article, this was a bad article, this article was*

awful. And for the one course I teach I have them using . . . an article review form and one of the questions is, "Was there bias in the article?" . . . And what we talk about a lot in that particular course is, well, was there anything in the article that made you think about something else you have read and was this treatment of the issue better in this article or in the other article that you read or have you read anything about this in the news lately . . .

. . . You're essentially saying that you . . . direct them about what to look for. But . . .

But it's not that difficult to direct them to look for facts in an article, you know, as opposed to opinion.

. . . there's a lot of students these days, at least . . . when they begin their careers in our English Composition courses that [have] the idea that one opinion is as good as another opinion. Opinion becomes . . . fact to a certain extent. In other words, . . . we're each entitled to our own idea . . .

I get some of that, but most of the students in that one course I teach have to be juniors or seniors. Maybe by then they've matured. They're tired of reading opinions that have no basis in fact.

(Computer Science, August 12, 1999)

The mathematics professor explored one other use of professional journal articles that, although not directly related to any specific writing assignment, could strongly influence a student's awareness of the construction and current status of disciplinary knowledge. His approach is designed to attack common student misperceptions of the material they learn as monolithic, autonomous, and permanent. To see disciplinary knowledge as something quite different may constitute a significant sea change in student perceptions of both their own expertise and what they read in textbooks. Geisler argues that textbooks create a break between "domain content" and the "rhetorical processes" through which such content is created (212-13).

. . . Last year I was teaching an advanced calculus sequence and I ran into a student in the library while I was reading a journal and she was shocked to learn that people were still working on this subject. She said you always . . . get the impression when you're looking at the book that everything has already been done.

That's the nature of textbooks.

I heard that before yet completely forgot it. As soon as she said that, I felt this is just a mistake on my part. I started going through back issues of math magazines and college math journals and

Xeroxing articles for them to look at. To say here we are, working on sequences and series and here's an article I just got in my mailbox yesterday that deals exactly with that, to show them that it's a living discipline.

That's the thing about textbooks. . . . I even talk to my students about this in College Writing II, that when you're reading a textbook what you're getting is like the duck on the surface. It looks very calm, but underneath the discipline is paddling like crazy. . . . I say, well this is information that the discipline as a whole has decided to agree on at this particular moment . . . it's being presented to you in a textbook as this . . . solidified mass of knowledge.

Yeah. This is a done deal and this is the way it is.

(Mathematics, August 6, 1999)

Some professors may describe undergraduates mainly as consumers of "content" in their majors, but it appears that many of their writing tasks seek to push undergraduates into practical application (learning how), as well as critical analysis (asking why). Textbooks, because they analyze information in a field and break it up into manageable chunks, often disconnect it from the processes that produce it. But professors can reconnect what textbooks tear asunder through writing assignments that encourage critique.

It's important to remember, also, that undergraduate writing can critique knowledge in relationship to its application and relevance to practice. Theorizing knowledge in a discipline primarily as basic research may be dependent on a specific academic context where the condition for knowledge production is leisure and freedom from the physical work of application, a problematic concept at a teaching institution. Aristotle explained that mathematics first arose among a priestly class who had such freedom ("Metaphysics" 500). In fact, it also may be reflective experience itself, seemingly freed from a practical context as we are "lost in thought," that serves as a model for separating why from that and how. Reflection also allows for actions to be consciously planned beforehand rather than improvised along the way, thus validating the idea of a priori causal principles that scientists discover but which those in the experiential world then merely perceive in their effects. Hasn't science more recently discovered the limitations of such a theoretical model of causality in the complex environments of real situations? If reflection on the validity of foundational knowledge in the disciplines does not seem to be a goal of undergraduate education in the major, that fact may not prevent students from learning to think critically through techniques of writing to learn, through producing documents simulating workplace genres in courses in the major, or through critiques or summaries of discipline-specific discourse. What role might general education courses outside the major play?

GENERAL EDUCATION AS A SUPPLEMENT TO SPECIALIST EXPERTISE

During the 1970s and 1980s SRU lived with a loosely structured set of general education requirements, under which students might select from a list of courses that at one point numbered more than 700 (Richardson). Every department felt, naturally enough, that at least some of their courses had interest and value to the general student population. Moreover, "gen ed" enrollments allowed departments to teach courses that a small contingent of majors could not sustain on their own. Still, faculty and administrators realized that the program had become a bloated adhocracy and struggled for years to replace it with a more tightly organized and coherent program. In the fall of 1991 the university put in place a liberal studies program under which students would meet requirements within each of seven blocks—Basic Competencies, The Arts, Natural Sciences and Mathematics, Challenges of the Modern Age, Cultural Diversity/Global Perspectives, Human Institutions and Interpersonal Relationships, and Our National Experience. Each block lists goal courses, most of which can be selected by the student, although a few are required of all; enrichment courses; and appropriate co-curricular activities. In working through the program a student can accumulate anywhere from 42 to 55 credit hours. College Writing I and II are required goal courses under the Basic Competencies block, along with courses in Speech Communication, Remedial Math, and Physical Education.

Although somewhat tighter and more focused than our old General Education program, the current Liberal Studies program is still quite inclusive in regard to the number of disciplines it may encompass. It defines "liberal studies" as including courses in almost all of the disciplines in which a student is not pursuing a major or minor concentration. It also reflects a faith in the potential positive impact of exploring other disciplines on the future professional practice of a student's major discipline, sometimes in general and sometimes in specific ways. Arguments for the relevance of the liberal studies program to the professional development of students appeared in several of our conversations. Sometimes those arguments took the form of a desire for direct and apparent links between liberal studies requirements and a student's major program, as in this exchange with the sport management professor.

I remember sitting there in class wondering, "I'm never going to use this again. Who decided that this was a course I needed." I can remember I took a French Revolution–Napoleonic Times class to satisfy a History requirement and I thought, "I want to teach PE and I'd like to be a coach. Now how is knowing anything about the French Revolution going to prepare me to win a national championship."

You should have listened to someone like Marv Levy. *[Former professional football coach with a master's degree from Harvard in history, best known for leading the Buffalo Bills to four consecutive SuperBowls.]* **Or Woody Hayes.** *[Former college football coach who had a long career at Ohio State University.]* **Wasn't Woody Hayes a big military science . . . ?**

He was. He was. I could not understand that when I was sitting in that class for the life of me. I think that . . . at the University of _____ as an undergraduate back in the early 70s, when I took the course work, there was not a real good correlation or there wasn't a lot of relevancy with those classes . . . what we're trying to do now is . . . establish a relevancy. In other words, in liberal studies, we have the students take a communication class that they will be able to use that communication skill . . . when they do public speaking or when they do some sort of writing or whatever later on . . . we spend a lot of time telling the students, when you choose, . . . choose something that's going to be specific for your needs. Don't just take a class to fill the block because you're going to be sitting there like me thirty years ago wondering, "Why in the hell am I learning this?"

(Sport Management, July 27, 1998)

We suspect that most faculty members in public comprehensive universities, both large and small, in 4-year "liberal arts" colleges, and in 2-year colleges have heard similar complaints from students. But our professors often found general education courses a more indirect, but enriching supplement to disciplinary specialization. For the health services administration professor, extradisciplinary interests appeared to have an invisible but nonetheless palpably salubrious effect on a health administrator's professional performance. His primary "real-world" experience as such an administrator occurred during a two-decade long career in the U.S. military, during which time he had worked his way up from medical platoon leader to medical company commander and finally chief operating officer in a small military hospital.

. . . the people that I've seen that are very good at their jobs . . . normally had some interest outside of what they were doing for

the military . . . and health care. Most people that I knew were actively engaged and also the top performers had some other interest and usually it was an interest outside of their area of concentration. So they may have been a fixed facility administrator or they may have been involved in the delivery of health care in a tactical environment, but when you asked them what they did for fun or enjoyment or to enrich their lives it may have been something like fly fishing . . . other friends . . . had interests, well in reading; something that does not particularly interest me is military history, but I have a number of friends that would read books like The Hunt for Red October *and things like that and found it enriched them professionally . . .*

(Health Services Administration, November 23, 1999)

Given the inclusion under the Basic Competencies block of a required "activity course" in physical education, it is actually conceivable that a budding health facility administrator could develop a passion for fly fishing while attending our institution. After reading this chapter, the health services administration professor reasserted the importance of the liberal studies program, not just for future professors but present students.

The discussion on the value of liberal studies paralleled a conversation I had with an excellent student in our program. Although she was very bright, and wrote very well, she didn't really enjoy going to school. When I asked her to reflect on what value her college education may have had for her beyond getting a better job she did affirm, with a dawning recognition, that her perspective on life was richer and deeper compared to her friends who had never progressed beyond high school. I'm used to dealing with students who are more geared to how can this college education get me a better job, contribute to the 40% improvement, say, in earnings that I'm likely to see over my lifetime and things like that.

(Health Services Administration)

The physics professor described a more direct connection between his liberal studies courses as an undergraduate and the current performance of his job, but just where and when the connection may occur was as unpredictable as the previous example. In the course of a lecture, it is sometimes examples from other contexts that help students understand best.

I think being able to draw on other things in the classroom for other disciplines is important, and being able to do that without struggle, you know, just have that stuff in your repertoire. You can't always imagine when stuff can be used, so if you got it available then you can use it when the opportunity presents itself...

(Physics, November 16, 1998)

Agreeing on the purposes or goals of "general" or "liberal" education, and on how such goals should be implemented, has been as difficult an ordeal at our university as it seems to have been at most postsecondary institutions. Should the program simply be an opportunity for students to dabble in a variety of disciplines, at first perhaps to assist them in choosing a major or career path, and secondly to satisfy various interests or curiosities? Should the program allow considerable selection of courses based on students' or professors' perceptions of their appropriateness to the major programs? Or are there definite tasks general education can accomplish that are beyond the reach of students' major programs? What are those tasks? How can they be accomplished?

All of these questions are embedded in something nearly all of the professors we interviewed commented on: the difficulty they had as undergraduates, or that their current students have, in seeing the value of required general education courses for professional or personal enrichment. Where do they fit in the parsing of expertise? These questions still remained after they read a draft of this chapter.

At our own institution, many of our students are "first-generation," meaning that theirs is the first generation in their families to enter into institutions of higher education. Frequently, like many college students, they have been motivated to enroll directly after their graduation from high school by the argument that college is necessary for anyone wishing to make a good living in 21st-century America. We also suspect, from our own limited conversations, that those same students' teachers could find an obvious problem with the sport management professor's proffered solution of selecting liberal studies courses according to their appropriateness to students' majors. A challenge that often emerged in our conversations entailed the demonstration, rather than the pronouncement, of those links that exist between our areas of study and our students' worlds, which often seem both indefinite and circumscribed. To borrow the everyday parlance of writing teachers, our students need to be "shown," rather than "told," what it means to have a wide-ranging intellectual curiosity and why possessing such a curiosity will have value for them.

For some of our interviewees, another way liberal studies or general education courses strengthened disciplinary expertise was by providing students with perspectives and practices usually unavailable to them in their major courses. For example, the Mathematics professor suggested that group work was something their majors needed to practice but seldom experienced in math courses because of deeply imbedded traditions governing the pedagogy of the field.

> ... *group work is a natural part of doing any job, and since we don't emphasize group work in our major classes I think that's a vital thing that they get out of other courses.*
>
> **Do mathematicians working outside of the academy. . . . Are they doing group work then?**
>
> *Yeah, you almost have to. In the least you need someone to bounce your ideas off of. Especially ... if you're really going to put a lot of money and a lot of work and really a lot of lives, you kind of hope they're going to talk to somebody to make sure their work is right. The other thing is, if you talk about a large-scale operation, it's too big for one person to do all the work on. So you really have to have a group doing little pieces and then putting all the pieces back together, making sure it really does describe ...*
>
> **... it wouldn't just be all the mathematicians going off into their cubicles and solving ... ?**
>
> *No, it wouldn't be; people have this image of a solitary figure bent over a desk, and it just doesn't work that way.*
>
> **But that's the way it works in math classes?**
>
> *Yeah, that's our fallacy, ... we teach them to do things one way and it's not the way things are going.*
>
> **It's kind of like a traditional model.**
>
> *Yeah, that is always the hard problem. It's that hazing mentality. When I was young I was hazed and I turned out all right ...*
>
> (Mathematics, November 12, 1999)

The elementary education professor was troubled that students couldn't take more courses outside their major, because of the necessity of at least ostensibly seeking to graduate people in 4 years, while several methods courses and various field experiences had to be included in the program. Having only 2 years of courses outside of education deprived students of the experience of smaller classes in another discipline, with "a set of people who also love to be there." Such courses, she felt, would help her students develop "intellectual curiosity" and a "passion" for what they taught, as well as enhance their ability to question commonly accepted approaches to teaching and curriculum design, rather than simply to mimic them. Liberal studies courses, by her lights, would encourage students to ask why as well as to learn how.

. . . last semester I had two students who, one had a philosophy major and an Elementary Ed major; the second student had a philosophy minor. . . . They approached my class very differently from other students, and I think situations like that remind me that I really want educators to be well rounded and to really love learning . . . if you don't have that intellectual curiosity then your classroom is so, you know, it's going through the motions. You don't always know why you're doing what you're doing.

Right. How would you say these philosophy minors approached your class differently?

Argumentative. And this was good. They really looked at articles they read, textbooks, class discussions; they were real quick to play devil's advocate. They were real quick to turn something around and question it. And they were very quick to disagree with me, which I encouraged. It's not a bad thing. Less passive, maybe. Other students seemed to just [say], "Tell me how to do it, Dr. _____." . . .

Yeah, all they want to know is how to do it, so we know what to do on Monday morning?

I have to admit that is a realistic thing. I think if you don't ask that question you're a bad teacher, but . . .

Of course, you should probably know why you're doing it too.

Some people really struggle. I think the philosophy people really wanted to know, why? Why not this? What about that? It was fun. It was a nice thing.

You sure wish they would go out and get into it . . . actually asking those questions and driving a few curriculum coordinators absolutely batty, right?

That's right.

(Elementary Education, November 18, 1999)

That liberal studies courses, and English in particular, could give students a sense of multiple perspectives and alternative modes of operation was also a strength articulated by the Mathematics professor. On the one hand, he was troubled by the acceptance of uncertainty and ambiguity in humanistic scholarship. "I get up in a meeting and I say I'm pretty sure this is true . . . opinions may lower a little bit. . . . It's okay to conjecture on something, but if that conjecture is your entire 20-minute talk, people will look at it funny." He clearly found the "rigor" and precision of his own field preferable. On the other hand, he let pass the interviewer's insistence that language invited ambiguous responses and was characteristically "irreducible to a number [or] an equation. . . ." Earlier in the interview, the professor had recalled an English class in which "aspects of homosexuality in *Huckleberry Finn*" had been discussed:

> Yeah. When you think of something like that, especially in literature, I don't think it does you any good to read it alone. You need to talk to someone afterwards.
>
> **. . . Would you say then, was there any way that these courses that dealt with ambiguity, uncertainty, and so on, is there any way that taking them helped you with math?**
>
> Yeah, although once again, while I was immersed in it I didn't notice it. I'd say that the big thing that you learn is to look at things from different sides. The biggest problem I have in doing my research was that once I planned a plan of attack, if it doesn't work out, I get stuck. It's like I can't turn around in the maze and work my way in another direction. But classes like that help you learn to say, "Okay, this approach didn't work. Now let's try it from over here." Just because in those classes you're learning to look at all different perspectives.
>
> (Mathematics, November 12, 1999)

Can expertise be ambiguous, collaborative, ad hoc, flexible? When can flexibility and an awareness of ambiguity serve useful professional and quotidian purposes? And how can those traits be acquired?

If we can return to this chapter's title, in thinking again of the distinction between "knowing that," "learning how," and "asking why," between the operational and the theoretical, between "men of experience" and artists and scientists, we are more and more convinced that some other formulations could be useful. Perhaps such formulations would more aptly describe the commingling of experience and theoretical expertise so often described by our conversants. That commingling could more aptly guide our search for the role writing plays and could play in the education of undergraduates. In other words, such an expert needs to be both thoughtful and pragmatic, theoretical and mundane. A creative reading of Book I of Aristotle's *Metaphysics* could use the concept of adaptation, which we developed in Chapter 4, to recognize practical contexts as places where critical thinking abounds, rather than as homes to unreflective, mechanical, or habitual action. Such a reading could also challenge the claim that teaching is a prerogative that belongs only to those with theoretical knowledge of first/causal principles (500). Perhaps there are important kinds of knowledge that practitioners have that need clearer articulation as expertise at institutions like our own.

Moreover, can expert knowledge derive from indirect contact with the everyday through simulation or case study or most any variety of narrative, and from the direct experience of apprenticeship or job or social interaction? Perhaps situations themselves draw from us more or less expert responses rather intuitively. These adaptations may evolve into a repertoire of ways of acting to best effect in particular situations. Maybe "learning how" differs from "knowing that" because it signifies *success* in application, and differs from "asking why" because it acknowledges, along with Lave and Wenger, that "abstract representations are meaningless unless they can be made specific to the situation at hand" (33). Maybe "learning how" can be done by undergraduates in both liberal studies and major courses. Aristotle admits that it is more effective for those with theoretical knowledge to have practical experience as well but his hierarchy betrays his allegiance to an academic model that has often acted as if all students were nascent professors who are unlikely to engage in application or teach undergraduates.

Our interviewees in the health fields spoke of going beyond lecture and "content delivery," not because they saw less importance in knowing or understanding discipline-specific foundational knowledge, but because they had become convinced it was most important for their students to acquire the "know how" to apply both information and theory to particular professional situations.

> *. . . So is there a primary way . . . in nursing . . . one communicates in the classroom, or is there a tradition of using a variety of pedagogies, or what?*
>
> *I think historically the emphasis was very much on lecture . . . there has been this feeling of . . . this enormous amount of information that was absolutely imperative, that the content you taught students, they would make life decisions, and maybe not every decision is life and death, but some of the tragedies that can occur . . . can be just sad and so you had this great feeling that "gee, students need to know every bit of this." But now the information has reached the point that it's impossible for your students to know everything they need to know, and it's reached the point where it's impossible for the faculty member to know everything that should be taught. So as that has happened I have moved away from the information transfer and the demand that students memorize and know that information to very much focusing on teaching students information access skills, information evaluation skills, and information utilization skills and problem solving. In other words, how to find what they need to know, how to evaluate the quality of the information they did find and then how to apply that information and not be as concerned with the specific content of what they've learned. As I said, part of that is definitely from the fact that the information has gotten so enormous it's impossible to keep up. And the other piece is the fact at Slippery Rock I'm teach-*

ing nurses, people who are already functioning in the field, who already have a good basic database . . .

(Nursing, November 21, 1998)

What about in terms of how would things like critical thinking and . . . analysis and those kind of skills figure into the type of work, or are those more associated with theoretical . . . ?

I think it's important, but it's important in terms of how can you apply knowledge. For example, a good part of the profession is information management. If you're working within finance . . . there's a . . . whole bunch of information, . . . in fact, in health care you're practically inundated with information . . . not information, what it is, you're inundated with data and your ability to select from just streams of numbers and then make, package those numbers so they convey relevant information to you or to your boss or to the decision maker you're trying to influence is important.

(Health Services Administration, July 1, 1999)

LEARNING NONSPECIALIST FUNCTIONAL EXPERTISE

As we considered that ubiquitous term *critical thinking*, our own first, perhaps commendable instinct in compiling our interview questions had been to consider that critical thinking could only be defined within the context of the disciplines in which it was to be exercised. We were still bound by the notion that such thinking would have to be based on a particular discipline's ostensible scientific method, its ways of asking why and discovering the cause. Toward the end of our first of two interviews with each professor, we had asked questions such as "What are the rules of evidence and modes of proof which are commonly employed in your discipline? Do students in your program discuss these rules and modes?" (see Appendix A). We had left out experience, whether of the vocational or social or even personally reflective variety. We had even left out that whole realm of academic experience not easily reducible to an articulated curricular feature, or a measurable outcome, or an easily categorized pedagogical practice.

Moreover, we had left out ourselves, and our colleagues in those times and places when they were not "disciplining" majors but instead functioning as teachers of a liberal study course available to all. So, during the second interviews, we asked "What was the role 'liberal' or 'general' studies courses played in your intellectual development? What role do you think 'liberal' or 'general' studies courses play in the intellectual development of students in your major program?" "Could you characterize what was different about the courses in your major program, when compared with courses you took as electives, or as part of a general education requirement?" was another question (see Appendix B). We now wish we had asked what they saw that was *similar* in those courses, or what they perceived were the purposes of courses their department offered in the liberal studies program. What were we doing in College Writing II, if not at least pretending that a form of textual criticism could be practiced that took into account not just a variety of disciplinary methods over which we and our students lacked a trained command, but also kinds of experience and perception that neither our discipline nor others had necessarily reified as worthy of study? Does "critical thinking" have to be discipline-specific in the mode of what commonly takes place during advanced graduate education? As we've already observed, along with Scholes, much undergraduate education seems to aim at replicating academics' own modes of knowing and discovering. But how many of our students, what percentage of the whole, will ever become academics?

Whether through theory or experience or some commingling of experience and practiced response, our respondents seek to immerse their majors in the practice of the professional lives for which they are supposedly preparing—in the disciplinary "lore," in "the recipes for manipulating nature" that have been integral to scientific applications since the renaissance at least (Longo 30). But the students who come to those same faculty as enrollees in liberal studies courses, and just about every department has at least a course or two listed in the program, may get much use out of something other than a survey of canned disciplinary knowledge or a smattering of practitioner lore.

One view of the liberal studies program that emerged from the interviews saw certain courses and disciplines as so integral to a contemporary grasp of both the physical and social worlds as to be unavoidable. These are the areas of study that make someone "well-rounded," rather than "narrowly focused," able to see the "big picture" and, as a consequence, to ameliorate a disciplinary perspective that might otherwise disable a practitioner. English can obviously be perceived in this way, since the myriad forms and functions of language are inescapable, regardless of one's area of study. And steering conversants in that direction provides at least momentary relief from what we in English sometimes see as the tight box of perceptions outside our field that our "content" is linguistic correctness (discussed in Chapter 7), on the one hand, and a desiccated, faintly ethereal sense of the literary canon on the other. Even after reading our manuscript, assumptions about the proper "content" of English studies remained.

> *I perceive that English professors really have a skill set that I don't have in that they have a whole taxonomy related to the use and expression of language that doesn't come easily to me. When I attempt to talk about what's good or bad about a student's writing, in some sense I kind of approach it from what is more of a gestalt. Maybe even more of an approach of, "I can't define what art is, but I know what I like," that sort of thing. And that's probably not a good way to try to get someone to become a better writer, just describing for them if you liked or did not like their effort and beyond that simply correcting the punctuation and the grammar, which too often I think I do and others do. And where I think English faculty could be helpful to those of us in other disciplines is offering kind of a structure or a methodology from which to approach or critique writing.*
>
> (Health Services Administration)

The professors representing mathematics and physics, the two disciplines among our conversations that could be considered as closely related to the medieval trivium (grammar, rhetoric, and logic) and quadrivium (arithmetic, music, geometry, and astronomy) as English, were also capable of regarding their fields as equally essential and inescapable. In fact, their departments both offer courses within SRU's liberal studies program that can boast of healthy enrollments: Concepts of Science within physics and Mathematics as a Liberal Art.

For the physics professor, his subject was clearly one that could be learned "for its own sake," regardless of a student's vocational concerns or ambitions.

> *I tend not to focus on application and career things. I tend to be more interested in the field because it's inherently useful, which may not always be the right, good approach for students.*
>
> **Now, when you say inherently useful, what do you mean by that? Some might . . . call the vocational part inherently useful, so . . .**
>
> *. . . We live in a physical world, so having some awareness of the environment in which you live is bound to help your survival. I don't know if that's too Darwinian or not, but . . .*
>
> **As opposed to those of us who might electrocute ourselves at the slightest drop of the hat.**
>
> (Physics, November 16, 1998)

The Mathematics professor, on the other hand, explained the extra-disciplinary usefulness of his subject in more direct and specific terms that had the effect of suggesting a very particular role for courses attempting to introduce non-majors to a discipline.

> You can't open a newspaper and not be inundated with facts and figures, statistics, graphs, conclusions based on probability, whether you want to admit to it or not.
>
> Yeah, that's one of the things that I find interesting . . . thinking about what students might need to learn who aren't . . . math majors, who take a math course. Let's say . . . one as part of a liberal arts core, . . . what do they actually need to be able to pick up a newspaper, for instance, and look at something like a scientific study, which, as you say, is based on probability and actually to understand what's going on there, as opposed to just jumping to a conclusion that I can no longer eat apples; it causes ulcers or something like that.
>
> Especially with a course like that, which is taken by people who are not interested in mathematics, . . . when you do a section on probability, basically what I want the overall feeling to be is how people lie with statistics. People bend the truth all the time. . . . You've got to beware that people are always using numbers just to commit you to their position, not necessarily that it's a reality.
>
> It's a form of persuasion and how you know about that, what we would call a particular rhetorical move, the more you can make a critical judgment about its validity.
>
> Right.
>
> (Mathematics, August 6, 1999)

What "expert knowledge" do students acquire in first-year writing courses? What "expert knowledge" can those same students obtain when they take just a course or two in physics or math or health education or computer science? Maybe this is part of the knowledge we were motivated to look for when we initiated our cross-campus conversations. For example, what can we learn that would allow us to make judgments concerning what is reported and discussed in discourse aimed at general audiences but derived from our colleagues' fields? Web sites, journalistic articles, television reports and programs, all contain material "borrowed" from the natural and social sciences, dealing with medicine or meteorology, stocks and salaries, culture and conflict. This discourse "leans" on expertise, which in turn "leans" on method, and yet it is meant for the "nonexpert" to read, interpret, and often apply. Within a semester, could a student learn enough of a discipline's observational scope and investigative methods to judge the import of a report of findings in terms, for instance, of personal health, of financial planning, or of public policy debate? If so, should the courses that provided such learning be offered before or after a course such as College Writing II? Should College Writing II be abandoned entirely in favor of some clustering of writing courses and liberal studies courses after the first year?

A field like nursing may seem as far removed from general education as a discipline can be, but the professor we interviewed in that area indirectly hints at the value of a health course that focused on teaching non-majors how to critically read medical information.

> *. . . I always refer to printed material as predigested, you know, everything from journals to books to whatever and so we walk into the Internet with a certain trustingness and the credibility is higher than it should be.*
>
> **Right.**
>
> *. . . probably one of the best examples is the research that just came out looking at the quality of information on the Internet related to children with diarrhea. These are very specific, well agreed on protocols for the treatment of children with diarrhea. And this particular researcher used those protocols as the gold standard and then checked a number of sites for major medical centers, seeing what they had on their web pages for consumers related to treatment of children with diarrhea and found that only one-third of the sites were actually accurate and up to date . . .*
>
> (Nursing, November 21, 1998)

How could political science or history or economics or physics, or English for that matter, construct and present courses for non-majors in a way that would enable students to respond in an informed and expertly critical manner to the "information" with which they are bombarded, whether it appear in a newspaper or film, on television or a Web site? We return here to the heart of Scholes' proposal for the future of English studies, but with the recognition that English may not be able to shoulder the burden of teaching a critical practice regarding "public discourse" without the assistance of an array of disciplines far exceeding the seven listed in the medieval liberal arts. During the past quarter century many in English studies, most ostensibly within literary criticism but also among compositionists, have been busily cultivating a sensibility that seems in tune with such a take on general studies. From another direction, some within the field of science and technology studies have advocated the development of a "social epistemology" that would allow science to "be scrutinized and evaluated by an appropriately informed lay public" (Fuller

25). Some of our liberal studies offerings are courses described as "challenges of the modern age." Could such a course be an example of where public discourse might be critiqued or composed?

Such a nonspecialist functional expertise could include a grasp of not just scope and methods, but also of limits, of that which the discipline cannot say or does not "know." "Characterized by fealty to both subject and method," Malinowitz has argued, "the disciplines don't simply describe knowledge, they legitimate it by creating zones and codes of acceptable scholarship that effectively bracket out all that is not always already the progeny of those zones and codes" (291). Some of our colleagues have taken note of the shortfall of various kinds of research within their disciplinary mainstreams. Would they be willing to share that sense of inadequacy with their pupils? To say, "This is what such a method can tell us; this is what it cannot tell us. Here is the 'x' factor, the areas that our study, at least so far, cannot explain, even though the professional practices associated with our study must cope with them."

Additionally, our colleagues could help their majors recognize an obligation to explain the workings of their discipline to those outside of it, as well as the inherent difficulties that occur when doing so. Some of the WTL assignments that our physics professor's students did were end-of-class free writes recording "the most important points . . . they learned and . . . major questions they have." Students did "different kinds of research projects" such as biographies and the linking of recent news items concerning physics to specific course material. One assignment combined "writing to learn" with a professional's eventual need to communicate with "a nontechnical audience," and could be said to encompass, consciously or unconsciously, the old argument that an effective way to learn is to attempt to teach, doubtless a practitioner's point of view with which Aristotle would disagree. The professor appears to want his students to experience something of the challenges he must face, explaining disciplinary knowledge to nonexpert audiences, and doing so by drawing from a broader learning than just a physics curriculum can provide.

Lately I've been having students write chapter summaries. Very short narrative summaries. To help them focus on the major points, because a lot of times we teach in a way that helps them focus on details and they lose sight of the big picture. I've been doing that in lower level classes and upper level. And it tends to be a little more challenging in the upper level classes, because the books are not as narrative in their writing, because they have a lot of equations and proofs and so it's quite challenging to use this book as a model to write a narrative summary. . . .

So the book isn't likely to provide that kind of information then itself?

The particular class right now that's a 300 level, the chapter actually has a summary, but it's a really condensed mathematical summary and it's not very helpful in writing this narrative. So I told the students you might need to go to the library, do a little bit of research to find out what this chapter is really about, what's it good for, why should I learn it. Because . . . this purpose might be to inform somebody what this is about who's never taken class, so you can't just take this mathematical point of view because nobody outside of class will understand it.

(Physics, November 16, 1998)

At a time when many are calling for increased accountability by science to the public sphere, such an assignment, tying theoretical knowledge to everyday environments, seems particularly appropriate. Ultimately, it acknowledges that even the most theoretical research (the "why") returns to specific contexts where its importance must be weighed in terms of practical considerations (knowing that, knowing how) regarding cost and benefit in comparison to other similar endeavors. Here may be where discipline specific knowledge meets the goals of general education requirements. Perhaps the relationship between writing and the rhetorical education that once served as the foundation for what we now call liberal arts education can help to define expertise in the realm of professional practice. Additionally, we are suggesting a kind of expertise that professionals can convey to others through general education, an expertise that allows critical thinking about knowledge generated within a discipline by those outside it.

Such a line of conversation is worthy of further exploration. We have initiated this cross-disciplinary talk in the spirit of learning from our colleagues, acknowledging that, in many areas of discourse, we are not master-workers but apprentices.

And what, again, of the place of English in liberal studies, and of the study of literature that has defined English for a century or more? Michel de Certeau has noted the difference between everyday and theoretical contexts and observed that "method" systematizes Plato's "art" or "activity," ordering "a know-how . . . by means of discourse" (65). Activity is rationalized through this process, while some "ways of operating . . . that have no legitimacy with respect to productivist rationality" remain unordered and largely unexamined (69). In the 19th century, he points out, when scientific method overtook humanistic and religious sensibility in the hierarchy of thought, the novel of realism became the "new representational space . . . populated by everyday virtuosities that science doesn't know what to do with and which became the signatures . . . of everyone's micro-stories" (70).

That could be one place where those of us in English can come in. Lacking the expertise to adequately consume and critically respond to the texts of scientific discourse, we have instead cultivated our abilities to read what lies outside the scope of that discourse—not just novels, poems, familiar essays and plays, but also films, journalistic reports and polemics, television serials, advertisements, and so on. In the glare of scientific dominance, our inadequacies have been long exposed, but our colleagues do not seem so shy as to be unwilling to expose some of their own. They admit to a curiosity about the materials of our classes, although their sense of what that material may be is frequently limited, as ours is of theirs. And although they may not articulate the motivations for their curiosity in the language of de Certeau, it seems worthwhile to probe deeper into those motivations through further conversations.

One motivation, we are certain, is the desire to help their students learn; both English teachers and those who write for the nonspecialist audience do have their ways of helping learning along. If what we teach is more than delivery of content, an academic form of "knowing that," perhaps it is awareness of the different forms for conveying information and for adapting modes of application dependent on context. Novels, for instance, can teach discipline-specific knowledge as well as the quotidian. Melville pauses at several junctures in his story of the white whale to tell us of the physiology, the behavior, and the variety of his animal subject. During the 1960s it's certain that many readers obtained their knowledge of the workings of the airline and automobile industries by reading the novels of Arthur Hailey. And one chemistry professor at Stanford, Carl Djerassi, has turned to writing what he calls "science-in-fiction" in order to "smuggle scientific facts into the consciousness of a scientifically illiterate public" (37-38).

In Clemson University's "Poetry Across the Curriculum" project, students in all disciplines use poetry to process the content knowledge of their coursework, as a way to bring ever more specialized knowledge out of its cave of isolation, to cross the great divide between the humanities and sciences, to recognize the continuing importance of humanistic concerns in the university of Excellence identified by Readings, and to discover and question the dominance of the information culture (Young 475-76).

If expert knowledge is more than discipline-specific theoretical foundations, perhaps expert knowledge is accessible even at the undergraduate level, both within practically oriented courses in the major and in the general education core. And a primary tool for the acquisition of an undergraduate expertise is writing, for it is writing, whether to learn, reflect or critique, that has the capacity to reveal the primarily linguistic nature of academic, disciplinary and professional knowledge, and hence to spark ongoing thought. In his dissection of the current plight of higher education Readings identifies the modern university as a political, autonomous society built on rational consensus (and more recently converted from cultural to corporate purposes). He would replace that "ruined" institution with a society built on dissensus that "preserves the social bond as a question" not "the answer" (187). Echoing but resisting Aristotle's claim that only those with theoretical knowledge (knowing why and the cause) should speak and teach, Readings notes that it is surprising how often intellectuals think only about the speaker and not the listener (186).

Readings wishes to put teaching at the center of university work as an "ethical practice" rather than a tool for transmitting scientific truth (154). Perhaps we could abandon the whole process of agonizing over agreement regarding the purposes and goals of general education or liberal studies and espouse dissensus, as opposed to an unstable, dereferentialized consensus, as our watchword. Writing as literate activity, as an inevitable mode of critical thinking, becomes a valued process rather than a product (Crosby 643). Essentially, both writing to learn and writing in the disciplines are validated as vehicles for academic expertise.

Readings substitutes teaching, "which takes place in language" and is "fundamentally relational," for the administrative, social, and economic relations of merit and the market (Crosby 642). Readings undoes Aristotle's hierarchy. He requires the speaker as well as the addressee to listen, leveling out authority. He recognizes that both the discursive formations and the varied lived experiences of participants in the dialogic relation of teaching and learning prevent transparent communication. He questions whether there exists some unifying consensus joining the supposedly autonomous subjective consciousnesses of rational subjects, the ideal of the modern university. "The listener is not an empty head, as in the line drawings that illustrate Saussure's account of communication" (155). The world of IDEAS becomes a WORLD of ideas. Readings prefers Bakhtin's dialogism to consensus. Conversation and presumably argument is not serial monologue but the receiver is another human being "full of inner words. . . . All his experiences—his so-called apperceptive background—exist encoded in his inner speech, and only to that extent do they come into contact with speech received from outside" (155).

What we seek to do here, with Readings help, is to concretely describe that often empty phrase "critical thinking" as a process, a process by which the undergraduate University of Excellence can recognize the negotiation and interpretation that accompany disciplinary dialectic, perhaps through writing and through the core of liberal studies. Such ongoing thought, or dissensus, along with a healthy dose in major programs of the perspective of practicing professionals with experience in nonacademic contexts, might develop in our students a nonspecialist, functional expertise capable of critical judgments about generalized research results. More generally, critical thinking as dissensus, as ongoing questions rather than agreed on answers, could help produce what our faculty appear to desire: that is, practitioners who are light on their feet because they have "know how," as well as general education students who can both understand disciplinary knowledge and its limitations, "knowing that" and "wondering why."

This book could be seen as one way of modeling Readings' dissensus. Our second set of interviews, through modified general questions and specific questions for particular interviewees, recognized the limitations of earlier formulations. By incorporating our colleagues' reactions to reading a draft of various book chapters, we seek to listen. Likewise, since we mentioned at the outset of this chapter the questions that drove us forward and our desire to "answer" them, we must now more correctly say we have not found an answer to the role of writing but rather a possible way of continuing to explore the role of liberal studies courses in the development of nonspecialist functional expertise.

It is clear from our interviews that theoretical questioning about the nature of things is not the only arena for written critique, but it often occurs wherever teachers want students to examine discipline-specific information, or to apply such information in practice, or to synthesize concepts or question research results. In response to Readings, we must add that such a statement is not a call for authoritative definitive conclusions, but for engagement in a continuing process of questioning in which the role of writing in the undergraduate curriculum and in the functioning of expertise is pursued. This questioning can take place in ways only limited by the imaginations of faculty across the curriculum.

Listening across disciplines, in other words, can be a catalyst to critical thought among faculty. When faculty share with students in their own and other disciplines the processes involved in generating, disseminating and challenging knowledge, the hierarchy between theory and practice can break down. Both students and professors learn to think critically about the existence of the knowledge base in their fields simply as "content." Readings does not think such an approach to critical thinking and writing will lead to skepticism or hopeless relativism. Rather, pedagogy is recognized as a relation and the teacher becomes a *rhetor*, not *magister* (158). The whole hierarchy between theory and practice, master-worker, practitioner, and/or mechanic is undone. Expertise is generalized, not by abstraction from context but by recognizing expertise in every context. Expertise is knowing that, learning how, and asking why.

Our conversation with faculty about the role of writing in their disciplines has left us confident that the undergraduate curriculum offers many possibilities for learning how to write that will survive translation across contexts within and outside the university.

Connecting Correctness and Style to Writing Instruction Within and Beyond Disciplines

> . . . the powers of [pupils] sometimes sink under too great severity in correction; for they despond, and grieve, and at last hate their work, and, what is most prejudicial, while they fear everything, they cease to attempt anything. . . . A teacher ought, therefore . . . to praise some parts of . . . performance, to tolerate some, and to alter others, giving . . . reasons why the alterations are made, and also to make some passages clearer by adding something of his own . . . since study is cheered by nothing more than hope.
>
> Quintilian (*Institutio Oratoria,* Book II, Chapter 4)

TEACHING WRITING AND TEACHING CORRECTNESS

This chapter exists and has been placed near the end of the book for two compelling reasons. The first is that some of our colleagues clearly equated teaching writing with teaching "correctness." The second is that, even after 30 years of process pedagogy by writing teachers, accompanied by learned assaults on the linking of writing to traditional grammar instruction by scholars within the fields of linguistics, composition, and education, we weren't in the least surprised by our colleagues' perceptions. No area of human endeavor may be more subject to the influences of the recent past, of intergenerational lore and tradition, and of institutional inertia than school teaching. "I know the stereotypes that mathematicians go through—that we just crunch numbers and all that," our mathematics professor remarked after reading an earlier draft of this chapter. "I hadn't really thought about it in terms of other departments." And when it comes to the equation of writing with "good grammar," the profession of English probably has no entity to blame more than itself.

> When I went to high school approximately 25 years ago . . . we would actually have instruction in terms of parsing sentences. I'm not sure that's done any more and, I think, just the lack of knowledge of sentence structure and things like that also affects students' willingness to write. It's not uncommon for me to have students who don't recognize whether or not they're writing in complete sentences and . . . that's very troubling.
>
> (Health Services Administration, November 23, 1999)

Teachers of English at the undergraduate level, whether they work at a 2-year college, a private liberal arts institution, or a public comprehensive university, are haunted by a centuries-old image of themselves as guardians of the language and enforcers of its inexorable "laws." It's not the only image that adheres to us but it is the one that seems to cling most persistently to our role as writing instructors. Within our culture's collective memory this image elicits what is at best a bitter-sweet aftertaste; people sense they should be grateful for the effort they think we've made, but mostly they just feel relieved to no longer have to subject what they say or write to such pitiless scrutiny. It is this indelible collective image, regardless of whether it has been actually validated by an individual's personal experience, that causes people to reflexively monitor the form of their expression whenever they find themselves in the presence of someone who has been identified as an English teacher.

A great many members of our profession loathe this image. Like all stereotypes, we recognize how reductive it can be, and how easily it lends itself to caricature. In the not so distant past, the likes of H.L. Mencken branded English teachers with such epithets as "grammatomaniacs" (cited in Corbett and Connors 350) and the virulently misogynist "schoolma'ams" (Mencken, *American Language*, passim). More recently, Steven Pinker argued that the so-called "rules" applied to English usage "survive by the same dynamic that perpetuates ritual genital mutilations and college fraternity hazing" (374). (It matters little that Pinker was more concerned with copyeditors and newspaper columnists than with schoolteachers. The chains that bind us in the public mind remain.)

As earlier noted, the knowledge that English teachers have helped perpetuate the image, both in the past and in the present, is at least as galling as the image itself. Mencken once mockingly reviewed a book by a Tennessee professor reporting a survey of teachers regarding the reasons why English should be taught. The "objective" receiving the most votes from his respondents was: "The ability to spell correctly without hesitation all the ordinary words of one's writing vocabulary." Number two read: "The ability to speak, in conversation, in complete sentences, not in broken phrases" (cited in Mencken, "Schoolma'am's Goal" 143).

> His jury was very carefully selected. It consisted of eighty teachers of such professional keenness that they were assembled at the University of Chicago for post-graduate study. Every one of them had been through either a college or a normal school; forty-seven of them held learned degrees; all of them had been engaged professionally in teaching English, some for years. . . . They represented, not the lowest level of teachers of English in the Republic, but the highest level. And yet it was their verdict by a solemn referendum that the principal objective in teaching English was to make good spellers. (Mencken, "Schoolma'am's Goal 145)

A 1959 study of English teachers found that, as a group, they were "far more conservative than the rest of the population" in their tendency to reject usages that had recently become acceptable in both practice and publication (cited in Lindemann 73). Moreover, "grammar-based instruction" persists up to the present day—might even be regarded as prevalent—despite supposedly overwhelming evidence of its ineffectiveness (Miles 758).

Beyond the damage that the "guardian of the language" stereotype does to our self-image, on a more altruistic plane writing teachers informed by recent scholarship also fear what "hyper-correctness" might do to our students' sense of themselves as developing writers, and to the commitment we hope they will make to that development. In this, we tend to agree with the advice Quintilian offered nearly two millennia ago. We expect that novice writers need encouragement and practice and a sense of hope in order to move forward, rather than persistent reminders of how their work falls short of a "standard" in terms of accepted usage or appropriate "style."

Moreover, empirical evidence accumulated within linguistics and educational studies over the past century suggests that assuming formal grammar instruction will contribute to the development of writing ability is almost certain to engender feelings of failure and frustration. A 1906 experiment led Franklin S. Hoyt to point out the absence of any "relationship between a knowledge of technical grammar and the ability to use English and to interpret language" (cited in Hartwell 179). Constance Weaver has summarized a 1950 *Encyclopedia of Educational Research* article as "concluding that the study of grammar has a negligible effect in helping people think more clearly . . ." (cited in Lindemann 74).

> In 1963 Braddock, Lloyd-Jones, and Schoer stated that "in view of the widespread agreement of research studies based on many types of students and teachers, the conclusion can be stated in strong and unqualified terms: the teaching of formal grammar has a negligible or, because it usually displaces some instruction and practice in actual composition, even a harmful effect on the improvement of writing." (cited in Hillocks 133)

And finally, in 1986, George Hillocks summed up his meta-analysis of research conducted over the previous 20 years by saying the studies simply did not provide "any support" for the idea that grammar instruction could improve students' written compositions. "If schools insist on teaching the identification of parts of speech, the parsing or diagramming of sentences, or other concepts of traditional school grammar (as many still do), they cannot defend it as a means of improving the quality of writing" (Hillocks 138)

It would seem, nonetheless, that all this research has had little impact on perceptions outside English studies, or even among a great many practitioners within the discipline, regarding the value of "traditional" grammar instruction, the nature of language change and usage standards, and the relationship of both to writing. Colleagues, professionals, politicians, and parents, still in the thrall of that "language guardian" image and of the equation of "good writing" with "good grammar," continue to expect us to behave in ways that both experience and scholarship push us to discard. For teachers of first-year composition, the frustration can double, since those courses are likely to constitute the last general writing instruction ever received by the majority of our students. That being the case, how could so many have apparently failed to "master" the "basics," as evidenced by continuous and seemingly egregious deviance in syntax, spelling, and punctuation? When the "freshman English" course was established by Harvard in the 1880s, probably the most significant motivating factor was the perceived ignorance of standards for English punctuation, spelling, and syntax (Crowley 68). This is a history we cannot rewrite and a tradition we cannot deny. Therefore, it is hardly surprising when many professors expect students to have full command of such usage once they've completed the first-year composition courses.

> ... I'm appalled as to the lack or inability of people to read and write at the level. It's like I don't see how some of our students could pass College Writing I and College Writing II with some of the crap they come through with us. It's difficult. It's like where do you point the finger? Do you point it to College Writing I or College Writing II? No, probably not, because. . . . Do you point it at high school? These students are coming out and they're getting passed over, so they're coming up to a junior or senior taking my classes and I'm basically the one saying, "You're not going to pass here, because this is not the quality. You can't write a memo or you can't put a sentence together."
>
> (Sport Management, June 12, 1998)

If we can't provide a quick and easy solution to this colleague's frustration, we can at least feel sympathetic regarding its source. Within the "disease" metaphor our own profession has often been guilty of encouraging (writing ability as something that can be "remediated"; tutoring in writing as an activity that often took place in "clinics"), it is not surprising that someone should regard nonstandard usage as a "symptom" with an identifiable "cause" that should suggest an observable "treatment" most effective when administered at a particular moment in the development of the "condition." A recent student evaluation of a College Writing II course taught by one of us acknowledged that it was not the professor's fault that students didn't know the difference between "its" and "it's." Nevertheless, if such a problem couldn't be addressed in a composition course, the student went on, then where could it be addressed? Who *is* responsible? The writing center, perhaps, where some students still think they can drop off a draft for proof-reading by one of the staff? After all, isn't the avoidance of error an important part of writing, a part that may even take precedence over other parts?

> ... I get a little frustrated with English as it's being taught here in terms of, I think some of the emphasis is on drawing people out so they express themselves. I do think that's very valid. . . . You do want to teach people how to express themselves. You do want to teach people how to argue persuasively and that sort of stuff, but if that's done at a sacrifice that people can't write and can't spell and if it's done to the exclusion of content development or what I think people should know. . . to write effectively, which is to put subject and verb together, to be able to recognize whether it's a sentence or a fragment, to be able to use correct tense, to be able to spell effectively, or at least to be smart enough to check spellchecker, to hit that in their document and realize that the spellchecker didn't catch this one.
>
> (Health Services Administration, July 1, 1999)

People still lay the responsibility for writing instruction directly at the feet of the English faculty, and they still equate good writing with an absence of error, of deviations from standard written English, and they still perceive that such qualities as self-expression and persuasiveness and "idea development" are subordinate to "correctness" in determining the value of a written document. As frustrating as it can sometimes be, as much as English faculty would like to "move on" and move away from the role of language guardians, and as much as we may believe that linguists and education scholars have clarified the role of "usage" and formal "grammar" instruction in the development of writers, we have to admit that the equation between "effective" writing and "linguistic etiquette" (Lindemann 68) is still current and a force within people's professional lives. Both students and professionals can be, and all too often are, seriously hurt by the careless presentation of their prose. Because the link between correctness and credibility is so strong in the minds of many academic and workplace readers, a misspelled word or an obvious agreement error can subvert a writer's communicative aims. And those readers' ignorance of the dynamics of language change, or of the gaps between classroom-centered "rules" and the accepted usages found in quotidian language, doesn't really alter our obligation to address these issues, rather than dismiss them, during our instruction and during the conversations we have both inside and outside our profession.

When I look at a written document and you see the basic grammatical errors that I'm talking about, I think it erodes whatever argument you want to present. Now, I also have to say, conversing in the field, I'm not sure how often . . . a written document is our vehicle for convincing. I think so much of it . . . is a very brief briefing or a verbal and a visual presentation. The problem with the writing becoming so critical then is if all you're presenting is 25 words, if two of them are misspelled, I think even though you haven't written a lot what you've said by that misspelling, I mean, is just . . . devastating to whatever argument you want to make.

(Health Services Administration, July 1, 1999)

Our own frustration might be eased a bit if we realize that the arguments against teaching traditional grammar, and those skeptical of its value for developing writers, are still recent in comparison with the customs and traditions such arguments seek to refute. Maybe we should think of English pedagogy as a big boat, filled with tens of thousands of writing teachers and millions of "stakeholders," one that has been heading in a particular direction since the 17th century. It is going to take a while to turn it around. Several scholars have pointed out that in the 17th and

18th centuries the most commonly known English grammar of today was developed by borrowing heavily from the Greek and Latin grammars that teachers were most accustomed to promulgating in the schools of the time. English sentences were often described in ways more appropriate to Latin than to the spoken vulgate (Lindemann 78-79). Grasp of a "standard" English tied to an often inaccurate grammar was perceived as essential to the conduct of science and to the upward mobility of those aspiring to membership in growing middle and professional classes (Pinker 373). That perceived need has been with us a long time, and it is hard for people to judge that it may have outlived its usefulness.

Perhaps the seemingly strong experimental evidence has yet to convince people of the ineffectiveness of traditional grammar instruction because, as Patrick Hartwell observed some years ago, "Studies are interpreted in terms of one's prior assumptions about the value of teaching grammar" (164). Moreover, teaching is such an ongoing, contingent and circumstantial activity that it isn't necessarily unhealthy to be skeptical regarding the results of experimental studies attempting to reach general conclusions about how instruction should be executed. The possibility exists that some teachers, through their own personal dynamism or other unforeseen variables, could demonstrate a correlation, if not a causal relationship, between formal grammar instruction and student writing ability. As Hartwell also observed, "Any experimental design can be nitpicked, any experimental population can be criticized, and any experimental conclusion can be questioned . . ." (164).

Seeking to end the debates over formal grammar instruction by citing professionally sanctioned knowledge may engender resentment rather than conviction. Just how we seek to teach writing has become, whether we like it or not, a public issue we cannot eliminate simply by invoking reified knowledge that removes "immediate social, material contingencies" from consideration (Horner 375). We can't forget that the "rules of grammar" have also been presented as professional knowledge; comprehending them supposedly qualified some people to teach English, whereas a lack of familiarity with them disqualified others. The association of the "rules" with writing effectiveness boxed teachers in then as well as now because of their general acceptance, especially when those same teachers were confronted with students whose incoming ability to produce standard written English varied widely. Insisting on a linear acquisition of linguistic competence, with grammar "mastery" supposedly preceding writing practice, has kept teachers from implementing even Quintilian's sage advice. Quintilian was, after all, just one teacher, albeit a particularly renowned and articulate one, and his advice could be characterized, and dismissed, as mere "practitioner lore," rather than a generally applicable knowledge developed through rigorous scientific method.

An approach that seeks to teach writing through imparting "rules" is, for many people, the only approach to teaching writing they recall with any clarity or vividness. If those people eventually evolved into effective writers within their particular disciplines, then it is quite natural for them to associate their success with their school experience, even if the actual roots of their ability may lie in activities quite separate from that experience. They also know that producing error-free, "standard" written English is a sine qua non of their professional lives. If formal grammar instruction won't get the job done for their students, then they want to know what will.

> ... I had written a paper and put a copy in my advisor's mailbox. And then he marked it up and put it in my mailbox and it was pretty red. He explained; you know, he wanted to make sure I didn't jump off a bridge, but the reason he marked it up so much is that it says a lot about you, how you write these things, and that, especially because I would be going into the job market, he wanted to make sure that things were done very well. So I wrote the paper up to his satisfaction, sent it in and got the referees' reports back. ... He pointed out to me that both referees' reports commented on how well written it was. That really said to me that people really do look out for that.
>
> (Mathematics, November 12, 1999)

Handbook usage may not keep up with common usage; traditional grammar may not reflect many of the ways English sentences are organized; the contribution of instruction in such grammar to student writing may be problematic at best. But as we speak to our colleagues we have to keep in mind the attractiveness of packaged familiarity. One fair criticism of the Platonic dialectic is that it effectively negates, but seldom replaces. When have we reached the end of a Socratic dialogue with the confidence that a term or concept *has been* effectively defined? We must move beyond debunking, and help our colleagues identify some specific alternatives to the pedagogies we insist will not work, alternatives that seem to fit the writing their students will do in their courses and at work, rather than ones that may strike them as mere "self-expression," as forms of verbal "navel gazing."

Regrettably, our first attempts at cross-campus conversations about writing never got very specific about what our colleagues or we meant by terms like *grammar* or *style*. We need to get that specific, we now believe; we need to create, rather than just discover, a common language that will help our colleagues feel more comfortable responding to student writing in the ways Quintilian envisioned.

SEEING MEANING AS STABLE OR VARIABLE

Conversations with some of our colleagues did suggest a tendency to associate both the functionality and the aesthetic quality of a written text with style, with prose sentences that are organized in particular ways and that correspond with a "standard" form of written expression. This tendency may, as we have already suggested, owe something to an exposure to writing instruction that strongly emphasizes the role of style (style as closely connected to an "accepted" or "standard" usage) in writing, at the expense of other canons in classical rhetoric, such as invention and arrangement. But an instructional emphasis on style is also driven by the assumption that written language merely represents a reality free of language. Many are convinced written language is simply a conduit for transmitting the "real" objects of disciplinary study to its audiences, a tool that can be wielded in much the same way when representing any number of distinct objects. Informed English teachers, exposed during the last three decades to the thinking of Saussure, Derrida and a multitude of poststructuralist critics, have moved far beyond such a representational conception of language. Nevertheless, when we speak of written language with colleagues in other disciplines, we cannot forget that quite often those colleagues will think of language as gladly representational.

For the nursing professor, "quality of writing" is inseparable from the qualities of clarity, readability, and conviction in the professional writing with which she is most familiar.

> **Okay, what do you mean by the quality of writing?**
>
> *Well, I've done peer review for a couple of journals in my field and there are some people who are just outstanding writers, that you read, you can understand even if there's a complex idea. You can understand what they mean the first time you read the sentence. You don't have to read the sentence two or three times to figure out what they're talking about. And I find that very important . . . in writing.*
>
> **It adds to the credibility for you?**
>
> *Very much so. If I can understand what they are talking about immediately. . . .*
>
> (Nursing, June 17, 1998)

In fact, our very position as the "go to" people of writing pedagogy may rest to some extent on a lingering belief in the one-to-one correspondence between word and object. Because it is not the object that influences the style in which it is described, but the style that reveals the object, then the professionals who have most diligently studied style, namely the English faculty, remain the most qualified to teach the style that can reveal just about any object. Only such reasoning, it seems to us, could justify countless academics placing the "preparation" of their multitudes of majors in our often trembling hands. And this trust extends beyond first-year composition, since the teaching of "technical writing," the writing that both promulgates and implements the knowledge gained through scientific inquiry, has become the nearly exclusive domain of English departments since the end of World War II (Longo 150).

Technical writing relies on what has come to be known as the "plain style," a way of forming prose that emphasizes both "accuracy" (a supposedly direct correspondence between the written language and the subject of the writing) and "correctness." Sometimes linked to the "attic" style of the ancient Athenians, the modern English "plain style" actually owes its origins, its promotion, and its considerable cultural clout to certain trends and personages of the English Renaissance and Enlightenment. In the 16th century, science became a more public, accessible activity through the publication of medical self-help books, "books on farming and animal husbandry, and . . . a variety of books on Renaissance technologies" (Tebeaux 151). In the 17th century, Francis Bacon, John Locke, and the Royal Society in London articulated the value of a "clear," functional language, stripped of unnecessary verbal and syntactical flourishes, that could "explain experience without resorting to occult, secret knowledge" (Longo 50). As John Locke said in his *Essay Concerning Human Understanding*:

> Vague and insignificant forms of speech, and abuse of language, have so long passed for mysteries of science; and hard or mis-applied words, with little or no meaning, have, by prescription, such a right to be mistaken for deep learning and height of speculation; that it will not be easy to persuade either those who speak or those who hear them that they are but the covers of ignorance, and hinderance of true knowledge. (cited in Longo 51)

The influence of "plain style" on professional and academic writing has been both profound and lasting. Locke's sentiments were echoed during several of our interviews, through expressions of preference for clarity and brevity in student writing.

> *. . . When I grade math students who are beginning to write like a mathematician the biggest problem is puffery. When they read something in a book they see a lot of big, important words so they think they have to sprinkle those throughout and what is better is*

> kind of the Hemingway technique—short, clear sentences. I would much rather read something that says "therefore" and reaches a conclusion than something that reads, "therefore, we must arrive at the following conclusion" and states it . . . it's just that, emphasizing the idea that it's better to be clear in what you say than to be saying a lot.
>
> (Mathematics, November 12, 1999)

We cannot be sure, as we read over the math professor's statement, just what books are encouraging students to employ "big, important words" in their writing, whether they are mathematical books or some other kind. But when he wishes to identify a model of the kind of style he prefers, the mathematics professor draws from his own experience with creative literature, specifically with a fiction writer celebrated for the clear exposition to be found in his novels and stories. Put another way, the example of a transparent, concise style in which he wants his students to write mathematics, the example he can readily draw on, is from the literature with which an English professor would be most familiar. Consequently, it could be a style someone in English may most readily teach.

Identifying writing drawn from professional practice but directed toward heterogeneous audiences as "technical writing" may also throw responsibility for teaching style back onto the English faculty. It isn't just that English departments have traditionally housed courses in technical writing; there is also the sense that professionals used to writing for each other could run into trouble when they seek to communicate with those outside their usual disciplinary group. When one of us defined technical writing in the way mentioned above, the computer science professor appeared to connect successful achievement of a "plain style" to practice communicating with audiences outside narrow academic and professional coteries.

> **Do your courses deal with the writing aspect of the documentation? Is it likely that at the work place, that person with the computer training would be working with technical writers to do that or would they themselves be the technical writer?**
>
> I would think depending on the student; usually students that major in information systems feel more comfortable, would feel more comfortable, doing the technical writing themselves than the computer science students. Usually, but not always, depending on their background . . . we do have courses that both information systems majors and computer science majors, and now the new information technology major will take that are labeled writing intensive . . . of all the programming courses, part of the outcomes

assessment is that students learn how to write coherent, clear, plain English documentation for all the code. . . . I have students write, and I know some other people write executive summaries so that they get in the habit of condensing whatever it is that their project is, whether it's a big network system project or just one program, so that their supervisor can read and understand the product without going through reading code.

(Computer Science, August 12, 1999)

Which is not to say that our colleagues were not aware of other, less desirable styles for their students' current academic and future professional writing that could be associated with writing in English courses. The health services administration professor clearly would not want his students adopting an expressivist mode he considered all too common in first-year composition. The mathematics professor's allusion to an overly elaborate "therefore, we must arrive at the following conclusion" may be drawn from other experiences in "English," such as instruction in the studiously polite style once featured in ninth-grade units on letter writing and in courses dealing with business correspondence. And the "flowery" style referred to by the nursing professor in what follows may also recall contact with reading or writing done in "English," of the belles-lettres variety.

. . . In the nonacademic setting, certainly those people in more responsible positions, who have a larger scope of responsibility, need excellent writing skills. They tend to be writing probably more from the executive management approach.

What do you mean? How would you distinguish that?

Well, when I look at something for executive management, I think that the clarity is extremely important and at the same time brevity is extremely important. A busy manager or busy executive who gets several memos from several different sites can only read so much in a day, so a memo that can put executive summary together and . . . highlight key points and draw attention and can clearly communicate an idea in very few words is much more successful than someone who tends to pick more words and tends to be more flowery . . .

(Nursing, June 17, 1998)

Such responses, although reflective of the popularity of "brevity" and "clarity" and "directness," of the "plain style," suggest one way that our colleagues manage, perhaps unconsciously, to embrace style of a particular character while continuing to hold the English faculty responsible for its implementation. Nevertheless, regardless of origins, or the most likely places where certain stylistic features may be found, the popularity of the features our colleagues extol are most directly explained through examination of the activities, epistemological preferences, and institutional positions of their own disciplines. Scientific inquiry and professional applications of such inquiry require written language that is stable in both its meaning and its usage, to limit linguistic interference with the "material reality" it is supposedly conveying (Longo 147). However, as composition specialists know all too well, language doesn't always do even the most adept writer's bidding. It isn't always stable, and Keith Hjortshoj remarks on the "fear" language can evoke among academics in a variety of disciplines.

> . . . most of the scholars who want to confine the disorder of writing to the margins of the freshman curriculum are themselves struggling, often desperately, to control written language, and making enormous messes in the process. . . . We are not supposed to point out that the most powerful texts in their fields probably emerged from piles of notes, incoherent thoughts, and disjointed drafts—not from tidy outlines, the deductive selection of thesis statements, and obedience to rules. (Hjortshoj 500)

Within our interviews, this wariness, this suppressed awareness of language's slipperiness and potential for treachery, did appear. But there were also times when our colleagues described ways in which either language or the material reality it "represents" must be altered or adjusted to fit the written conventions or methodology of their discipline, or to fit the expectations or needs of particular audiences. The health education professor did not just see brevity and skillful condensation of material as some general stylistic good, but as qualities of writing that answered the needs of certain significant audiences within his profession.

> *One reason we stress the article review. The IMRAD [Introduction, Methodology, Results, and Discussion] model is still the template used for grant acquisition. You still have to identify the problem, what you produced supporting that observation, what you think you could bring to bear on the problem, and how much money you think it's going to cost, and also put together an evaluation protocol. Since a lot more RFPs [Requests for Proposals] want more than just lip service in terms of how you are going to evaluate what you accomplished, what you think you've achieved. And that writing forces you to be tight and concise. . .*
>
> (Health Education, July 16, 1998)

One immediate and future task of our conversations, it would seem, is to help colleagues bring these two levels of consciousness about writing together, to link what happens when writing occurs in their disciplines, both generally and personally, with what is therefore bound to happen when they ask their students to write. Our physics professor, for example, took note of something that has been described by a number of scholars; that is, the difference between the way scientific activity has been "written up" and the way it may have actually been conducted.

> . . . *the scientific method in practice tends to not be as linear and structured and orderly as the scientific method you might see in a ninth grade science book, where you make an hypothesis and you test the hypothesis and there's this feedback. Because, to be honest, when you're doing research, when you're discovering knowledge, the discovery process is not linear at all, but there are tangents, there are dead ends, there are; . . . it's just not linear. So I think there's a lot of philosophers and scientists have written about this—that even though there's this scientific method that serves as a guideline, . . . the way that research really goes, is you proceed in whatever way that helps you accomplish your immediate goals. . . . It's kind of like anything goes, you do whatever you need to do to solve the problem at that moment and that little problem hopefully is going to relate to the big problem that you're working on. But in terms of the actual dissemination, the way that stuff gets written, I think that the kind of format that articles have evolved into is very logical. . . .*
>
> (Physics, June 22, 1998)

In mathematics, our professor discussed how the need to help an audience comprehend a mathematical concept or proof might directly challenge the truth value or general application of that same concept or proof. We found this exchange fascinating, as most academic disciplines rely on examples or illustrations to effectively convey their knowledge. And yet, examples and illustrations contextualize that knowledge. We can only grasp some generalized "truth statement" through a particular instance that belies the abstractness of the statement.

> *. . . in the last interview . . . we talked about how people have to learn how to explain . . . proofs; for instance, if they're working, so that their boss or somebody else will actually understand it, right? Generally, how do people do that? Do you have any ideas?*
>
> I have vague ideas, but I haven't done that much outside to have definite things. The biggest aid is proof by picture. Technically, it's not allowed; your proof has to be logical and based on definitions

and things like that, but definitely the best way to get the idea across is to have a picture of the situation.

When you say technically not allowed, you mean among mathematicians?

Yeah. When you want to prove something is true that means it's true under all situations. As soon as you draw a picture that is one specific situation. So it can't qualify as a for-all statement.

That's interesting. And basically what you're saying is when you address a nonexpert audience, that doesn't understand the math, then you would have to make it specific; you have to apply it to the situation.

Yeah. Lots of pictures and lots of examples. I always tell my students, especially the ones that I know are going on to be teachers, that you should never have a definition without an example to follow it.

(Mathematics, November 12, 1999)

For us, the need to communicate seemingly identical "material realities" to distinct audiences, whose prior knowledge of a discipline and its vocabulary may vary considerably, poses the greatest challenge to the idea of language as unerringly representational, and to the belief that "plain style" can successfully suppress the semantic drift to which words inevitably succumb. If there is a direct correspondence between words and objects of study, and such a premium placed on finding the precise word that most exactly represents an object, then what happens to those objects when the words are changed to fit a particular audience? Does the knowledge change as well? (We know these questions may strike our readers from English studies and other areas of the humanities as obvious and "old hat." But when they are put in the context of recalling past conversations with colleagues from other disciplines, and of rehearsing new ones, we believe they are quite relevant.) Some of our interviewees described disciplinary and classroom writing that was meant to simplify material. In simplifying, do we also alter? Why are popularizations of knowledge, or even textbooks, not satisfactorily precise or detailed enough for the scholar, as they apparently are for the general reader? The Nursing professor tells her students to consciously simplify the language in an executive summary, while the mathematics professor suggests mathematicians must substitute rough translations for the Greek symbols used in proofs, when explaining the proofs to non-expert audiences. But if both renderings of the material do not change the material itself, then what difficulties require alterations for the benefit of novices in the first place?

If you're not clear and precise, you're not going to be persuasive. And that's where that executive summary comes across. And I even tell them to do a grade check on it and to keep it low, because the people who are reading fast or skimming will get more of the information, even though they can read at a 15th-grade level, if it's written in a fifth-grade level. They're going to get more of the information if they're skimming through it very quickly.

(Nursing, November 21, 1998)

Then another problem is, of course, let's say they do a proof and the job that they're working on . . . is an operations research analysis, then they have to describe the proof that they did for an audience of non-mathematicians, let's say a boss, and they can't even use the word Epsilon, in that case. They have to indicate they are doing distances and measuring distances or whatever.

In doing the proof you would say, for this distance Epsilon there's going to be another distance Delta and such that whatever happens. When you're presenting to someone who's not a mathematician you basically want to say, that if they're going to be this close in the beginning then we know they're only going to be this close at the end.

(Mathematics, August 6, 1999)

Another variation involved formats that demanded just words or phrases, or a few sentences, whereas others required more expansive exposition. How might these different formats alter word choices and sentence structures? And is there enough wiggle room within the "plain style" to accommodate the alterations and still accurately represent the subject under discussion?

The executive would tend to write more in sentences. The practicing nurse does not write in sentences. There are phrases and fragments that are part of the style. Yeah, so the ability to communicate an idea clearly goes across everywhere. It's just the style that fits the various areas . . . changes. But what I found, quite honestly, is that if you are totally grounded in writing those phrases and fragments and the style that's written for medical records, you don't necessarily immediately translate to writing in a style that might be appropriate for a term paper.

(Nursing, June 17, 1998)

Regardless of these conundrums, the "plain style" is so pervasive that it may be one of those "culturally generated" global writing strategies Carter suggested English faculty could teach before students moved on to more localized contexts for writing (281). In fact, it is probably safe to say that "plain style," so valued within and integral to American culture, *has been* taught, under various labels and using various approaches, in first-year writing courses for the past several decades. From Strunk and White to innumerable handbooks, the gospel of "transparency," urging writers to get out of the way so the subject and the reader can commune with minimum interference, has been forcefully preached. Clearly, we have believed we can help current and future student writing exhibit these exalted values. And our colleagues in other disciplines have often believed we could do so single-handedly.

Whether we can or cannot (we ourselves are skeptical), it is important to remember that the deeper researchers have delved into writing in academic and professional settings the more obvious it has become that every act of writing is "situated" within a particular, ever evolving, context. Just as every act of teaching is unique, and generalizations about teaching methods must be made with caution, so every act of writing is in some way unique, and the appropriateness of a particular, identifiable style to that writing must be offered with caution. Paul Prior even suggests that it may be best not to think of writing as singular acts at all, but as an ongoing element in what he labels "literate activity." "Literate activity, in this sense, is not located *in* acts of reading and writing, but *as* cultural forms of life saturated with textuality, that is strongly motivated and mediated by texts" (Prior 138). Texts inherently connected to an activity are formed through their use within the activity. A particular style cannot be disconnected from the purposes and uses spawning the texts that feature the style.

That insight was borne out when our interviewees touched on stylistic concerns specific to their own disciplinary practice, concerns that composition courses populated by students with a variety of vocational and academic interests could not be expected to address. The nursing professor described three distinct approaches to "charting" a patient's condition and therapeutic progress; all three seemed to us to make their own particular stylistic demands on a writer. One involved supplementing data fed into a computer from machines monitoring physical functions.

We're still picking up a lot of data you can't pick up from a machine.

Would you still be, like reporting phrases the patient has himself communicated to you.

> *The machine might record exactly how many breaths the patient had in a minute. The nurse might be describing things like, "The patient is breathless. They run out of air before they run out of sentence."*
>
> (Nursing, June 17, 1998)

Another was known as "problem-oriented charting," or by the acronym SOAPI (subjective, objective, assessment, plan, implement). In this approach, a patient's "subjective complaints" are combined with or contrasted to the "objective things" that could be described about a patient, in order to arrive at a diagnosis and subsequent treatment. A third approach is called "the critical path," which compares a patient's condition or symptoms at a particular moment with a model of where the patient should be at that point in treatment.

> *... If you looked at a whole group, if you had that regimen, you said, "This is what we expect." So we expect a patient that has a total hip replacement to be able to stand unassisted in two days. So if we have a patient who can't stand unassisted in two days then we know we're getting behind here. There's something wrong.*
>
> (Nursing, June 17, 1998)

The critical path approach and other approaches that ask for nurses to employ the language of patient charting, we deduced from our conversations, require a grasp of a set of acronyms for conditions or procedures that would strike non-health professionals as obscure and occasionally comical.

> *A critical path looks at . . . a particular condition or problem, like heart attack or a total hip or something, not a patient, but a problem, okay, and says, "On the first day, any patient with this problem should have these meds, these lab tests, these activities, this diet and we should look at these things on that patient. . . ." It's an interdisciplinary tool that then is used to track a patient. Once we design that tool, then we take a patient and say, "They're on the total hip track or they're on the CABAGE path. . . ."*
>
> **How did they get that name for that kind of thing?**
>
> Coronary Artery Bypass Surgery.
>
> **Coronary . . . Artery . . .**
>
> Bypass Graft, I guess. CABAGE.

> **Bypass . . . Graft. [Laughing] Okay. That's one of those terms that . . .**
>
> Yeah, just like TURPH is Treated Urethral Prostate. . . . I think probably one of the most commonly recognized . . . is an SOB. . . .
>
> **[Laughing]**
>
> A patient who is SOB means they are short of breath.
>
> (Nursing, November 21, 1998)

In physics, the style of writing may vary depending on the course or professor. The professor we interviewed required synopses and other, more extensive writing assignments, but added that he was "the exception in the department and not the norm." In many other courses, students would have to "fill in the blanks in the laboratory instructions, to write down the results and a little synthesis, but they wouldn't have to do anything more that a couple of sentences. . . . Lots of the instructors don't give any questions that are qualitative and so they would never have an opportunity to write in complete sentences. Everything would be in the form of a mathematical proof—that has its own kind of logic. . . ." (Physics, November 16, 1998). Our mathematics professor said that the aforementioned "proofs" were the primary form of writing math majors performed, and one that made style demands no composition teacher could be expected to master or assist others in learning.

> . . . I remember one student who would write her proofs out longhand in English paragraph form. That's not how mathematicians write. We have our own language as far as shorthand symbols go, but if you wrote proof that was all symbolic, you'd get a bad grade on that. If you write it out in paragraph form, you get a bad grade on that. You're supposed to be able to marry the two.
>
> **It has to be a . . . mix of sentences, paragraphs, and symbols, mathematical symbols.**
>
> Right. If you're going to take a function, you're going to say something like, take a function F of X symbolically. You are not going to say, "Take a function, and call that function F," because it's too wordy. That's not how mathematicians write. What I tend to tell people is that we want short sentences and no ambiguity. You need to be clear in what you're saying. . . . If you look at this paper here, the introduction is paragraph form, but when you start to define things, you have offset equations, and then when you actually get into a proof, you start to see, to make sure symbols and words are written out.

> **What's interesting here, and what I see, is that the symbols are like part of the sentence.... You'll have like a phrase, like, suppose that and then given, but that is followed by a set of mathematical symbols, which is followed by a period indicating that's the end of the sentence.**
>
> These are sentences. These are things you could take and translate into longhand English.... You could write out long hand, given Epsilon greater than zero, pick a Delta less than the minimum of Epsilon and X minus Y. You wouldn't write that out longhand. The Epsilon, Delta, minimum part all have their own notations and so that's what you should be using in your sentences, but it better be a sentence...
>
> (Mathematics, August 6, 1999)

The material to which we were referring during the interview was from the 1989 *Proceedings* of the American Mathematical Society. We cannot use a sentence from that article to further illustrate what the professor was saying, but he did provide us with an article of his own from which we can use this example:

An analytic way to describe the functions is as follows:

a function $f: R^+ \rightarrow R^+$ is metric preserving if, and only if, $f^{-1}(\{0\}) = \{0\}$ and for all $a, b, c, > 0$ such that $|a - b| \leq c \leq a + b$ we have

$$|f(a) - f(b)| \leq f(c).$$

("Metric Preserving Functions" 373). Aside from the sentences that must be a mix of normal verbiage and mathematical symbols, students writing proofs must also master the Greek alphabet and know the kind of entity that a particular Greek letter represents.

> ... One of the things I brow-beat our majors about is you've got to read the symbols like you're reading words. A large case Greek Epsilon looks a lot like a letter E. One of the things that drives me crazy is when students say, "Let E be greater than zero," because it's not an E, it's an Epsilon. While it might be a small distinction saying it that way, Epsilons are used for only one purpose. When you keep repeating, that's an Epsilon, hopefully that's going to reinforce what they're used for... Epsilon's what we use when talking about some sort of distance. It's something that should become automatic.
>
> (Mathematics, August 6, 1999)

These considerations of discipline-specific style demands should not, of course, be taken as an argument that first-year composition courses are incapable of teaching "plain style" to some good effect. It is more an observation on our part that students' education in style and correct usage won't stop there, and that there may be more in the stylistic universe of even "functional" or "technical" or scientific writing than can ever be encompassed by attention to "plain style."

A simple truth compositionists cannot ignore, and must help colleagues in other fields understand, is that learning a discipline involves learning a language, a way of "representing" and expressing inseparable from the objects of disciplinary study. Moreover, the uniqueness of both acts of writing and the styles each act might demand is responsible for a phenomenon many teachers, compositionists, and writing program administrators have doubtless observed—the tendency of even seemingly accomplished writers to lose stylistic control when momentarily overwhelmed by new information. Academic discourse in general, and discipline-specific discourse in particular, can be like a "second language" to students, one that demands the learning of "common phrases," "content words" and "collocations (words that co-occur)" (Myers 614). Joseph Williams and Gregory Colomb observed the challenges faced by students with high SAT scores at no less an institution than the University of Chicago. They have, in turn, urged teachers at "every point in the curriculum" to "be aware of what to expect in the way of 'incompetent writing'— summary rather than analysis, inappropriate imitation of obvious and concrete features of a professional style, slavishly following cues in the assignment, stylistic and other breakdowns" (Williams and Colomb 108).

On reflection, this phenomenon seems quite understandable. Written composition is first of all a working toward meaning, rather than a simple "capturing" of meaning through selection of the most accurate words arranged in the clearest way. And when we are unsure of the elements through which we are expected to construct our meaning, then a struggle with syntax and with word choice seems inevitable. Some writing, as everyone who has written must know, has to be seen as "rough" and "preliminary" drafts, steps on the way to an acceptable clarity and coherence. The mistake lies in seeing such writing as something else, and judging it accordingly.

> ... *I do think that the shortcomings the students possess are magnified when you present them with new knowledge and ask them to write within the discipline. And I think then what you see are, in addition to their grammatical and punctuation problems, you see problems using unfamiliar terms ... or using those terms properly within a health care context.... So in that regard the new knowledge causes problems, but it's really just a further reflection of the previous symptoms I mentioned.*
>
> (Health Services Administration, November 23, 1999)

In light of Williams' and Colomb's observations, and our own experience as writers, we can only ask the health services administration professor not to be so certain that the "grammatical and punctuation problems" he describes are separate from the "new knowledge" his students are absorbing.

CONNECTING STYLE TO WRITING WITHIN AND BEYOND DISCIPLINES

When it comes to teaching usage or style, being aware of what does not work and of the harm one might do can lead to a form of paralysis. "I've often been taken aback," writes Kate Ronald, "by the sheer vacuousness of my editing suggestions in the face of a student's desire to tell a real story or explore a true dilemma" (259). The easy way out is to fall back on to that old nostrum that "writing just can't be taught," which frequently translates into "style can't be taught." Mencken used to cynically claim that the ability to write was a matter of genetic predilection, even arguing in one essay that attempting to get the vast majority of people to do it well was like training a dog "to walk on its hind legs" ("Literature" 198). Of course, he seemed to unconsciously contradict himself later in the same essay, observing that one of his favorite examples of philistinism, Warren G. Harding, could display charm and clarity when addressing a subject he knew well. The ability to express something in an interesting manner, Mencken added, was "possessed by all literate persons above the age of fourteen" ("Literature" 199-201).

In other words, we can help students gain a mastery over the language of their subject matter, but are understandably hesitant in the attempt simply because the intimate connection between knowledge and style, as well as the specificity of all expression, makes such assistance damnably difficult. In our colleagues' cases, believing there is not the time to spend on usage or style may add to this sense of paralysis. As will a suspicion that spending the time would prove too painful for both teachers and students.

> *I think each term paper is individually graded by a faculty member who's in a hurry because it's the end of the term and they have a lot of responsibilities. And so I don't think that kind of process builds writing skills for our students.*
>
> (Nursing, November 21, 1998)

> *In my international health class when I give an essay question, I rarely correct the spelling; I rarely correct for incomplete sen-*

> tences. I'm basically looking, can they even carry the argument of the content. Normally what I do is grade very, very easily because most of them kind of fail horribly at it.
>
> (Health Services Administration, July 1, 1999)

A century of specialization and an eon in which the scholarship of most disciplines has habitually ignored the impact of language on subject matter may also leave our colleagues feeling out of their depth when it comes to matters of "correctness" and style. For instance, we know that the word *grammar* is hardly used in a precise way by any one of us. Often, "good" grammar simply means the absence of what the reader perceives to be stylistically unacceptable. At the same time, and despite all the supposed "rules" and conventions we've absorbed through schooling and experience, it is difficult for many of us to articulate just what has gone wrong and how it might be modified into acceptability.

> My former students think that having to do as many as I used to require helped them in some of their grant writing skills. Helped them become a more clear writer, but at the same time . . . I didn't have the same types of assessment or feedback sheet that they now have. I guess I was eyeballing. I knew what I wanted; I just didn't have it written down.
>
> (Health Education, July 16, 1998)

One way to begin may be to distinguish between "grammar" and "usage" in the way that linguists do, with "grammar" meaning "formal systems . . . scholars have developed to explain and analyze language" and "usage" meaning "socially sanctioned styles of language appropriate to given situations and audiences" (Lindemann 68). This distinction would allow faculty to recognize that grammar can't be "bad," but that usage can be "inappropriate." What a student writes in a journal or an outline or a draft may be okay, but not okay if carried over into a supposedly completed paper or presentation, memo or report. Absorbing the term *usage* would also help faculty grasp that some of their expectations for student writing may be specific to their discipline, and dependent to an extent on the student's current relationship to disciplinary knowledge.

The danger here lies with the tenacious hold the association of "grammar" with acceptability and correctness has on many people. We're not very clear on what grammar is, but we sure know "good grammar" or "bad grammar" when we see it. Hartwell tried to get around this difficulty by identifying 5 different meanings for grammar. Passing these on may be initially confusing, but at the same time they could help colleagues recognize the different ways they've used the term in the past, or heard it used by others. *Grammar One* is the "tacit, unconscious, 'knowing how'" (Hartwell 169) that allows most of us to be able to distinguish what is and is not an English sentence. This meaning is the one compositionists are using when they insist that native speakers have known English grammar since the age of five, regardless of their schooling. *Grammar Two* encompasses the linguists' attempts to model "the competence of a native speaker" (Hartwell 170). *Grammar Three* is the "usage" we referred to previously, including not just appropriate word form and place but also the conventions governing punctuation, spellings, and so on, whereas *Grammar Four* is "the 'rules' of the 'common school grammars'" (Hartwell 174), such as the prohibition against splitting an infinitive, or beginning a sentence with a conjunction.

Grammar Five can be defined as the "grammatical terms used in the interest of teaching prose style" (Hartwell 178), and this meaning of the word defines the site of a still unresolved controversy among writing teachers. We've disagreed among ourselves for years about whether students need to know the meaning of such terms as an "absolute" or a "nominative," in order to successfully manipulate written language—that is, to consciously modify their style. Maybe the most important point we can make is that compositionists' true linguistic expertise rests in our awareness of the existence of these various definitions and distinctions, rather than in an encyclopedic knowledge of the "rules" that supposedly regulate English. Additionally, our expertise rests in our awareness of a variety of traditions regarding the teaching of style, rather than in an allegiance to the one tradition with which our colleagues might be most familiar.

In these first interviews we have conducted, these first attempts at cross-disciplinary conversation, our questions and other displays of curiosity may have at least helped some colleagues see they possess a knowledge of their own discipline's stylistics we could not possess ourselves. They also possess, the interviews reveal, some tacit awareness of alternatives to formal grammar instruction that can help students improve style and eliminate usage errors. Those alternatives include reading, particularly the reading of professional materials of the kind students will eventually be expected to produce. They include the use of machine-driven scans of a document's spelling and usage (often maddeningly, but predictably, labeled "grammar checks"), the creation of opportunities for revision, for rewriting as well as proofreading, sometimes with the assistance of peers, and of opportunities for practice in the manipulation and construction of sentences.

In terms of eliminating "error," or getting students to employ standard written English, we know some of our colleagues have concluded that the usual response, laboriously correcting deviations from standard usage via the application of pen and ink to student papers, was something they had neither the time nor the patience to execute. (The suspicion remains that some also regarded such close work to be the province of a student's writing or composition teachers.) Those of us who have studied written composition or rhetoric also know that teachers from Quintilian to the present-day have often found the "red-inking" of student papers to have little noticeable impact or to be visibly counterproductive. Experience convinced our nursing professor that computer software could do a better job of helping student writers than could teachers responding directly to written work or even conferencing one-to-one concerning deviations. In fact, she made this observation on two occasions—following her reading of a draft of this chapter, and during her second scheduled interview for the study.

> I had it [profitable correction] not from people but from software. I had somebody who made me write in college, an English teacher who made me come to her office and made me write. She did do some correction. I think what she was confused about, I'm wanting to say what she couldn't put together, was the level of thinking I could do and the quality of the writing. For example, I remember I turned in the term paper at the end of the year and she said if you have compound sentences you'll get a "C." I wrote the paper, gave it to somebody else to type, because I couldn't spell, and never proofed it because I couldn't spell so I got a "C." And she wrote a big long note because she was upset about this "C." Probably, overall, the content of the paper and the research I had done, she probably was looking at more work than she saw for the majority of students. That's the way life always was for me. I didn't question it. Just, you know, you can't spell and the world penalizes you for that. But I thought the best correction of those problems [came] not from people but from machines, and I think the reason is that the machines are so dang consistent and so objective.
>
> (Nursing, Draft Response Interview)

> ... I learned a great deal of writing skills from Right Writer, which was a software program that did grammar tracking much more thoroughly and much more specifically than I see in, for example, Word, and it was an extremely valuable process to use that over a period of two or three years on almost anything I wrote. I would like to see us use more of those tools because I don't think that students get feedback that is consistent and over time and helps them build writing skills.
>
> (Nursing, November 21, 1998)

Writing teachers who have gained a lot of experience with "grammar checks" during the last several years would caution against students relying too heavily on this technique. It is the very "consistency" and "objectivity" of these tools that make their help frequently problematic, since appropriate usage in one writing context may be quite inappropriate in another, as well as damaging to clarity and suasiveness. On the other hand, the proliferation of "teacher-created" rules (Why no compound sentences?) has confused many student writers for decades as they have moved from one instructor to another. Computer software can at least help students track stylistic tendencies in their writing that may be inappropriate in contexts they frequently encounter. Such tracking can lead to creation of style lists that can aid writers looking for the aforementioned tendencies as they or their fellows proofread their work.

We asked our interviewees directly about the impact reading in their courses might have on student writing. It was not surprising, therefore, that reading figured most prominently as a way to influence students' writing without resorting to correction or evaluation. Sometimes this influence might be general and a result of lifestyle changes that were, at least, subject to the assignments and exhortations of teachers.

> *. . . more of what's given me any kind of verbal ability is the fact that I read an awful lot. When I was a kid, I would read comic books. I would read the Oz series by L. Frank Baum. I read all kinds of science fiction and I read for pleasure. . . . I think if I were to poll my class I think maybe three out of 30 or 1 in 10 would read for pleasure or would tell me that . . . they had read in the past year five books beyond what they had to read for class.*
>
> (Health Services Administration, July 1, 1999)

> *. . . When you and I grew up, I mean, you fight your father or one of your siblings for the sport section every day. Now the kids don't read the sport section. They watch ESPN Sports Center or they get on the Internet and dial into the Sports Center web page. . . . At least on the net they still have to read it. But there's [are] so few of the students that read the paper. I try to get them . . . just doing something as simple as that.*
>
> (Sport Management, July 27, 1998)

As their students progressed into upper level courses, professors did believe that reading professional materials could have a direct effect on writing and thinking patterns (Elementary Education, November 18, 1999).

> *. . . The other thing is, you choose textbooks that have lots of good examples of readable proofs.*
>
> **So at least they've got some models.**

> Right. Our introduction-to-proving-things course, the book that I use has a section called "Proofs to Grade"; they are other people's proofs and your choices are (A) everything is perfect, (C) it's good but needs a little bit of work, and (F) the student is clueless. That's the reason I chose that book. I love those problems because it let's them see mistakes without being the person to make the mistake.
>
> (Mathematics, November 12, 1999)

The sport management professor felt that writing material similar in form and subject matter to what they were reading would assist comprehension.

> ... the one journal I was showing you, the Sport Business Journal, is a much more of a technical, it's sort of the Wall Street Journal for sport managers. I know that when I require; this will be the first semester we require students to use it; I know that when we first get into it they're going to think it's way over their heads but I believe that since we are now going to be writing more, doing more with that type of journal, then the reading will . . . sort of follow along.
>
> (Sport Management, July 27, 1998)

Having discussed the meaning of Hartwell's *Grammar One*, we might also help our colleagues see the value of students reading their own writing out loud. If students, through both speaking and reading, have developed a tacit knowledge of English grammar and of how the language is encoded in print, then reading out loud can help them match their writing to unconscious templates (Hartwell 176). Such "out-loud" reading might work best, however, if done in pairs or groups of three because students will often correct their writing orally, as they read, without realizing that the same adjustments need to be made on the page as well. Our own experience tells us students often do not make many distinct errors in usage, spelling, and punctuation, but just a few errors that appear repeatedly. As students read aloud with each other, they can make lists of those common difficulties, a strategy we have already suggested could be stimulated by "grammar check" software, and can begin to look for the same specific difficulties while proofing.

Quintilian's sense of how to respond most effectively to student work assumes the necessity of revision, and a realization that writing should usually be considered as work in progress, rather than a finished display of knowledge or inquiry. Revision can be initiated and encouraged through student–teacher conferencing, which can serve to discover what the student knows and can express forcefully, as opposed to merely identifying what has gone awry in a piece of writing.

> . . . I skipped over regular English and went into honors English and then distinguished myself by, I think the first five or six papers, getting . . . , it was slash grades, it was an F over an F+. Usually the content warranted the F+ and then the grammar warranted the F. And then the instructor called me in and said, . . . because I did a paper, I forget the poem. It was about motorcycle riders. He called me in and he said tell me about this poem. So I got real expansive and I was talking about it and I said you really want to know what happened and he said, yeah, because he said it was a much better paper. I said I ride a motorcycle. This was when I was 18 or 19. I said, I understand what the people in the poem are doing. . . .
>
> (Health Services Administration, November 23, 1999)

Our nursing professor described how carefully and extensively she comments on student papers, but usually these comments are made on papers she has graded (November 21, 1998). The experience of composition teachers, as often discussed in the professional literature, is that such thorough responding bears more fruit if "meant to motivate and guide revision, not justify an assessment" (Tinberg 34). We suspect the nursing professor hopes her responses will stay with the student and carry over into future writing. Still, the experience of actually successfully revising a paper for both content and style, and subsequently receiving a higher grade than might otherwise have been expected, may do the most to encourage students to carefully revise their own writing in future, especially when a supportive teacher is no longer available.

The key here, we might move our colleagues to understand, is to help students see their own writing as evolving, rather than an immediate failure, full of missteps and blind alleys, or an equally immediate and possibly unanticipated success. Our mathematics professor appeared to grasp the importance of sending such a message, while combating earlier messages that mastering particular activities in his discipline is usually done in brief, intense bursts that lead quickly to other, more sophisticated work.

> **. . . Have you thought about how best you can get your students to learn how to write proofs and what kind of ideas have you gotten from them?**
>
> The best is the usual; practice, practice, practice.
>
> **Just have them do a lot of them?**
>
> Yeah. What is hard is to keep their confidence up and correct them all the time. Because they can't help, in the beginning especially, to make mistakes. They can't help doing that, but you don't want them to think, oh, I'll never learn how to proof things.

How do you do that?

Myself, pretty badly. Basically, I keep pointing that out to them. Yes, things are getting corrected, but on the other hand, things are getting better. The other is that this is not something that you learn in a week.

You point out basically that this is developmental. This takes a while.

Yeah. Of course, they've never seen that before in a math class. Everything is a nice, compartmentalized subject. You're going to spend a week on linear equations and then you're going to spend a week on this. So you're given a week to get it and then you're going to move on. Proofs aren't that way. You don't do it in a week. . . .

(Mathematics, November 12, 1999)

An observation by the health services administration professor suggests that drafting and revision need to be encouraged among his students, and maybe even built into his writing assignments.

> *. . . I honestly feel that for many written assignments, students do it [in] one draft; they do it at a time that is not particularly convenient to them, but time that is available, maybe between working two jobs, which many of my students do, or when time is available in a 30-hour work week, in an 18-credit-hour academic semester . . . So I think what we're seeing are products really of opportunities to write that are not necessarily conducive to the writing process . . . in that kind of environment, people . . . don't really attend to effective structures for writing, or for persuasion or for many of the things that we would like them to do.*

(Health Services Administration, November 23, 1999)

As composition teachers, we are acutely aware of the difficulties a paucity of time creates for the effective development of student writers. For us, perhaps one of the lingering attractions of traditional grammar instruction is that it can be easily delivered through class lecture, while seeking to help students eliminate error and refine style through close attention to their own writing is painstakingly slow and time consuming. And, as our physics professor has pointed out, the pressure to deliver "content" in disciplines other than English often encourages teachers to keep writing activities to a minimum. "So the act of me using writing so heavily in my classes means that I've given up other things, whether that means some chapters or sections or what" (November 16, 1998).

A common strategy employed by composition teachers to increase the amount of revision students perform involves having students complete collaborative assignments, as well as engage in peer review of each other's writing. Such activity ensures that others will read student work more frequently than could be the case if only the instructor does the reading. After examining an earlier draft of this chapter, the computer science professor recalled one effective collaborative assignment in her classes that has the added virtue of an external check of the effectiveness of the resulting written work.

> They [students] know that the compiler won't read their program properly unless it's written in the correct syntax. In some students' programs they have the right code but in the wrong order. Like if you write a paragraph where the sentences are out of order. They, in turn, because I have them work in pairs or as a member of a team and so they're reading each other's code because they have to, they divvy up the program and then they have to put it together so that it becomes one workable whole. If they have problems I suggest to them that they show it to somebody else; well, if they're working on a team they have to. And so that way helping each other debug their code is useful for them because it helps improve their own writing. Actually they told me that it did. They were surprised. They said they thought what they would just do is eliminate a lot of work and they wouldn't have to pay attention to that other part, that other module. But they found that they ended up working on the program together. They figured since they were working together as a team they felt more comfortable having a peer evaluate their work. Whereas if they were working as an individual on something, even if I told them they could have someone else check it, they wouldn't do it.
>
> (Computer Science, Draft Response Interview)

For our colleagues to engage in the kind of drafting and response implicit in Quintilian's advice may require a happy confluence of transformed perceptions. One is that they perceive we have abandoned traditional grammar instruction not out of faddishness or distaste but because of genuine conviction based on both scholarship and hard experience. A second is that they recognize the value of drafting and facilitative response for themselves as writers, and a third is that they understand that same value for their students. In other words, they have to conclude students will benefit professionally from adopting the same processes their professors follow when composing. How those transformations might come about we honestly do not know. One reason to hope is that, in our institution, professors generally believe their main professional purpose is to teach, and that the conditions under which they work encourage them to place that purpose above others.

> . . . I give them a lot of feedback. I mean, even in a class of 72, I would assign 10 of these in a semester, and I'll read 5 of them by each student, so they would get some opportunity to improve. If I was at a research university, I'd be answering a lot of these questions very differently because I think the space that you're in professionally really influences where you go in your attitude and actions.

> **At a research institution, how many of the courses that you teach do you think would be taught by grad assistants instead . . . ?**

> It could be a lot and if you had a class with 800, clearly you're not going to be able to read five papers from each student a semester. It would change things immensely.

> **Could there, do you think there are classes that large?**

> There are classes that large, probably that don't require any kind of writing. At the big schools they have classes bigger than 500—calculus, chemistry, physics. It's not an ideal way to learn.

(Physics, November 16, 1998)

One more alternative to traditional grammar instruction alluded to in our interviews is the development of students' control of style and standard usage through increased "awareness of their linguistic options" (Lindemann 84). During the past 30 to 35 years, composition teachers have often attempted to accomplish this task through various kinds of sentence combining and sentence construction activities. Studies investigating the effectiveness of student work with sentence combining have been largely positive, "with about 60 percent . . . reporting" results indicating "significant advances on measures of syntactic maturity" (Hillocks 142-43); that is, measures indicating students produced lengthier, grammatically controlled sentences featuring an increased variety of phrase and clause constructions. Moreover, some studies have recorded increases in syntactic maturity even though no grammar instruction accompanied the sentence combining work (Hillocks 142). Robert J. Connors concluded just a few years ago that he could "find no work that genuinely 'disproved' the gains created for students through sentence practice" (119).

Such results indicate that students could perform sentence-combining activities even if neither the teacher nor the students had a strong command of transformational or traditional grammars. Sentence combining exercises usually provide practice in melding shorter sentences closely related in subject matter into larger ones through the strategies of "embedding, deletion, subordination, and coordination" (Connors 103). They have been easily adapted to technical writing in a variety of subjects, although someone familiar with such exercises might be needed to assist teachers who are not (DeGeorge, Olson and Ray). Additionally, sentence-combining won't just teach "syntactic operations across phrasal and clausal boundaries" but can also help students become familiar with words and collocations specific to academic writing within particular fields (Myers 615).

Another technique, known as "sentence construction," has students "observe some phenomenon, generate a basic sentence, and add details about the phenomenon using various syntactic structures but particularly final free modifiers" (Hillocks 146). Again, this kind of sentence manipulation is adaptable to any subject matter, and can even work from sentences the students themselves have generated within their own writing. It is also important to note that sentence combining and sentence construction activities are reflective of particular qualities of English "plain style."

> In the plain style, clausal units are left intact and unaltered to produce asymmetry. The result is full clauses and verb phrases that carry a heavy predicative load. Predication, in turn, tends to presuppose and depend on sequencing, or arrangement in a set order, whether that of events or steps in a process. (cited in Tebeaux 170)

Our computer science professor began her career as an English teacher and is convinced of the value for programmers of a familiarity with the syntactical variation to be found in English sentences. Traditional grammar may not be up to the task of creating such familiarity, simply because it "focuses on taking language apart, not on putting it together" (Lindemann 79). Sentence manipulation that does provide experience in construction rather than dissection, especially when the subject matter is derived from the student's own work, seems much more promising.

> ... the training I had in grammar and linguistics was very valuable to me in learning computer programming because there are rules, there's grammar, there's syntax in programming and if you don't follow the rules the program won't run. . . . The Cobol programming language has been sometimes called "life on the hyphen" because if you leave out a hyphen, the whole thing, you know, there's a "fatal error." And . . . there are clauses and there are sentences and sentences end with periods.
>
> (Computer Science, August 12, 1999)

In the end, the question of how students should learn to manipulate and enhance written language has to be answered with evidence concerning how well students write. It is our suspicion, based on what we have seen of state and school district curricular guidelines, that by the time our students reach college most have received at least some traditional grammar instruction, and many have sat through weeks, months, and years of such instruction. Has it made a difference? While we have merely highlighted those few approaches to teaching style and increasing "correctness" to which our colleagues already seemed predisposed, the literature of our field is rich with alternatives to the "grammar" and "rules" approach—examining models of clarity and obfuscation, writing parody and more sober modes of imitation, experimenting with levels of diction, presenting information to distinct audiences, and so on (Lindemann 178-181). A recently emerging area of study known as "corpus linguistics," developed from the computer's ability to identify and analyze frequencies, patterns, and placements of words, phrases, and collocations, has generated still more pedagogical approaches, such as sentence templates (Myers 621-23). "I have long provided such templates to second-language students," Sharon Myers wrote recently, "but ask them to express meanings specific to their fields of study, rather than individually personal examples, . . . (since it is academic prose that they are in class to write)" (621).

Sharing these alternatives to what some call "the basics" may go a longer way toward dispelling the "language guardian" image than mere denial of the effectiveness of traditional grammar. We have to help our colleagues in other disciplines understand that abandoning what seems most familiar to them about English composition is not the same as abandoning concern for a student's writing style or ability to use standard written English. Many in composition studies have shunned the alternatives of sentence-combining, imitation, and cumulative sentences during the past two decades because our own discipline has been defining itself as "anti-formalism," "anti-behaviorism" and "anti-empiricism" (Connors 110-16). Unfortunately, imposing such forced choices on ourselves has also created an impression among colleagues in other disciplines that composition teachers do not care as much as they should about style and standard usage. We would rather, through cross-disciplinary dialogue, leave behind the "either-or" arguments that sometimes characterize intradisciplinary discussions and embrace a "both–and" approach that can yield a greater variety of potentially efficacious teaching approaches.

Perhaps an even greater challenge than helping others see alternatives to "grammar" instruction may lie in helping others see writing ability as ever evolving, situational, and integrally tied to knowledge acquisition. Composition courses will always be the place where writing *is* the main focus (David, Gordon and Pollard 525-27). But although composition teachers can help students understand the nature of written language and experiment with the variety of ways it can be produced, we cannot inoculate those same students against any future occurrences of linguistic awkwardness or confusion. Writing is an instrument for stretching—for developing empathy, for understanding knowledge, for questioning ways of knowing. Writing induces intellectual and emotional growth; neatness and presentability are not constants in the growth process. To see written language as a matter of "rules" or absorbed etiquette may be a matter of innocence or evasion. To absorb its slipperiness, its messiness, and its chameleon nature into our concepts of teaching can be both a shock and a liberation. We hope our future conversations can help us get that idea of liberation across to our colleagues; but gently . . . gently.

8

Further Steps in the Search for Eloquence

> Socrates . . . separated in his discussions the ability of thinking wisely and speaking gracefully, though they are naturally united. . . . Hence arose that divorce, as it were, of the tongue from the heart, a division certainly absurd, useless, and reprehensible, that one class of persons should teach us to think, and another to speak, rightly . . .
>
> Cicero (*De Oratore,* Book III, C. XVII)

One could say that, as compositionists, we began our conversations with colleagues from other disciplines because our own concentration within English studies is one of "discontent." As supposed teachers of written eloquence within the contemporary academy we teach *how*, not *what or why*. We must either relegate ourselves to sharing an expertise confined to techniques of process and style ("speaking gracefully"), or move outward into the disparate worlds of the "contented," where we must always live as sojourners, not as masters. With the Socrates of Plato's *Phaedrus*, we can embrace a rhetoric of truth-seeking, or "content," because one of appearances "is ridiculous and is not an art at all" (132). But as compositionists within the academy, we seem to have no clearly contented place; we do not "fit in" because we cannot accept the inadequacies of a superficial conception of written rhetoric. And so we have chosen to wander beyond our offices and buildings, to see if we can somehow connect content knowledge with eloquence, context with writing, and even body with mind. For face-to-face talk with our colleagues across disciplines serves as the nourishment that preserves our human embodiment, while resisting the tendency to separate matter and form, substance and appearance. It is in tune with our situated perspective that finds truth as much in hearing from every quarter as in making universal claims. Such an integrated humanity allows us to avoid the fate of Plato's grasshoppers, those lovers of discourse who sing without need for food or drink, but in a language unknown to all but themselves (*Phaedrus* 131). At a primarily undergraduate teaching institution like our own, the need for language intelligible to both faculty and students across disciplines seems as self-evident as any premise or axiom.

However, identifying our "discontent" is not the same as saying we have no knowledge of our own to bring to these conversations. Ours is the sometimes unsettling and paradoxical knowledge of linguistic power and limitation, elusiveness, and changeability, a knowledge suggesting that the seeming clarity and stability of our colleagues' disciplinary discourse may rest on a suspension of disbelief not unlike that which sustains narrative and dialogue. The discourses of disciplinary knowledge have engendered epistemic processes, social interactions, and material results that are marvels of our world. But not without a self-awareness that encourages questioning, disputation, and change; hence our concern that the role of those processes in the building of the knowledge base is so absent at the undergraduate level; and hence the concern articulated by our colleagues regarding not just the content but also the style and form of each field's knowledge. They know their students must write and write well. They understand the need to help students meld eloquence with knowledge, if the discipline they teach is to have applicability to their students' professional lives. They also wrestle with what compositionists have already learned about teaching the uses of language. We trust our conversations can convince our colleagues that the fruits we bear have both more allure and more danger than a regard for language as mere tool, or as a conduit for knowledge neither substantive nor integral to knowledge making (Lakoff and Johnson 11).

When we raise our awareness of how language and knowledge coexist, then we also raise our awareness of the difficulties inherent in expressing knowledge, beginning with teaching. Michael Leff pointed out another of Cicero's insights, that the orator (and in our day the expert, the professional, and the professor) "must adapt to the language of the crowd precisely because he [*sic*] has to adapt to its imperfect understanding" (20-21). Plato would add that the intellectual honesty necessary to a rhetoric committed to truth demands the speaker also acknowledge and adapt to the imperfect understanding of the self. In short, knowledge expressed is also knowledge rendered unstable by the variances in understanding of both speaker and audience. This observation, both melancholy and liberating, originated with the sophists, Plato's predecessors and nemeses in ancient Athens. And what we are perhaps introducing to our colleagues is what Leff called a "modern sophism," one that "implies an educational reform that would emphasize the study of concrete practice in place of generalized methodology" (28). It is in concrete practice where one encounters the messiness of knowledge making in every discipline, the counter currents present at every moment and the persuasion necessary for arrival at what is always provisional disciplinary consensus. In concrete practice one also encounters the messiness of consensus about using such knowledge in practical ways. Universality may be an ideal toward which we strive, but particularity is the circumstance under which we commonly live. Carefully considering how language and knowledge shape expression simply drives home that reality in an unavoidable manner.

Within our conversations, once the inseparability of knowledge and linguistic form is accepted, either tacitly or openly, then it isn't just the "experts" in written composition who begin to perceive themselves as hopelessly swamped, would-be polymaths and polylinguists. We are all in the same interdisciplinary boat, gunwales either above or below the water line, depending on one's level of optimism. For academics, this can be a disconcerting state of affairs, acknowledged less out of bravery than with grudging apprehension. Can we abandon our old sense of expertise as founded on a discrete, stable knowledge thoroughly grasped?

Cross-disciplinary conversation can intensify our apprehensions, but can also allay misery. It can even help us reconceive ourselves, so we are less a departmentalized faculty and more an integrated orchestra of educators, providing students with a cohesive curricular melody. As English composition professors, we have probably had the greater motivation to seek out our colleagues, since our place in the academy increases our sense of the need for interdisciplinary contact. Regardless of the longevity of first-year composition courses, Fleming rightfully wonders what the late 20th-century "revival of rhetoric" has actually wrought, beyond the creation of several dozen new PhD programs. Aside from first-year writing courses that pre-existed the movement, where can rhetoric's influence on the undergraduate curriculum be clearly discerned (173)? Can we realize Scholes' vision of the centrality of rhetoric in the undergraduate curriculum? The receptivity of our colleagues suggests that even before our interviews they were uneasy, like us, about their own teaching, about their students' learning, about the sometimes troubling lack of connection between disciplinary knowledge-making and professional practice at a variety of levels. As seen in Chapter 7, the lingering use by many writing instructors of a "current-traditional" approach (a rhetoric that emphasizes correctness and style almost exclusively) to issues of appropriate usage demonstrates an obvious rift between knowledge-making and practice within our own relatively new field of composition studies (Miles 756-57). Our colleagues were uneasy, too, about the necessity of writing in performing professional practice, and about the responsibility for ensuring that students can execute practitioner writing effectively on graduation. To echo our sport management and health services administration professors' questions: "Just where do you point the finger?" "Whom shall we blame?"

Both Scholes and Fleming argue for a much more thorough undergraduate education in rhetoric than what we have currently. The most challenging question that remains, however, is how to implement such an education, one that defies the neat compartmentalizations of knowledge that have enabled scholarship and determined curriculum for the past century or so. Our dialogic approach, we admit, is only a tentative step toward an answer, a toe in the water. It may be that the previous four chapters are a discovery of what could be considered a contemporary liberal arts quadrivium, an indication that no college curriculum should fail to teach the ability to analyze and adapt genres, as well as distinct forms of argumentation, the relationship between discourse and expertise, and appropriate usage and style. It is also hard to imagine English departments inculcating such a four-sided rhetorical curriculum on their own, especially when so much of it will be put in practice through a graduate's professional activity, with its particular audiences, genres, and methods. Can a first-year writing sequence and an introductory literature course, the 9-credit hours SRU's liberal studies program grants our department, suffice? We know this allotment is generous compared to that of many other institutions; it would require a breathtaking naivete to imagine our faculty granting us an even greater slice of the undergraduate curricular pie.

> *Liberal Studies has a long way to go, and probably will always have a long way to go in terms of trying to, not justify because I don't think you have to justify every single thing you do, but it obviously has to market itself. There's just such a disconnect right now between some of the things the kids want out of college and what the liberal studies are all about. And I think we're going to see this play out in our reorganization. The pressure of getting Harrisburg to cut back on the number of courses that a kid needs to get a 4-year degree here. They're throwing out the 120 [credit hours] number now. We're saying where is that going to come from. The professional prep faculty are saying, "Well we're going to have to cut hours from liberal studies."*
>
> (Health Education, Draft Response Interview)

No; the conclusion is inescapable that all faculty are teachers of language and discursive practice and that the rhetorical education roughly outlined here must, and currently does, rest mostly in their hands. We are not yet convinced by the arguments for completely abolishing the first-year-writing requirement that have been presented by Sharon Crowley and others. Not only do those courses provide freshmen "a small class with a supportive environment where they get a good deal of individual attention" (cited in Crowley 256), but they also provide a curriculum in which writing is the main subject, and where considerable time can be devoted to such important matters as invention, drafting, and revision (David, Gordon and Pollard). We do have "content," as indicated by our suggested quadrivium, by the recent investigation of composing processes, and by Thomas Miller's deceptively simple heuristic for civic discourse—"who gets to speak what to whom about what" (39).

Still, we have some hard questions to answer regarding the *extent* of our first-year writing requirement, and regarding whether all our efforts bring about the best results if concentrated in the first year of an undergraduate program. Moreover, we agree with Crowley that the requirement's effect of associating writing almost exclusively with English tends to obscure the impact of various disciplinary contexts on writing, as well as to perpetuate our roles "as literacy gatekeepers" (243).

> *You're the expert in English. So your interpretations of the implications for grammar, for teaching grammar or for language, I wouldn't question those.*
>
> (Nursing, Draft Response Interview)

Our initial conversations are, first of all, an admission that, like modern-day dentists with their use of ever-improving prophylaxes, one of our primary tasks is to put ourselves out of certain jobs. Both we and our colleagues have to admit that to recognize the inseparability of form and content is also to recognize that many issues involving usage and style, genre, argumentation, and discursive expertise cannot be addressed anywhere but within the instruction of a student's major program. Initiating our conversations puts us in agreement with Catherine Blair "that the English faculty's all-purpose writing expertise is in actuality limited to their own culture and that their practice of textual criticism does not make them experts qualified to teach writing in other contexts" (386). Those of us who are composition specialists have the task of helping our colleagues see *why* this is so, and see how our knowledge, experience, and practice can assist, as well as *not* assist, their instruction. It is also important to remember that often the whys and the hows of this task are not predetermined, but are discovered through the process of the conversations on which we now briefly reflect.

> *Obviously I do a lot of thinking about teaching composition in nursing because they're going to use it. I never thought about teaching composition in itself. I would have thought you were*

teaching composition. I didn't realize I was. Until you raised the questions. We even have outcomes that say we're teaching people to communicate in writing. And I just see it as we're teaching nurses to communicate and never step back.

(Nursing, Draft Response Interview)

Fleming, borrowing directly from Quintilian, mentions three evolving stages of self-consciousness through which a student of rhetoric must pass: nature, art, and practice (181). Within cross-disciplinary conversation the interlocutors can pass through similar states. The "nature" stage, characterized by Quintilian as student "ability" (Fleming 181), can be refigured by us to represent a recognition of the pervasiveness of persuasive, or rhetorical, elements in the production of disciplinary knowledge, elements that become evident when a practical, student-centered, and situated approach to teaching and learning is adopted. We approached our colleagues with an awareness that such elements have to be present in their discipline as well as our own, and with the inference that a full education in their discipline should include an awareness similar to our own, regardless of the name such awareness is given. (Because we are having conversations, "rhetoric" need not be the operative term. Given the connotations of deliberate manipulation that have adhered to that word across the centuries, it may be sometimes preferable to avoid it. For like the contemporary uses of the terms *spin* and *image* in broadcast media, the connotations of "rhetoric" rob persuasion of its substantive merits among some audiences.) This recognition of persuasive processes in every discipline is often momentary, and needs to be frequently regained, because professional training and habits of mind can lead us to ignore the contested nature of disciplinary truths, and to take notice of other textual elements first and foremost. The pressures of time continually lead our colleagues to emphasize the need to cover "content" as quickly and thoroughly as possible.

So the recognition of pervasive persuasiveness requires frequent conversational work but also necessary work, because so much depends on it. Without such work a corollary recognition of linguistic power, limitation, and malleability cannot occur, because the sense of imperfect speakers and audiences is lost. Aristotle's fixed hierarchy of knowers, with the pure thinkers at the top, hardly seems to apply to the professional lives of our colleagues and others in their fields. To be more specific, unless we recognize the persuasive elements in disciplinary discourse, we cannot make such pedagogically important connections as those noted in Chapter 7, linking what happens in the disciplinary writing of faculty members themselves, along with that of fellow practitioners, to the writing assigned to students.

Failing to recognize the persuasiveness of discourse shaped by imperfect speakers and audiences makes it difficult, if not impossible, to move on to Fleming's next stage of rhetorical self-consciousness, that of "art," defined as "a theoretical vocabulary providing the language user . . . with a way to isolate, analyze, and manage communication goals, resources, acts, and norms" (183). Without a sense of discourse shaped always by the "context," what could be an art is reduced to technique, to a "tool box" employed in crudely schematic ways that inevitably expose the novice trapped inside. Seasoned by our conversations, we cannot resist asking a troubling question concerning the possible sources of Fleming's "theoretical vocabulary." Does it come solely from classical, traditional, and contemporary rhetorical studies? Does it come solely from the composition community, even though the great bulk of "practice" to which such a vocabulary might be applied must occur in our students' major courses and later professional lives? We already wondered in Chapter 5 how the language of argumentation employed in a first-year composition course can be reinforced in the subsequently experienced major programs of our students. Isn't there more students should know, and know how to do, than acquire the current content knowledge of their discipline, because so many of them will enter their professions directly after graduation? Don't those disciplines have something to offer in developing students' vocabulary and self-consciousness about the role of language in the practitioner's work?

In responding to our chapter drafts, the health services administration professor suggested that at some point we should "transition the conversation or dialogue into practice techniques," as an adjunct to this book. This transition might take the form of an "addendum," a "workbook," or the second part of a "two-part series."

> *You have the dialogue and then have . . . like a workbook or something like that that has some suggestions for how people can take advantage of comments in the dialogue. In fact, you can even refer back to interviewees' responses and say, "Here's a way that you might construct that in terms of a writing exercise." I know in my comments I talk very specifically about some of the writing exercises I do because of the tie-in to the discipline, such as the scenario analysis or the strategic decision timeline. But in fact if someone hasn't seen that done before they might not have any idea of how to apply that to their discipline. So what you might do is engage your respondents to offer an example or offer tips that they found to be effective in improving students' writings.*
>
> (Health Services Administration, Draft Response Interview)

In this colleague's comments we can perceive the tension between "technique" and "art" that makes us both intrigued by and wary of the program he advocates. The initial forms suggested—addendum, workbook, or second part of a series—seem like entities existing quite separate from the dialogues. But as our colleague gets further into elaborating what is on his mind the whole process begins to sound more and more *like* our dialogues, only this time between practitioners *within* a discipline, rather than between various "disciplined" faculty and composition teachers. 'Tis a consummation devoutly to be wished, for it is the professional practitioners who can best devise writing opportunities that prepare their students for the composing practices found within their fields. Our conversations can serve as models for negotiations or discoveries of both theory and practice that, to return to Leff's language, are "concrete" rather than "generalized." Moreover, as universities seek to devise various course and program assessment strategies, the conversations about forms of rhetoric and writing practiced within disciplines that occur among English compositionists and their colleagues in other departments, and among colleagues within the various disciplines, could aid the discovery of strategies that accurately reflect student achievement and preparedness for professional practice.

"Sophistic rhetoric," argues Leff, "sacrifices theoretical coherence for the power of coherent practical action. It seeks to arm us in the effort to encompass and explain particular situations" (35). One important thing we learned from the draft response interviews that followed our composition of Chapters 4 through 7 is that we cannot address our own specific professional concerns, such as those regarding the nature of genre and argumentation, or style and usage, without creating at least a momentary sense of exclusion among some of our respondents from different disciplines. Discipline-specific terminology can be less of a barrier the more we continue to talk with and listen to each other.

Our main interviews also revealed, as we explain in Chapter 6, how our respondents are sometimes troubled by the way the most privileged academic discourse within their disciplines tends to deny access to their own students. This denied access engenders crises in disciplinary teaching by forcing questions about what should be taught, and in what manner, to be of the greatest assistance in enabling the future professional practice of our students, most of whom will not be academics. Again, only an awareness of the malleability of language and the situatedness of discourse can provide a remedy. We can share practice, both across and within disciplines, but we cannot abstract practice itself into a compendium of universal dicta and generalized procedures. When Fleming suggests that rhetorical art requires a healthy belief in the efficacy of human agency, we are in full agreement. But when he adds that it also requires "some way to reliably separate form and content" (183), then we begin to back away, fearful that art will devolve into a set of abstracted techniques, the transferability of which is problematic. To reduce art to technique is to separate mind and body, turning practice into mindless, rather than mindful, execution—the mere manual labor Aristotle associates with not artful thought but "acting like fire burns." With reference to rhetoric, it is to imply that the *same* thing can be said in different ways, rather than to acknowledge how meaning inhabits every change not only of word but also of gesture, and with each ear that hears and eye that sees. Moreover, it changes not because our knowledge is so unreliable, but because contexts are so rich and there are so many points of view from which more can be learned. We prefer to think students must engage in the practice of communicative arts appropriate to their discipline throughout their undergraduate education, rather than relegating writing *as an end* to English faculty, when it functions *as a means* for others. Such engagement is possible if we and our colleagues continue to both speak up and listen to each other.

But if not dicta and procedures, then what do our interviews suggest colleagues in different disciplines can gain from contact and conversation with compositionists and each other, and even perhaps from reading some professional writing about rhetoric? (Aside from the possibly different view of language and discourse we have already discussed.) Regarding classroom genres, compositionists draw on years of experience developing writing assignments, like journals but certainly not limited to journals, as well as responding to and evaluating writing at various stages of development. Only professors and practitioners within particular fields can have a necessary awareness of genres appropriate to learning and practice in those fields. But as compositionists we can certainly help in the creation of the discursive circumstances that will heighten the value of student writing activities, especially if we, in turn, are willing to increase contact with professionals and organizations outside our discipline, and to incorporate the knowledge gained from such contacts into our own discussions with students (Segal et al. 84-85). Administrators must also become aware of the implications of incorporating writing thoroughly into each major, if class sizes and teaching loads are to make such a commitment possible. The incentive for doing so is certainly real.

Oral and written communication is consistently at the top of lists of important qualifications employers say they are seeking when hiring. In August 2000, *Time* magazine named Clemson University one of its "colleges of the year," after specifically choosing writing as its criterion for judging colleges. Clemson's leadership in technical communication seems due, at least in part, to Art Young's joint appointment in the Department of English and the School of Engineering. The $1 million gift that funded Young's appointment and the $1.5 million gift that established Clemson's Center for Professional Communication, along with the honors the university has received, certainly indicate the importance of writing for not only educators, but also the public at large. Young's conception of the activity on his campus as a whole seems akin to the one we are advocating: "WAC [Writing Across the Curriculum] and CAC [Communicating Across the Curriculum] got the conversation going about teaching that wasn't happening 13 years ago. More people on campuses are talking about teaching and the value of teaching. . . . In some ways, it is similar to the Middle Ages' community of scholars' talking, reading and writing about issues" (Denny).

We hope that the fullness of the excerpts from our conversations, and the arrangement of the book itself as a colloquy, reinforce the value of such conversation while going beyond the consideration of writing as a tool alone, or the implication that English doesn't itself have much to learn from practitioners in other disciplines. This point is well made by one of the students interviewed by *Time* at Clemson, acknowledging the inseparability of form and content in the real contexts of her professional architectural practice: "They really try to get you out there in the real world where we learn to describe our design verbally, because if we can't do so, we can't sell it" (Denny).

In asking our respondents to read drafts of our chapters we were pleasantly surprised by their tolerance for the variety of distinctions we made in Chapter 7 concerning grammars, usages, and styles. We may also assist them in articulating already tacit understandings of alternative strategies for building student command of usage and style, alternatives to the strategies they may vaguely or vividly recall from their own schooling. Moreover, we can continue to reinforce a sense of writing ability as continuously evolving, and as tied to knowledge acquisition, rather than as some distinct "skill" or tool students either possess or lack by the time they enroll in upper division major program courses. For our part, as compositionists we have been reminded of the rhetorical importance of careful proofreading as a concluding step in the writing process—the message it sends about credibility in every field. The emphasis on invention and argument that has occurred in our own discipline, important as that is, may sometimes lead to less than full attention to the proof-reading step, or to a treatment of that task as a matter of process but not rhetoric. The abandonment of traditional grammar instruction, and a necessary tolerance for some surface error as students learn more sophisticated modes of expression, or overcome differences in writing experience or background, are moves that seem unavoidable to us. But these decisions can be misinterpreted by our students and colleagues; we must make sure they are not and that our colleagues' legitimate *rhetorical* concerns regarding appropriate usage are also ours.

As for argumentation, it would seem we are more likely to share common ground with our colleagues across disciplines, and to contribute rhetorical insights, when the discussion turns to aesthetic, "ethical," and emotional appeals, rather than to issues of admissible evidence and acceptable inferential reasoning. We must recognize increasing specialization within fields and subfields, as well as current time and class size constraints on the teaching of contested and marginalized views. As we saw in Chapter 6, specialized discourses have divided those within as well as across disciplines, making the learning of various modes of logical argumentation, especially in the scholarly discourse of a field, problematic at the undergraduate level. Discourse aimed at audiences not clearly identifiable with particular disciplines and professions may remain the primary concern of composition courses, including those offered beyond a student's first year, with the caveat that little discourse is devoid of the truth claims made through processes of disciplinary inquiry. We see a role for our colleagues across disciplines in educating all our students regarding the strengths and limitations of various modes of inquiry, a role that can hardly be fulfilled in writing courses offered outside the contexts of their disciplines. Composition teachers may offer up language and method for recognizing effectively persuasive strategies in all manner of discourse, but only our colleagues, and by extension their students, can modify what we offer to fit particular modes of inquiry and practice.

In the rhetorical education of "citizens," we also believe that people are not separately "professionals" or "citizens," but often both at once. For the separation of ethical and moral considerations from "pure" questions of science, through the distinction between sciences and the technologies they engender, is not unlike the separation of worker from citizen or body from mind that recognition of the situatedness of all practice puts into doubt. Despite the currency of notions like "information worker" and "global economy," professional people are not just knowledge-givers, receivers, and users, but also persuaders and those subject to persuasion. The idea that knowledge is totally clear, neutral, and neatly complete, merely to be transferred, is itself a powerful rhetorical move because of the naturalness and even necessity of seeing clearly in our daily lives. Yet a closer look also teaches us the selectiveness of our perceptions and how often we substitute what we think we know for what we might actually see (Fendrich B11).

Those of us in composition studies can always call attention to the "naturalness" of imperfect speakers and audiences, working on each other through a perpetual dance of persuasion akin to the metaphorical turns we have taken throughout this book. But only our colleagues beyond our expertise can identify the steps most often found in their particular disciplines, what each highlights and hides, and how their combination may make a claim more or less stable. From these myriad identifications evolves the "art" of disciplinary discourse, and Fleming's final level of discursive self-consciousness, a practice based on recognition and agency

(181). Such a practice would ideally recognize disciplinary discourses as not just the single currently accepted voices of truth within the field, but also parts of a whole cross current of conversation. Working identifiable levels of rhetorical self-consciousness into our students' major programs, while shaping a liberal or general studies program that is aware of the spectrum of rhetorical practices and traditions, seems the most feasible way to provide our graduates with a full education in writing effectively and reading critically. But how can such a scheme be implemented unless we have composition faculty and faculty within what Fleming calls the "vocationally oriented curricula" (185) communicating with each other in a substantive and ongoing manner? In Chapter 3, we explored the importance of both speaking and listening, and of a broader, situated definition of truth based on hearing from every point of view, rather than proving others wrong.

In several chapters, but particularly in Chapter 6, we agonized over the value of our current College Writing II, given the impossibility of anticipating the genres, the contexts, the audiences (Schwegler 29), and the modes of argumentation a heterogeneous set of first-year students may encounter as they become more deeply immersed in their major areas of study. Following the conversations that have been the subject of this book, we are inclined to think such a course may not belong in a student's first year, or even function as a liberal studies program requirement. It may better function as a required course within each student's major that explores the concerns we have just enumerated. There may need to be a transition period during which the course remains the province of composition teachers in consultation with a discipline's faculty, and vice versa. But the ultimate goal would be to have a course on the conventions, demands, and limitations of a discipline's discourse firmly located within the department that teaches that discipline.

Such a transfer in responsibility would not necessarily mean a reduction in work for English faculty, or a shrinking of their department's size. Major and minor programs in writing (already in place at SRU) could offer upper division courses that "investigate recurring textual and discursive practices" in "activity fields" such as editing and publishing, legal writing, media and political writing, and writing for community organizations (Schwegler 30). Students in other programs might even substitute this course as a degree requirement until such time as their own major's course in disciplinary discourse practices is firmly in place. In addition to one required first-year composition course, the English department could also offer electives at the same level, such as one focusing on civic discourse. Heavy enrollment in such a course wouldn't be surprising, as there may be plenty of students attracted by the ideas and activities experienced in the remaining required course, or simply interested in producing increasingly effective writing about public controversies.

Within our own institution, we might characterize our interviews as a beginning, as one important step toward the kind of innovation described above. What should we do next in terms of our own "professional development" and that of our colleagues? Do we resurrect the WAC reading groups we once had and hope for a sustaining transfiguration? (See Chapter 2.) "I wonder if we should start those reading groups up again," said our physics professor during his draft response interview. "I don't think that I even have time to organize one but I would just like to be part of one because it's healthy to, even if it's just once a month." Or does writing within or about disciplines require something different than what we had before, even though our faith in "talk" has clearly grown during the ensuing years? Were the books that were the focus of those groups something of a distraction, a detour that kept all of us from discussing what really concerned us about teaching and writing and our students' futures? Did they place writing faculty in the uncomfortable position of supposedly possessing expert knowledge about specific disciplinary discourse outside their field, while denying what we had to learn? Do we hone in on our individual classrooms, or think more broadly about instructional and curricular innovations? Surely we must do both. We know that we have learned much from our conversations and that they must continue, and that more ways must be found to expand participation among the faculty within and beyond English.

> *If you want to be able to incorporate writing effectively into your course work, you really have to think about it. It's not just happenstance. You have to make a commitment to do it because it takes—I can't count the hours—but it takes thought, and so you have to budget that into whatever your workload is; it has to be a priority. And institutions can help make that a priority through organization.*
>
> (Physics, Draft Response Interview)

At undergraduate institutions where teaching loads are high, the gift of time may be one of the most important ingredients but the necessity is clear. We have argued that the academic world can reflect on and anticipate the nonacademic world that our students already occupy in many guises. Adaptations of classroom writing, and innovative writing assignments that engage students in simulated and real world environments, could prepare undergraduate students for professional contexts. Acknowledging the situatedness of practice means recognizing our own institutional situatedness as well. Signature programs and university resources, obstacles to implementation, opportunities for collaboration among colleagues and with the community outside the university, all these elements vary, as do institutional cultures. Just how participation is expanded at our own university and others like it is best determined locally. But we believe a good starting point is the one we have described here. Conversations among trusted and committed colleagues at one's own institution, undertaken in a spirit of reciprocal speaking and listening, with recognition and respect for the expertise of each discipline regarding its own writing methods and practices, seems the best guarantee for success in the search for disciplinary and interdisciplinary eloquence. We do believe the method described here can be successfully adapted across contexts, and that the resulting insights can be made relevant in other institutions' cross-disciplinary conversations on the role of writing in undergraduate education.

Appendix
Schedule of First Interview Questions

The Role of Undergraduate Textual Awareness in Disciplinary Instruction:
Searching for a Cross-Disciplinary Conversational Model

Dr. Neil Cosgrove
Dr. Nancy Barta-Smith

1) How would you characterize your discipline?
2) Can you briefly describe some of the ways your discipline is practiced in academic and nonacademic settings?
3) Do you make distinctions between academic and nonacademic practitioners in your discipline? How would you describe those distinctions?
4) Do you regard the students who complete your undergraduate program as practitioners in your discipline?
5) How do your courses prepare a student to become a practitioner in your discipline? What other purposes do your courses serve?
6) How do you expect your students to *apply* what they've learned in your courses once they've left them? What forms do you think those applications will take?
7) What specific professional materials do you read as an academic in your discipline? What professional materials would a nonacademic practitioner of your discipline read?
8) What do you find persuasive when reading professional writing within your discipline? Do you think students find these elements equally persuasive? If not, why not?
9) What are the rules of evidence and modes of proof which are commonly employed in your discipline? Do students in your program discuss these rules and modes?

Appendix
Schedule of Second Interview Questions

The Role of Undergraduate Textual Awareness in Disciplinary Instruction: Searching for a Cross-Disciplinary Conversational Model

Dr. Neil Cosgrove
Dr. Nancy Barta-Smith

1) Could you describe how your discipline interacts with other disciplines?
2) What was the role "liberal" or "general" studies courses played in your intellectual development? Could you characterize what was different about the courses in your major program, when compared with courses you took as electives, or as part of a general education requirement?
3) What role do you think "liberal" or "general" studies courses play in the intellectual development of students in your major program?
4) Could you list the different pedagogies you use when teaching a course to your majors, and how frequently you use those pedagogies?
5) In general, what is the relationship between reading and writing in the courses you teach? What are examples of the major genres of writing in your field? Does reading any of these genres inform/affect how students write? What are examples of the major genres of writing students produce in courses in your field? Does writing in these genres affect how students read?
6) How important is researcher credibility to the persuasiveness of arguments made within your field? Does communication within your discipline contain elements other than reasoning and professional credibility that can move a researcher or practitioner to accept a claim?

Appendix

Transcript Analysis Sheet

Interviewer_____   Interviewee_____

Date of Interview_____

Correlation of Passages to Projected Subject Matter

(Give page and line numbers in the appropriate block. A passage may be cited in more than one block.)

Subject Area	Passages						
A. Chapters							
1. Grammar (Style, Correctness)							
2. Rhetoric (Issues Regarding ethos, audience, etc.)							
3. Logic (Critical Thinking, Disciplinary Argument)							
4. Expert Knowledge (Career Paths, Why vs. How)							
5. Conversing about Language (Meaning & Perception)							

Appendix C

Subject Area	Passages											
B. Modes of Conversation												
1. Difficulties												
a. Assume Knowledge												
b. Semantic Dissonance												
c. Negative Responses												
d. One-way Commun.												
e. Contradictions												
2. Successes												
a. Repeating to Confirm												
b. Agreement												
c. Recall Earlier Discuss.												
d. Free Exchange												
e. Coining Common Lang.												
C. Related Issues												
1. Student Meta-Awareness												
2. Disc. Knowledge Creation												

Trasnscript Analysis Sheet 235

Subject Area	Passages											
3. Role of Liberal Studies												
a. Prof's. Discipline												
b. Other Disciplines												
4. Genres												
a. Classroom												
b. Professional												
c. Transitional												
5. Student Growth												
a. Commun. Abilities												
b. Cognitive Abilities												
c. Professional Skills												
6. Possible Mutual Assist.												
7. Writing as Operation												
8. Others												
a. Connecting to other Disc.												
b. Teaching Methods												

Appendix
Technical and Scientific Writing

ASSIGNMENT 4

Students will produce two papers related to a professional, technical, or academic field of their choice. Each paper should be around three to four typewritten, double-spaced pages in length.

1. The first paper will introduce a basic process or concept to a reader who is not familiar with the field.
2. The second paper will discuss communication practices within a particular field—their purposes, processes, conventions, and forms or genres. The student may review and categorize several kinds of writing within an academic or professional field, analyze one piece of representative writing in the field, or interview a professional as to the role of writing in the acquisition or application of knowledge in the field.

Appendix E

College Writing II

EVALUATING THE FIRST POSITION PAPER

This paper provides your first opportunity to clearly articulate conclusions regarding a public issue or question that engages you. You should try to base those conclusions on evidence derived from reading and personal experience, evidence that leads readers, through some traceable logic, to the position you have reached. As you write, acknowledge your debt to reading that has provided you with evidence and ideas. In this paper, simple attribution will do (According to . . . So-and-so says . . .). Place a works cited page at the end of your paper, indicating any source you used to develop your content. Follow MLA style in listing your sources, as illustrated within your text.

There are a few significant differences between this paper and the *Second Position Paper* you will submit in the course. I expect you will be more consciously persuasive in the later paper. The documentation of your source material will need to be more precise, through the use of in-text parenthetical citations as well as a works cited page. I expect (rather than just hope) you will feel more confident and controlled while writing that later paper, after your experience reading numerous arguments, taking part in class discussions, doing team-shared writing and successfully completing the first position paper.

Characteristics of an "A" Paper:

* Your position is clearly stated and prominently placed.
* Your evidence is substantial, effectively integrated into your reasoning and relevant to both the issue and your conclusions.
* Your reasoning is carefully explicated, easy-to-follow and convincing.

- Your paragraphs are clearly linked, your sentences are fluent, and your words are apt.
- Any deviations from standard written English are either intentional and appropriate, or so few in number as to not distract the reader.
- Your source material is clearly attributed and the entries in your works cited page are complete, while closely following the MLA form for each kind of source.

Characteristics of a "B" Paper:

- Your position is clearly stated but the reader may have to search for it, or it is occasionally obscured.
- Your evidence is *adequate* and relevant, but may not always fit your conclusions.
- Your reasoning is traceable, but could use more thorough explication.
- Your paragraphs, sentences, and word choices are functional and workmanlike. But they may not pull the reader forcefully towards the desired conclusions.
- All deviations from standard usage are not equal. In a "B" paper, they may be occasionally distracting.
- Your source material is clearly attributed but your works cited entries may deviate from the appropriate MLA form.

Characteristics of a "C" Paper:

- Your position is there, but must be inferred by the reader.
- Your evidence is relevant to both the issue and your position, but you could have used more of it.
- Your reasoning may be flawed, easily refutable or hard to follow.
- Paragraphs and sentences seem untended—in clear need of further revision. Word choices are stale and/or inexact.
- Deviations from standard usage are more frequent and may occasionally create confusion in a reader.
- Material from sources is not attributed; works cited entries do not follow appropriate form and are missing required information.

Characteristics of a "D" Paper:

- You are still groping your way through the issue, and have reached no discernible conclusions.
- Your evidence is thin and often irrelevant—you needed to do more reading and/or reflection.

* Your reasoning *is* flawed, hard-to-follow and occasionally obscure.
* Meaning occasionally breaks down because of muddy, confusing sentences and word choices. Reader confusion is more than occasional because the writer is still teasing sense from the material. Frequent deviations from standard usage are another result of the writer's groping.
* The works cited page may be missing, or the final characteristic of a "C" paper is present.

This information is meant to assist and guide you in producing the best possible writing. Most "C" and "D" papers result from writers failing to devote the time needed for completing the task, and therefore submitting what is still a rough draft. Obviously, some papers will possess characteristics found at two or three different grading levels. That's where the professor's judgment comes into play. Grading is *always* a matter of subjective judgments. If you ever question mine, don't keep it to yourself, allowing your resentments to fester. Talk your disagreements over with me, outside of class and when we have time to adequately reconsider your writing together.

Appendix F

College Writing II

SECOND POSITION PAPER CHECKLIST

If the final draft of your second position paper has all of the qualities listed below, it will receive an "A." The degree to which a paper is deficient regarding these qualities will determine if a lower grade must be given, as well as what that lower grade will be—a "B," "C" or "D." As you revise your work it is suggested that you refer back to this checklist frequently. Bring it with you when you share a draft with team members, or with a writing center tutor.

_____ The writer's position regarding the issue is clearly stated.

_____ The reasoning that has led the writer to her/his position is carefully explained.

_____ This reasoning is supported by ample evidence that is clearly related to both the reasons and the conclusion.

_____ The position statement, reasons and evidence have been organized within the paper in a way that allows the reader to easily follow the structure of the argument.

_____ Evidence and/or reasoning derived from a particular source is clearly attributed to that source, using parenthetical citations following MLA style.

_____ The paper is accompanied by a works cited page which faithfully follows MLA style.

_____ The paper has been carefully edited to eliminate or avoid distracting deviations from standard usage, punctuation and spelling.

References

Aristotle. "Metaphysics." In *The Works of Aristotle, Volume I.* Translated by W.D. Ross. Chicago: Encyclopedia Brittanica, 1952. 499-626.
———. "On Generation and Corruption." In *The Works of Aristotle, Volume I.* Translated by H.H. Joachim. Chicago: Encyclopedia Brittanica, 1952. 409-41.
———. "Rhetoric." In *The Works of Aristotle, Volume II.* Translated by W. Rhys Roberts. Chicago: Encyclopedia Britannica, 1952. 585-675.
Bakhtin, M.M. *The Dialogic Imagination: Four Essays.* Edited by Michael Holquist. Translated by Caryl Emerson and Michael Holquist. Austin: University of Texas Press, 1981.
———. *Speech Genres and Other Late Essays.* Edited by Caryl Emerson and Michael Holquist. Translated by Vern W. McGee. Austin: University of Texas Press, 1986.
Baldwin, James. *Thought and Things: Functional Logic or a Genetic Theory of Knowledge.* Vol. 1. New York: Macmillan, 1906.
Barnet, Sylvan and Hugo Bedau. *Current Issues and Enduring Questions: A Guide to Critical Thinking and Argument, with Readings.* Fifth Edition. Boston/St. Martin's, 1999.
Bazerman, Charles and James Paradis, Eds. *Textual Dynamics of the Professions: Historical and Contemporary Studies of Writing in Professional Communities.* Madison: University of Wisconsin Press, 1991.
Berkenkotter, Carol and Thomas N. Huckin. *Genre Knowledge in Disciplinary Communication: Cognition/Culture/Power.* Hillsdale, NJ: Lawrence Erlbaum, 1995.
Berlin, James. *Rhetorics, Poetics, and Cultures: Refiguring College English Studies.* Urbana, IL: National Council of Teachers of English, 1996.
Blair, Catherine Pastore. "Opinion: Only One of the Voices: Dialogic Writing Across the Curriculum." *College English* 50 (1988): 383-89.
Broughton, John M. and D. John Freeman-Moir. *The Cognitive Developmental Psychology of James Mark Baldwin: Current Theory and Research in Genetic Epistemology.* Norwood, NJ: Ablex, 1982.
Carter, Michael. "The Idea of Expertise: An Exploration of Cognitive and Social Dimensions of Writing." *College Composition and Communication* 41 (1990): 265-86.
Cicero. "De Oratore." In *Cicero on Oratory and Orators.* Translated or edited by J.S. Watson. Carbondale: Southern Illinois University Press, 1970. 5-61.
Coe, Richard M. and Aviva Freedman. "Genre Theory: Australian and North American Approaches." In *Theorizing Composition: A Critical Sourcebook of Theory and Scholarship in Contemporary Composition Studies.* Edited by Mary Lynch Kennedy. Westport, CT: Greenwood Press, 1998. 136-47.
Connors, Robert J. "The Erasure of the Sentence." *College Composition and Communication* 52 (2000): 96-128.

Corbett, Edward P.J. and Robert J. Connors. *Classical Rhetoric for the Modern Student.* Fourth Edition. New York: Oxford University Press, 1999.

Crosby, Christina. "Writer's Block, Merit, and the Market: Working in the University of Excellence." *College English* 65 (2003): 626-45

Crosswhite, James. *The Rhetoric of Reason: Writing and the Attractions of Argument.* Madison: University of Wisconsin Press, 1996.

Crowley, Sharon. *Composition in the University: Historical and Polemical Essays.* Pittsburgh, PA: University of Pittsburgh Press, 1998.

Crusius, Timothy W. and Carolyn E. Channell. *The Aims of Argument: A Rhetoric and Reader.* Third Edition. Mountain View, CA: Mayfield Publishing, 2000.

David, Denise, Barbara Gordon, and Rita Pollard. "Seeking Common Ground: Guiding Assumptions for Writing Courses." *College Composition and Communication* 46 (1995): 522-32.

deCerteau, Michel. *The Practice of Everyday Life.* Translated by Steven F. Rendall. Berkeley: University of California Press, 1984.

DeGeorge, James, Gary A. Olson and Richard Ray. *Style and Readability in Technical Writing: A Sentence-Combining Approach.* New York: Random House, 1984.

Denny, Robin. "Clemson University Named *Time* Magazine's Public College of the Year: Clemson Featured in Magazine's 2001 Edition of The Best College for You." *Clemson University.* 17 August, 2000. 13 January, 2001. <http://clemsontigersfansonly.com/genrel/082200aaa.html>

Devitt, Amy J. "Integrating Rhetorical and Literary Theories of Genre." *College English* 62 (2000): 696-718.

Dias, Patrick, Aviva Freedman, Peter Medway, and Anthony Pare. *Worlds Apart: Acting and Writing in Academic and Workplace Contexts.* Mahwah, NJ: Lawrence Erlbaum, 1999.

Djerassi, Carl. "Useful Work." In *Profession 1999.* Edited by Phyllis Franklin. New York: Modern Language Association, 1999. 36-48.

Edwards, Derek. *Discourse and Cognition.* London: Sage, 1997.

Fendrich, Laurie. "The Importance of Perceptual Drawing in the Age of the Keyboard." *The Chronicle of Higher Education.* 17 November, 2000. B-11.

Fish, Stanley. "Being Interdisciplinary Is So Very Hard to Do." In *There's No Such Thing As Free Speech And It's a Good Thing, Too.* New York: Oxford University Press, 1994. 231-42.

Fleming, David. "Rhetoric as a Course of Study." *College English* 61 (1998): 169-91.

Freadman, Anne. "Anyone for Tennis?" In *The Place of Genre in Learning: Current Debates.* Edited by Ian Reid. Geelong, Australia: Deakin University, Centre for Studies in Literary Education, 1987. 91-124.

Freedman, Aviva. "'Do As I Say': The Relationship between Teaching and Learning New Genres." In *Genre and the New Rhetoric.* Edited by Aviva Freedman and Peter Medway. London: Taylor and Francis, 1994. 191-210.

Fulkerson, Richard. "Technical Logic, Comp-Logic, and the Teaching of Writing." *College Composition and Communication* 39 (1988): 436-52.

Fuller, Steve. *Philosophy, Rhetoric, and the End of Knowledge: The Coming of Science and Technology Studies.* Madison: University of Wisconsin Press, 1993.

Gallagher, Shaun. "Body Schema and Intentionality." In *The Body and the Self.* Edited by Jose Bermudez, Naomi Eilan, and Anthony Marcel. Cambridge: MIT/Bradford Press, 1995. 225-44.

Geisler, Cheryl. *Academic Literacy and the Nature of Expertise: Reading, Writing and Knowing in Academic Philosophy.* Hillsdale, NJ: Lawrence Erlbaum, 1994.

Geisler, Cheryl, Edwin H. Rogers, and Cynthia R. Haller. "Disciplining Discourse: Discourse Practice in the Affiliated Professions of Software Engineering Design." *Written Communication* 15 (1998): 3-24.

Gill, Judy. "Another Look at WAC and the Writing Center." *Writing Center Journal* 16 (1996): 164-78.

Halliday, M. A. K. and J.R. Martin. *Writing Science: Literacy and Discursive Power.* Pittsburgh, PA: University of Pittsburgh Press, 1993.

Hartwell, Patrick. "Grammar, Grammars, and the Teaching of Grammar." *College English* 47 (1985): 105-27. Rpt. in *Rhetoric and Composition: A Sourcebook for Teachers and Writers.* Third Edition. Edited by Richard L. Graves. Portsmouth, NH: Boynton/Cook, 1990. 163-85.

Herreid, Clyde F. "Mom Always Liked You Best: Examining the Hypothesis of Parental Favoritism." Clyde Herreid, Nancy Schiller and Scott Hollander. The National Center for Case Study Teaching in Science. 8 April 2002. 13 June 2002. <http://ublib.buffalo.edu/libraries/projects/ cases/coots/coots_prologue. html>

Herreid, Clyde F. Personal Interview. 11 June, 2001.

Hillocks, Jr., George. *Research on Written Composition: New Directions for Teaching.* Urbana, IL: ERIC Clearinghouse on Reading and Communication, 1986.

Hjortshoj, Keith. "The Marginality of the Left-Hand Castes (A Parable for Writing Teachers)." *College Composition and Communication* 46 (1995): 491-505.

Horner, Bruce. "Traditions and Professionalization: Reconceiving Work in Composition." *College Composition and Communication* 51 (2000): 366-98.

Institutional Research. *Academic Information and Data: 2000-01.* Slippery Rock, PA: Slippery Rock University, 2000.

———. *Selected Demographic Characteristics of Students and Faculty: 2000-01.* Slippery Rock, PA: Slippery Rock University, 2000.

Journet, Debra. "Boundary Rhetoric and Disciplinary Genres: Redrawing the Maps in Interdisciplinary Writing." In *Genre and Writing: Issues, Arguments, Alternatives.* Edited by Wendy Bishop and Hans Ostrum. Portsmouth, NH: Boynton/Cook, 1997. 56-66.

Keller, Evelyn Fox. *A Feeling for the Organism: The Life and Work of Barbara McClintock.* New York: W.H. Freeman, 1983.

Kuhn, Thomas S. *The Structure of Scientific Revolutions.* Second Edition, Enlarged. Chicago: University of Chicago Press, 1970.

Lakoff, George and Mark Johnson. *Metaphors We Live By.* Chicago: University of Chicago Press, 1980.

Langer, Jonas and Melanie Killen. *Piaget, Evolution, and Development.* Mahwah, NJ: Lawrence Erlbaum, 1998.

"Latest National Research Council Data on PhDs Granted in English and Foreign Languages." *MLA Newsletter* 31.2 (Summer, 1999): 1.

Laurence, David and Elizabeth Welles. "More Data from the October, 1998 Job Information List." *MLA Newsletter* 31.2 (Summer, 1999): 2.

Lave, Jean and Etienne Wenger. *Situated Learning: Legitimate Peripheral Participation.* Cambridge, UK: Cambridge University Press, 1991.

Leff, Michael C. "Modern Sophistic and the Unity of Rhetoric." In *The Rhetoric of the Human Sciences: Language and Argument in Scholarship and Public Affairs.* Edited by John S. Nelson, Allan Megill, and Donald N. McCloskey. Madison: University of Wisconsin Press, 1987. 19-37.

Lindemann, Erika. *A Rhetoric for Writing Teachers.* Third Edition. New York: Oxford University Press, 1995.

Longo, Bernadette. *Spurious Coin: A History of Science, Management, and Technical Writing.* Albany: State University of New York Press, 2000.

Mackinnon, Jamie. "Becoming a Rhetor: Developing Writing Ability in a Mature, Writing Intensive Organization." In *Writing in the Workplace: New Research Perspectives.* Edited by Rachel Spilka. Carbondale: Southern Illinois University Press, 1993. 41-55.

Malinowitz, Harriet. "A Feminist Critique of Writing in the Disciplines." In *Feminism and Composition Studies: In Other Words.* Edited by Susan C. Jarratt and Lynn Worsham. New York: Modern Language Association, 1998. 291-312.

Mathematics Professor. "On Metric Preserving Functions and Infinite Derivatives." *Acta Mathematica Universitae Comenianae* 67 (1998): 373-76.

McLeod, Susan and Elaine Maimon. "Clearing the Air: WAC Myths and Realities." *College English* 62 (2000): 573-83.

Mencken, H.L. *The American Language: An Inquiry into the Development of English in the United States.* New York: Knopf, 1963.

———. "Literature and the Schoolma'am." In *Prejudices: Fifth Series.* New York: Octagon, 1977. 196-202.

———. "The Schoolma'am's Goal." In *Prejudices: Fifth Series.* New York: Octagon, 1977. 141-46.

Merleau-Ponty, Maurice. *Merleau-Ponty: Notes De Cours Sur L'Origine De La Geometrie De Husserl.* Paris: Presses Universitaires De France, 1998.

———. *The Phenomenology of Perception.* Translated by Colin Smith. London: Routledge & Kegan Paul Ltd., 1989.

———. *The Visible and the Invisible.* Edited by Claude Lefort. Translated by Alphonso Lingis. Evanston, IL: Northwestern University Press, 1968.

Miles, Libby. "REVIEW: Disturbing Practices: Toward Institutional Change in Composition Scholarship and Pedagogy." *College English* 62 (2000): 756-66.

Miller, Carolyn R. "Genre as Social Action." In *Genre and the New Rhetoric.* Edited by Aviva Freedman and Peter Medway. London: Taylor and Francis, 1994. 23-42.

Miller, Susan. *Textual Carnivals: The Politics of Composition.* Carbondale: Southern Illinois University Press, 1991.

Miller, Thomas P. "Rhetoric Within and Without Composition: Reimagining the Civic." In *Coming of Age: The Advanced Writing Curriculum.* Edited by Linda K. Shamoon, Rebecca Moore Howard, Sandra Jamieson and Robert A. Schwegler. Portsmouth, NH: Heinemann, 2000. 32-41.

Myers, Sharon A. "ReMembering the Sentence." *College Composition and Communication* 54 (2003): 610-28.

National Center for Education Statistics. *Digest of Education Statistics: Participation in Education, Undergraduate Education, Chapter Three.* 2000. 8 August, 2001. <http://nces.ed.gov/pubs2001/digest/ch3.html>

Nelson, John S., Alan Megill, and Donald N. McCloskey. (Eds.) *The Rhetoric of the Human Sciences: Language and Argument in Scholarship and Public Affairs.* Madison: University of Wisconsin Press, 1987.

North, Stephen M. et al. *Refiguring the PhD in English Studies: Writing, Doctoral Education, and the Fusion-Based Curriculum.* Urbana, IL: National Council of Teachers of English, 2000.

Odell, Lee and Dixie Goswami, Eds. *Writing in Nonacademic Settings.* New York: Guilford Press, 1985.

Ohmann, Richard. *English in America: A Radical View of the Profession.* New York: Oxford University Press, 1976.

Oliver, Kelly. *Subjectivity without Subjects: From Abject Fathers to Desiring Mothers.* Lanham, MD: Rowman and Littlefield, 1998.

Pemberton, Michael. "Rethinking the WAC/Writing Center Connection." *Writing Center Journal* 15 (1995): 116-33.

Pinker, Steven. *The Language Instinct: How the Mind Creates Language.* New York: Harper-Collins, 1995.

Plato. "Phaedrus" and "Gorgias." In *The Dialogues of Plato.* Translated by Benjamin Jowett. Chicago: Encyclopedia Britannica, 1952. 115-41 and 252-94.

Prior, Paul A. *Writing/Disciplinarity: A Sociohistoric Account of Literate Activity in the Academy.* Mahwah, NJ: Lawrence Erlbaum, 1998.

Quintilian. *On the Teaching of Speaking and Writing: Translations from Book One, Two, and Ten of the Institutio Oratoria.* Edited by James J. Murphy. Translated by J.S. Watson. Carbondale: Southern Illinois University Press, 1987.

Raymond, James C. *English as a Discipline Or, Is There a Plot in this Play?* Tuscaloosa: University of Alabama Press, 1996.

Readings, Bill. *The University in Ruins.* Cambridge, MA: Harvard University Press, 1996.

Richardson, Darlene. *Consultant's Report on the Liberal Studies Program at Slippery Rock University.* Unpublished Report. 9 May, 1997.

Ronald, Kate. "REVIEW: How to Tell a True Teaching Story." *College English* 62 (1999): 255-64.

Rottenberg, Annette T. *Elements of Argument: A Text and Reader.* Sixth Edition. Boston: Bedford/St. Martin's, 2000.

Russell, David R. "Rethinking Genre in School and Society: An Activity Theory Analysis." *Written Communication* 14 (1997): 504-54.

———. *Writing in the Academic Disciplines, 1870-1990: A Curricular History.* Carbondale: Southern Illinois University Press, 1998.

Russon, Anne E., Robert W. Mitchell, Louis Lefebvre, and Eugene Abravanel. "The Comparative Evolution of Imitation." In *Piaget, Evolution, and Development.* Edited by Jonas Langer and Melanie Killen. Mahwah, NJ: Lawrence Erlbaum, 1998. 103-44.

Scholes, Robert. *The Rise and Fall of English: Reconstructing English as a Discipline.* New Haven, CT: Yale University Press, 1998.

Schroeder, Christopher. "Knowledge and Power, Logic and Rhetoric, and Other Reflections in the Toulminian Mirror: A Critical Consideration of Stephen Toulmin's Contributions to Composition." *Journal of Advanced Composition* 17 (1997): 95-107.

Schwegler, Robert A. "Curriculum Development in Composition." In *Coming of Age: The Advanced Writing Curriculum*. Edited by Linda K. Shamoon, Rebecca Moore Howard, Sandra Jamieson and Robert A. Schwegler. Portsmouth, NH: Heinemann, 2000. 25-31.

Segal, Judy, Anthony Pare, Doug Brent, and Douglas Vipond. "The Researcher as Missionary: Problems with Rhetoric and Reform in the Disciplines." *College Composition and Communication* 50 (1998): 71-90.

Shamoon, Linda K. and Deborah H. Burns. "A Critique of Pure Tutoring." *Writing Center Journal* 15 (1995): 134-51.

Slippery Rock University of Pennsylvania. *A Selected Topics Self-Study prepared for the Commission on Higher Education of the Middle States Association of Colleges And Schools, 2000-01*. Slippery Rock, PA.

Smith, Dorothy. *The Everyday World as Problematic: A Feminist Sociology*. Boston: Northeastern University Press, 1987.

Spilka, Rachel, Ed. *Writing in the Workplace: New Research Perspectives*. Carbondale: Southern Illinois University Press, 1993.

Sudman, Seymour and Norman N. Bradburn. *Asking Questions: A Practical Guide to Questionnaire Design*. San Francisco: Jossey-Bass, 1983.

Tebeaux, Elizabeth. *The Emergence of a Tradition: Technical Writing in the English Renaissance, 1475-1640*. Amityville, NY: Baywood, 1997.

Tinberg, Howard B. *Border Talk: Writing and Knowing in the Two-Year College*. Urbana, IL: National Council of Teachers of English, 1997.

Toulmin, Stephen E. *The Uses of Argument*. Cambridge, UK: Cambridge University Press, 1964.

Toulmin, Stephen, Richard Rieke, and Allan Janik. *An Introduction to Reasoning*. New York: Macmillan, 1979.

Wagner, David L. "The Seven Liberal Arts and Classical Scholarship." In *The Seven Liberal Arts in the Middle Ages*. Edited by David L. Wagner. Bloomington: Indiana University Press, 1983. 1-31.

Walvoord, Barbara E. "The Future of WAC." *College English* 58 (1996): 58-79.

Walvoord, Barbara E., Linda Lawrence Hunt, H. Fil Dowling Jr., and Joan D. McMahon. *In the Long Run: A Study of Faculty in Three Writing-Across-the-Curriculum Programs*. Urbana, IL: National Council of Teachers of English, 1997.

Weaver, Richard M. *Language is Sermonic: Richard M. Weaver on the Nature of Rhetoric*. Edited by Richard L. Johannesen, Rennard Strickland, and Ralph T. Eubanks. Baton Rouge: Louisiana State University Press, 1970.

Williams, Joseph M. and Gregory G. Colomb. "Chapter 5: The University of Chicago." In *Programs That Work: Models and Methods for Writing Across the Curriculum*. Edited by Toby Fulwiler and Art Young. Portsmouth, NH: Boynton/Cook, 1990.

Winterowd, W. Ross. *The English Department: A Personal and Institutional History*. Carbondale: Southern Illinois University Press, 1998.

Young, Art. "Writing Across and Against the Curriculum." *College Composition and Communication* 54 (2003): 472-85.

Author Index

A

Abravanel, Eugene, 94, *249*
Aristotle, 15, 28, 103, 117, 135, 140, 146, 162, 169, *245*

B

Bakhtin, M.M., 8, 31, 67, 97, *245*
Baldwin, James, 6, 94, *245*
Barnet, Sylvan, 127, *245*
Bazerman, Charles, 22, 76, *245*
Bedau, Hugo, 127, *245*
Berkenkotter, Carol, 2, 8, 67, *245*
Blair, Catherine Pastore, 125, 219, *245*
Bradburn, Norman N., 41, *250*
Brent, Doug, 2, 6, 11, 131, 223, *250*
Broughton, John M., 5, *245*
Burns, Deborah H., 95, 96, *250*

C

Carter, Michael, 8, 197, *245*
Channell, Carolyn E., 127, *246*
Cicero, 1, 215, *245*
Coe, Richard M., 2, *245*
Colomb, Gregory G., 201, *250*
Connors, Robert J., 27, 106, 182, 211, 212, 213, *250*
Corbett, Edward P.J., 27, 106, 182, *246*
Crosby, Christina, 179, *246*
Crosswhite, James, 11, 32, 107, 126, 128, 129, *246*
Crowley, Sharon, 19, 104, 184, 219, *246*
Crusius, Timothy W., 127, *246*

D

David, Denise, 214, 219, *246*
deCerteau, Michel, 177, *246*
DeGeorge, James, 212, *246*
Denny, Robin, 224, *246*
Devitt, Amy J., 66, 67, 98, *246*
Dias, Patrick, 2, 5, 6, 7, 78, 88, 104, *246*
Djerassi, Carl, 178, *246*
Dowling Jr., H. Fil, 11, *250*

E

Edwards, Derek, 11, 34, 38, 40, 52, 54, *246*

F

Fendrich, Laurie, 225, *246*
Fish, Stanley, 61, *246*
Fleming, David, 217, 220, 221, 222, 225, 226, *246*
Freadman, Anne, 97, 98, 101, *246*
Freedman, Aviva, 2, 5, 6, 7, 78, 88, 101, 102, 104, *245, 246*
Freeman-Moir, D. John, 5, *245*

Fulkerson, Richard, 107, 125, 126, 127, 128, 129, 130, 131, *246*
Fuller, Steve, 175-76, *246*

G

Gallagher, Shaun, 100, *247*
Geisler, Cheryl, 2, 86, 143, 161, *247*
Gill, Judy, 95, *247*
Gordon, Barbara, 214, 219, *246*
Goswami, Dixie, 76, *249*

H

Haller, Cynthia R., 2, *247*
Halliday, M.A.K., 22, *247*
Hartwell, Patrick, 184, 187, 204, 207, *247*
Herreid, Clyde F., 72, *247*
Hillocks, Jr., George, 62, 184, 211, 212, *247*
Hjortshoj, Keith, 193, *247*
Horner, Bruce, 187, *247*
Huckin, Thomas N., 2, 8, 67, *245*
Hunt, Linda Lawrence, 11, *250*

J

Janik, Allan, 115, 128, *250*
Johnson, Mark, 3, 36, 216, *247*
Journet, Debra, 10, *247*

K

Keller, Evelyn Fox, 33, *247*
Killen, Melanie, 5, *247*
Kuhn, Thomas S., 135, *247*

L

Lakoff, George, 3, 36, 216, *247*
Langer, Jonas, 5, *247*
Laurence, David, 4, *247*
Lave, Jean, 141, 170, *248*
Lefebvre, Louis, 94, *249*
Leff, Michael C., 32, 216, 217, 222, *248*
Lindemann, Erika, 184, 186, 187, 203, 211, 212, 213, *248*
Longo, Bernadette, 190, 193, *248*

M

Mackinnon, Jamie, 89, *248*
Maimon, Elaine, 22, *248*
Malinowitz, Harriet, 155, 176, *248*
Martin, J.R., 22, *247*

McCloskey, Donald N., 22, *249*
McLeod, Susan, 22, *248*
McMahon, Joan D., 11, *250*
Medway, Peter, 2, 5, 6, 7, 78, 88, 104, *246*
Megill, Alan, 22, *249*
Mencken, H.L., 182, 183, 202, *248*
Merleau-Ponty, Maurice, 6, 8, 63, 101, 102, 111, *248*
Miles, Libby, 183, 218, *248*
Miller, Carolyn R., 66, 93, *248*
Miller, Susan, 125, *248*
Miller, Thomas P., 219, *248*
Mitchell, Robert W., 94, *249*
Myers, Sharon A., 201, 212, 213, *248*

N

Nelson, John S., 22, *249*
North, Stephen M., 4, *249*

O

Odell, Lee, 76, *249*
Ohmann, Richard, 104, *249*
Oliver, Kelly, 36, *249*
Olson, Gary A., 212, *246*

P

Paradis, James, 22, 76, *245*
Pare, Anthony, 2, 5, 6, 7, 11, 78, 88, 104, 131, 223, *245*, *246*, *250*
Pemberton, Michael, 67, 95, *249*
Pinker, Steven, 182, 187, *249*
Plato, 31, 215, 216, *249*
Pollard, Rita, 214, 219, *246*
Prior, Paul A., 66, 187, 188, *249*

Q

Quintilian, 181, 187, 188, *249*

R

Ray, Richard, 212, *246*
Raymond, James C., 4, *249*
Readings, Bill, 135, 136, 179, 180, *249*
Richardson, Darlene, 163, *249*
Rieke, Richard, 115, 128, *250*
Rogers, Edwin H., 2, *247*
Ronald, Kate, 202, *249*
Rottenberg, Annette T., 127, *249*
Russell, David R., 2, 22, 67, 99, *249*
Russon, Anne E., 94, *249*

S

Scholes, Robert, 4, 7, 8, 91, 217, *249*
Schroeder, Christopher, 104, 107, 129, *249*
Schwegler, Robert A., 226, *250*
Segal, Judy, 2, 6, 11, 131, 223, *250*
Shamoon, Linda K., 95, 96, *250*
Smith, Dorothy, 34, *250*
Spilka, Rachel, 76, *250*
Sudman, Seymour, 41, *250*

T

Tebeaux, Elizabeth, 190, 212, *250*
Tinberg, Howard B., `24, 118, 208, *250*
Toulmin, Stephen E., 107, 115, 126, 128, 130, 132, *250*

V

Vipond, Douglas, 2, 6, 11, 131, 223, *250*

W

Wagner, David L., 27, *250*
Walvoord, Barbara E., 11, 22, *250*
Weaver, Richard M., 109, 111, 113, *250*
Welles, Elizabeth, 4, *247*
Wenger, Etienne, 141, 170, *248*,
Williams, Joseph M., 201, *250*
Winterowd, W. Ross, 4, *250*

Y

Young, Art, 178, 179, 224, *250*

Subject Index

A

Academic
  definition of, 40
Academic literacy, 143
Action research, 3, 10, 16
Activity system, 67, 98
Activity theory, 28
  actions and operations in, 6
  Russian, 5, 8, 67
Adaptation, 94, 98, 125, 169, 227
  as goal of imitation, 100
  evolving, 170
  of classroom experience to research, 48
  role of perceptual clues, 102
Adaptation, 16, 61, 83
Agora, 13, 32
American Educational Research Association, 112
American Mathematical Society, 200
Anthropology
  interpretive, 8
Appeals
  aesthetic, 108, 110
  functional, 115
  logical, 115
  pathetic, 108
  variety of. *See* Logic

Apprenticeship, 72, 95, 96, 177
  in classroom, 97, 101
  in physics, 48
  reading in, 97
Argument
  and credibility, 118
  and emotion, 106
  and multiple perspectives, 61
  and probabilities, 107
  anecdotal, 126
  context dependent nature of, 131
  contextual nature of, 107, 112
  deductive, 106
  in composition courses, 105
  inductive, 106
  modes of disciplinary, 23
  pejorative connotations of, 36
  relationship to power, 104
  teaching in the major, 226
  teaching of, 104
  Toulmin model, 105, 127
  types of disciplinary, 43
  universalizing, 124
  use of syllogism in, 125, 126, 128. *See* Logic
  variety of appeals, 27
Art
  definition of, 221

Subject Index

Article Review
    use of IMRAD in, 82
Assessment, 10, 25
    developing strategies for, 222
    sustaining interest in, 22
Assignments, 84, 96, 101, 176
    "filling in the gap" papers, 71
    case studies, 80
    collaborative, 96, 210
    journals, 87
    portfolios, 89
Athens, 32, 217
Attic style. *See* plain style
Audience, 225
    acceptance of arguments, 107
    non-expert, 152
    paragon, 107
    positing a universal, 107
    universal, 107, 111
Autobiography, 83

B

Basal readers, 54
Bloomsburg University, 22

C

Canon of methods
    in English courses, 178
Canon of methods, 7, 8
Case studies
    in law, 101
    teaching, 80
    use in composition, 80
Charting, 114, 197
    critical path, 198
    Problem oriented, 198
Children's Literature, 59
Cicero
    dilemma of, 1, 13, 62, 125
Clarion University, 22
Classrooms
    dynamic character of, 95
Cognition
    development of, 16
    five-stage continuum of, 95
    nature of, 5
    origin of cognitive schemata, 100
    situated, 8

Cognitive psychology, 5
Collaboration, 7
    across disciplines, 7
    among faculty, 35, 54
    role of conversation in. *See* Conversation
Communicating Across the Curriculum, 224
Communities of practice, 64
Compartmentalization
    Academic, 51
Composition
    classes, anti-democratic, 104
    conditions of employment, 4
    first-year requirement, 29, 219
    teaching positions in, 4
Composition and rhetoric
    approach to argument, 129
    methods in, 8, 15
Composition and Rhetoric, 26
    as liberal arts, 32
Computer Science
    fluidity of credentials in, 151
Conferences
    student participation in, 90
Conferencing, 207
Conventions
    of discourse communities, 22
Conversation, 12, 217
    and disciplinary jargon, 222
    and shared experience, 56
    as method, 12, 61, 218
    creating consensus through, 54
    drawbacks of consensus in, 54
    dynamic nature of, 34
    how to foster, 51
    humor in, 58
    interruptions in, 54
    need for continuous, ongoing, 227
    on pedagogy, 73
    recognition in, 32
    use of affirmative statements in, 55
    uses of repetition in, 55
Corpus linguistics, 213
Correctness
    and social mobility, 187
    as content, 181

attitude of writing teachers toward, 62
rhetorical effect of, 186, 224
Credibility
establishing. *See* ethos
Critical path charting, 198

D

Developmental psychology, 26
Dialectic, 27, 124
and causal inquiry, 136
and interpretation, 179
and negation, 188
as general art, 135
defined, 137
Dialogism, 28, 67
Disciplines
as activity systems, 67
Discourse
and expertise, 218
as art, 225
as rationalizing activity, 108, 135, 177
as second language acquistion, 201
civic, 219, 226
diversity of, 124, 178
kinds of professional, 42
public, 107, 126, 174, 175, 176
role in professionalization, 10
situatedness of, 6, 221, 222
transparency of, 9
Dissensus, 179, 180
Diversity
role of liberal studies in teaching, 168
Doctoral programs
and teacher training, 46
Dualism
mind/body, 3, 5, 6, 8

E

Editing software
and correctness, 205
Einstein's thought experiment, 57
Elementary Education
graduate degrees in, 150
methods in, 49
reading and language arts in, 49

Embodiment, 216
of disciplines, 32
phenomenology of, 100
English
as liberal art, 5
English Departments
divisions within, 4
English teachers
conservative attitude toward usage, 183
Ethnomethodology, 8
Ethos, 117
and correctness, 186, 224
and institutional affiliation, 119
and media, 137
and real world experience, 120
as responsibility of gatekeepers, 123
how to establish, 118
in research, 118
relationship to institutional status, 118
Evaluation
in the workplace, 89
Evidence
experience as, 144
in nursing, 44
rules of, 43, 104, 113, 131, 171, 230
Executive summary, 84, 192, 195, 196
Expertise
and correctness, 139
and liberal studies courses, 137
and recognition, 146
and warrants for argument, 131
and writing, 178
functional, non-specialist, 176, 180
hierarchy of, 136, 140
in practitioners, 139
in undergraduates, 28
limits of, 125
of English faculty, 125
role of writing in, 152
Expressive writing, 2, 22, 35

F

Fermat's Last Theorem, 42, 58
First-year-writing
need for, 219

Form and matter
    relationship between, 3, 217, 219, 223, 224
    separation of, 3, 216
Forms of evidence, 116

G

Game theory, 75
General education
    goals of, 177
    role in teaching argument, 163
General Education
    enrollments in, 163
General Studies
    curriculum, 29
Generic writing, 86
Genre, 64
    as dynamic and evolving, 67
    as typical practice, 66
    boundary, 10, 84
    classroom, 11, 28, 86
    classroom and practitioner, 69, 85, 223
    classroom, similarities to practitioner, 82
    complexity and situatedness of, 13
    defined as speech and writing, 67
    in Mathematics, 65
    meaning of, 31, 45, 64, 66
    practitioner, 28, 76
    principles of classification, 66
    published, 70, 73
    role in successful publication, 66
    role of, 8
    teaching of, 28, 67
    theory of, 28, 67
    transitional, 5
    usefulness of tables of, 70
    varieties in professional practice, 63
Genre knowledge
    importance of, 67
Global strategies
    in textual analysis, 8
Graduate degrees
    and credentialling, 149
Grammar, 13, 27, 29, 138, 188, 205, 208, 213, 219, 224
    and Latin, 187
    as substitute for writing, 209
    distinguished from usage, 188
    five meanings of, 203
    in classical trivium, 173
    instruction, research on, 184, 187
    rules of, 187
    software applications, 205, 207
    traditional, 181, 184, 186
    transformational, 211
    value of instruction in, 184

H

Health Services Administration, 35
Heuristics
    in nursing, 44
Humanistic concerns, 178
Hypocriticism
    and literary study, 4

I

Imitation
    and genre, 80
    behaviorist notions of, 100
    deferred, 36
    in apprenticeship, 49
    role in mentoring, 96
    true, 36
indexicality, 38
Inductive reasoning
    confusion with deduction, 126
Informatics
    in nursing, 84
Information literacy
    and evaluating web sites, 121
    and online databases, 123
Interdisciplinarity
    necessity of, 9
Interrupted case study method, 72
Interview questions, 40
    strategies for asking and answering, 52
Interviewees
    responses from, 29
Interviews
    follow up, 25, 47
    goals in conducting, 23
    interpretation of results, 30
    miscues in, 61

Subject Index

J
Journal writing, 87

L
Kairos, 134
Knowledge
 as contested, 132, 138, 220
 marginalized, 225

L
Lamination, 99
Language
 and representation, 189
Learning how
 definition of, 137
Liberal arts
 trivium, 27
Liberal tudies, 163
Literacy
 definition of, 51
 effect of reading on, 13
Literary models
 use in teaching composition, 2
Literary study, 4
Lock Haven University, 22
Logic
 formal, 107, 108, 115, 116, 124, 128
 formal and informal fallacies, 106, 126, 131
 formal, in analysis, 130
 formal, in composition textbooks, 125

M
Mathematics
 difference between pure and applied, 42
MBA model
 of graduate education, 150
Mentoring
 in teaching, 95
Metaphor, 3, 31, 33, 36, 185, 225
Meta-reflection
 in journals and logs, 86
Methods
 types of, transitional, 5
Mode of proof
 in Computer Science, 44
Modern Language Association, 4

Modern sophism, 217
Modes of Conversation
 successes and failures in, 26
Modes of proof, 104, 113, 116, 124, 131, 171, 230
Motivation
 importance of among conversants, 51

N
National Center for Case Study Teaching in Science, 72
National Council of Teachers of English, 112
National Endowment for the Humanities, 21
National Security Agency, 58
 employment of mathematicians by, 43
Nursing
 role of graduate education in, 150

O
Objectivity
 degrees of, 111
Ontogenesis, 8
Operations research, 151
 in mathematics, 93
Ordinary language, 11, 12
 humor in, 58
 philosophers of, 36

P
Pedagogy
 as relation between student and teacher, 180
 as scholarship, 46
 meaning of, 45
Pennsylvania WAC Association, 21
Perceptual logic, 114
Perspectives
 multiple, 33, 34
Persuasion
 as a matter of degree, 107
 as an art, 124, 134
Phenomenology, 6, 26, 30, 34
Physics
 kinds of research, 41
 laboratory practices in, 41

rigor of graduate degree, 151
scholarship of teaching, 46
Plain style, 190, 191, 192, 195, 196, 197, 201, 212
  and Renaissance thinkers, 190
  as standard, 189
  need for in establishing objectivity, 193
  transparency of, 9, 108
Play
  artful, 93
Poesis, 135
Poetry Across the Curriculum, 178
Political writing
  in elementary education, 75
Portfolios
  and preparation for workplace writing, 89
Power relations
  how to avoid, 10
Practitioner
  definition of, 40
Professional organizations
  in elementary education, 50
Professional training, 32
Professionalization
  of undergraduate students, 10
Professionals
  interviews of types of, 16
Progressive disclosure, 72
Proof
  modes of, 43
Proofreading, 204
Proofs
  in mathematics, 112, 199
Psychology
  discursive, 38
Public comprehensive university, 182

Q

Qualitative research
  accessibility of, 141, 144
Queuing theory, 75

R

Reading
  content area, 49
  disciplinary specific, 39
  impact on writing, 206
  narrative, 49
Recognition, 12, 37, 179, 228
  in cross-disciplinary communication, 49
  of common experience. *See* Conversation
  of interdisciplinary contexts, 32
  reciprocity in, 11
Repair
  as strategy for continuing conversation, 52
Reproducibility, 111
Research
  assumed transparency of write up, 138
Revision, 204
Rhetoric, 27
  as an art, 28
  centrality of, 217
  difference from spin and image, 220
  interdisciplinary character of, 61
  relationship of context to meaning, 223
  role in argument, 216
  role in knowlege production, 220
  Sophistic, 222
Rhetorical education
  implications for class size and teaching load, 223
  of citizens, 225
Rhetorical limits
  knowledge of, 125
Rhetorical studies, 8
Rhetorical theory, 26
Science
  rhetorical nature of, 139

S

Scientific method, 194
Scientific persuasion, 64
Self reliance
  challenge of in teaching students, 49
Self-reliance
  in Physics, necessary trait in students, 47
Semantic dissonance, 51
Sentence combining, 204, 211, 212

Sentence construction, 212
Shippensburg University, 22
Slippery Rock University
　enrollment decline in 1990s, 17
　faculty job security, 18
　financial challenges, 17
　history of WAC program, 21
　history of Writing Across the
　　Curriculum, 21
　student characteristics, 18
　WAC reading groups, 22
　work load, 19
Social science
　standard research format, 14
Spill log, 77
Sponsorship proposal, 77
Sport Management, 34
STAR system, 128
State System of Higher Education, 17, 154
Stereotypes
　of English teachers, 182
Structuration theory, 8
Style, 28, 29, 215
　loss of stylistic control in learning, 201
　relationship to knowledge, 202

T

Technical and Scientific Writing, 23, 59, 63, 237
　field-related assignment in, 67
Textual analysis
　identification with literary study, 64
Textuality
　in contemporary life, 197
Toulmin model
　as heuristic for invention, 130
　in analyzing arguments, 130

Transcripts
　methods of analyzing, 26
Transferability
　of writing instruction, 7
Translation, 92, 93, 101, 125, 180
　as a model for adaptation, 91
True imitation, 94
Truth
　pursuit of, 33
　universal, 33

U

universities, 8
Universities
　public comprehensive, 32
University of Excellence, 179
Usage, 182, 202, 206, 211, 217, 240, 242, 243

V

Validity
　in surveys, 41

W

Word problems
　as situations, 92
　in mathematics, 38, 39
Writing, 176
　as action and operation, 12
　as end in English Departments, 6
　contextual nature of, 197
Writing Across the Curriculum, 106, 153, 224
　and missionary position, 11
　and social theories of knowledge, 105
　reading groups, 227
Writing in the Discipline, 2, 85, 154
Writing to learn, 85, 154

Printed in the United States
28173LVS00001B/136

9 781572 735767